The 1945 Revolution

The 1945 Revolution

William Harrington
and
Peter Young

DAVIS-POYNTER
LONDON

First published in 1978 by
Davis-Poynter Limited
20 Garrick Street London WC2E 9BJ

Copyright © 1978 by William Harrington
and Peter Young

ISBN 0 7067 0210 7

Printed in Great Britain by Bristol Typesetting Co. Ltd,
Barton Manor, St. Philips, Bristol.

FOR 'TAFFY' THOMAS

A*

Contents

Illustrations

Never Again – You Lucky People

After the 1945 general election Tommy Trinder, the comedian who was topping the bill in the longest running show ever at the London Palladium, hailed a cab: 'Number 10 Downing Street'. The cabbie dropped him at the stage door of the Palladium.

'What's this then?' asked Trinder.

'Isn't this where you want?'

'No.'

'You mean you *really* –'

'Yes.'

'You're not kidding?'

'No.'

So off they went to Number 10, where the comedian went up to the door, knocked and announced when it opened: 'I'm Tommy Trinder. Mrs Attlee's expecting me.' As he went in the cabbie, watching with arms folded, bawled: 'Blimey! Now I've seen the bloody lot!'

Mrs Attlee wanted to ask Trinder to organize a charity show and also, with her husband, to thank him for all his work towards the largely unexpected Labour victory. During the election campaign he had been a crowd puller among crowd pullers. His meetings were all jammed to the doors. He had helped Herbert Morrison, who was running the campaign in the London area, by speaking on the same platforms as Aneurin Bevan and Hannen Swaffer, the Labour journalist who commented on seeing Trinder's performance for the first time: 'It's either genius or sheer bloody ignorance.'

Trinder, whose catch-phrase was 'You lucky people', was not a member of the Labour Party nor did he embrace its broad philosophy. He had only one subject: State Medicine, about which he felt passionately. As an entertainer he had done hundreds of Sunday afternoon shows for hospital charities. It just did not seem right to him that a hospital should have to raise funds that way, to ask for them. Britain had spent, and was still spending, millions on death and destruction. He reckoned that kind of money could be put to much better use. There was no doubt that it could be found, as it had been for the war, if only the will was there. To him the Labour Party was the only one with a National Health Service in its programme – in fact, the Conservative manifesto had it too – and it seemed the party to vote for.

Saying so was a courageous act at a time when it was not customary for entertainers to declare their political views. His campaigning did not endear him to his employer, Val Parnell, who came to him in his Palladium dressing room and complained: 'I see you've been making political speeches again.'

'That's right.'

'Well, you'd better stop it.'

'Why? Am I in breach of contract or something?'

'Yes.'

'Are you going to sack me?'

'Yes.'

'Good. I shan't have to come to work tomorrow,' quipped Trinder.

Of course he was not in breach of contract. Val Parnell quietened down a bit when Trinder asked: 'What are you going on about, anyway?', reminding him that his old man, Fred Russell, had been an Edinburgh MP.

Other employers were not quite so tolerant towards those wanting a National Health Service. Dr David Stark Murray, long an ardent campaigner, at the time vice-president of the Socialist Medical Association, was sacked by Surrey County Council for daring to stand as the Labour candidate for Richmond. The sacking was not revealed at the time because he chose to ignore it, turning up for work just the same and leaving his car plastered with 'Vote for Murray' stickers in the Council car park. He was told to remove it. He did not. Others less exalted also had to pay for their political beliefs in 1945.

People had just come through more than five years of war. Statistically, for Britain it had not been as bad as the First World War. Fewer had been killed, fewer maimed in the Services. It had been a more active, mechanical war, fought on many fronts, not confined to a miserable slogging over stretches of a muddy no man's land. At home more people had been more involved in 'total war'.

Their lives had been disrupted. They had endured separation, scarcities, the strain of bombing. Up against it, they had worked hard, over long hours, in difficult conditions. Their vitality was lowered, their lives lacked variety.

One London housewife summed up the mood of May 1945:

It was almost worse than during the war. First of all we had this tremendous feeling of elation. It's over. I remember standing outside Buckingham Palace on VE Day [8 May] with the cheering crowds. Seeing the King and Queen and Churchill. We had to walk the seven miles home to Roehampton. Bonfires on the way and people dancing in the streets. The elation lasted for a week or two and then there was a feeling of flat disillusion, the kind of thing that happens after a party. The morning after had come. Everything was scarce and getting scarcer. The troops were browned off. This was the mood the people were in when the election was called [23 May].

People felt they deserved something more than they had been used to. There had to be a better way of doing things. To the veteran Welsh Socialist Jim Griffiths the simple question on everybody's lips was: 'After all this – *what*?'

Victorious but tired, people looked back on the devastation and dislocation caused by the war and asked themselves who had been responsible for it all. It was not only members of the Peace Pledge Union who blamed the Conservatives. Or Left-wingers like Nye Bevan's wife, Jennie Lee, who believed the war had its roots in class conflicts rather than national rivalries. Older men remembered names like Baldwin. Had he lied at that last election? Preached disarmament and then proceeded to rearm? To be followed by Chamberlain and the Men of Munich. You did not have to be Left-wing to argue that Germany had been allowed to rearm because the Conservatives had a greater fear of Bolshevik Russia. In the 1930s it was the Conservative Ministries that connived at the aggressions of the dictators and turned a deaf ear to the appeals of the Chinese Nationalists, the Ethiopians, the Spanish Republicans and the Czechs. They committed an unforgivable sin in the eyes of thousands of British people who cared little about Socialist doctrines, but cared a lot for their country's honour. The 'phoney war', that unreal time before Dunkirk, was remembered with its gentlemanly forbearance that we could not bomb German factories because they were private property.

Yet there were those still prepared to defend Munich, like Commander Agnew, the MP for Camborne: 'The Conservative Party does take the responsibility and thank God for the Munich settlement. My view of the Munich settlement and that vital year of grace and delay before the avalanche of force was loosed upon us is that it enabled us to get just those fighter aircraft which saved this country probably in the Battle of Britain.' Commander Agnew's majority was to be cut from well over 6,000 to under 600.

To Chamberlain Czechoslovakia may have been a faraway country of which he knew nothing, but appeasement was no abstraction to the electors. As Somerville Hastings, the Labour candidate for Barking, told a meeting: 'Don't think foreign policy has nothing to do with West Ham. Foreign policy came to West Ham in the shape of rockets and bombs.'

Harold Nicolson, the National Labour MP who was more adept at recording public opinion than dealing with it, wrote to his son Nigel at the end of May, 1945:

But times are not normal. People feel, in a vague and muddled way, that all the sacrifices to which they have been exposed and their separation from family life during four or five years are all the fault of 'them' – namely the authority or the Government. By a totally illogical process of reasoning, they believe that 'they' mean the upper classes, or the Conservatives, and that in some manner all that went well during these five years was due to Bevin and Morrison, and all that went ill was due to Churchill. Class feeling and class resentment are very strong. I should be surprised, therefore, if there was not a marked swing to the Left.

Even after being united for six years against a common enemy, the nation was still divided by its pre-war experience. To Lady Winterton the view from Shillinglee Park, Sussex, was rosy:

There was tremendous progress between the two wars. We had nearly done away with our slums, and we should have quite done away with them if the war had not come along. There is no doubt that the standard of living rose considerably. Before the war it was difficult to tell the girl who earned £3 a week as a typist from the girl who was having a season in London which was probably costing her father £1,000 unless you looked at them both very closely. They were both smartly dressed and both had polish on their nails.

A similar kind of gloss could have been put on the period by an economic historian taking a broad view. Statistically things were not so bad. For most, the twenty years between the wars had been a period in which their standard of living improved. The majority of people were employed. Their wages and salaries fell but so did prices. Cheap imports, improved methods of mass production, the development of chain stores like Woolworth's where sixpence (2½ new pence) was the top price, and easy credit all helped those in work to become relatively prosperous. Real national income per head rose by one third. The mass of the people though did not see and remember it so dispassionately. Statistics are made up of individuals. Whether you were below or above average depended upon who and where you were. There were two nations.

The prosperous one was mainly in the soft, suburban South and the brashly developing Midlands, where new light industries turned out consumer goods to be bought by the middle classes, adding distinction to their villas, semi-detached or otherwise, and by the better-off workers in the sprawling municipal housing estates. In the North, the prosperous places were isolated towns and suburbs like Altrincham, Wilmslow and Harrogate with a life style far different from that in the terraced houses separating the cotton mills of Oldham or in the back-to-back dwellings of Leeds.

The comfortably off were the salaried and professional classes. A teacher in the 1930s could put down £25 deposit on a new semi-detached, three-bedroomed house with bathroom and garage and pay the remainder off on a four-and-a-half per cent mortgage. A typical house cost about £450, a year's salary. Earning that kind of money you were somebody. A small family car like an Austin 7 or Ford 8 could be bought for £125. The working man's equivalent was the bicycle, motorbike or, for his family, the motor-cycle combination, often bought on hire purchase. Rates of interest for this new form of credit were also attractively low. The twenty-fold expansion of hire purchase between the wars enabled people to furnish their homes with three-piece suites and carpets and status items from the limited range of available domestic gadgets: wireless sets, vacuum cleaners and electric irons.

The relative prosperity of the many, however, was bought at the expense of a sizeable minority. To them the memories of the twenties and thirties were still vivid and bitter: the wasted years, the return to the unprosperous peace after the First World War, unemployment, lockouts, the General Strike of 1926, the slump of 1929-31, cuts in wages, hunger marches, the slow death of towns like Jarrow and the degradation of men left to decay at firmly shut factory gates, on street corners and in dole queues. Between the wars, South Wales, Northern England and Scotland, where the traditional industries of coal mining, textiles, iron and steel, heavy engineering and ship-building were located, suffered badly. When young people in these areas left school there were precious few opportunities for them and all too often the prospect of signing on at the labour exchange, collecting their dole and joining the demoralised army of cloth-capped, mufflered men who grew old before their time.

The enterprising ones moved. Miners, heavy engineering employees and textile workers left the old declining industrial areas and went to the Midlands and the South-East, where they soon adapted their skills or mastered the new techniques needed in the mass production of cars and other consumer goods. In doing so they reversed a 150-year-old trend. Ever since the beginning of the Industrial Revolution migration had been in the other direction, to the North and West. Where there was muck there had been 'brass'. When those areas were feeling the worst of the Depression people flocked to work for the new industries that were sited near their prosperous home markets. Ironically, many of these were in places that during the early 1940s were to bear the brunt of the German air attacks.

Money followed money. Where consumers had money to spend it was worth building factories or providing services, which attracted people wanting work, who in turn earned more money to spend. At the top of the pre-war economy was this prosperous circle, beneath it the distressed areas spiralling downwards into decay. When demand for their products – ships, locomotives, boilers, cotton goods and so on – went down, workers were laid off or put on short time, earnings fell, traders and professional men providing services suffered, rents and rates got into arrears and nothing seemed to be able to stop the rot. None of our politicians, Conservative, Labour or Liberal or any National mixture of them, had been able to relieve the Depression. The Prime Ministers of the period – Baldwin, MacDonald and Chamberlain – had been dwarfed by the economic problems. There was nobody of the stature of Roosevelt to bring a new deal.

That came unintentionally from an unexpected quarter: Nazi Germany. The war with Hitler brought to the British people full employment and a prosperity that some had only dreamed of. There was a levelling down from the top and a levelling up from the bottom. The value of the common man as a member of society and in hard cash terms was recognized. People were wanted, exhorted to work long hours to make the aircraft and tanks and munitions that were so desperately needed. The enemy was all too real, just across the Channel. The situation was far too precarious to be left to private enterprise. The Government stepped in to organize the war effort, to talk to the trade unions, to modernize industry, to bring in varying degrees a centralized control, an allocation of materials and men and money. The example was set early in the war by that crusading individualist Lord Beaverbrook, who as Minister of Aircraft Production prodded and bullied the manufacturers and their sub-contractors into achieving do-or-die targets.

When Goering's Luftwaffe rained bombs on London and other cities and towns the Government had to step in to help, to evacuate children, to provide private and communal air raid shelters, to find accommodation for those made homeless. At the outbreak of war Citizens' Advice Bureaux had been set up and the Food Office soon became a landmark in every town. When the U-boats severely cut our imports the Government brought in rationing so that what food and clothes were available should be shared fairly and not according to the length of one's purse. The few might be able to dine well in the West End but the many could get a wholesome midday meal at a reasonable price in the non-profit British Restaurants established by local authorities in disused chapels, requisitioned premises and 'temporary' accommodation. Social justice had to be seen. In mid-September 1940 Harold Nicolson wrote in his diary: 'Everybody is worried about the feeling in the East End, where there is much bitterness. It is said that even the King and Queen were booed the other day when they visited the destroyed areas. Clem [Davies] says that if only the Germans had had the sense not to bomb west of London Bridge there might have been a revolution in this country. As it is, they have smashed about Bond Street and Park Lane and readjusted the balance.'

Warfare led to welfare. By 1945 people wanted a great expansion of the Welfare State. Hitler's bombs blasted the holes for the new structure of society and its foundation stone was laid in late 1942, just after Montgomery's victory at the battle of Alamein and 'the end of the beginning', with the publication of the Beveridge Report. Sir William (later Lord) Beveridge was a Liberal, former civil servant and between the wars Director of the London School of Economics. He was very much the professor of popular image, an elfin-featured man with a reedy piping voice. 'You must remember we are the most *educated* democracy in the world', he liked to say. As a person he appealed to headmasters and headmistresses. He lacked the common touch. When he was made a peer he said he really hadn't expected it and he didn't really need it and was perfectly happy to be plain 'Sir William'. It was his Report that gave him a popular name.

Arthur Greenwood, then Minister without Portfolio and Minister of Health in the Labour Government of 1929-31, appointed him in mid-1941 to chair a committee that would carry out a comprehensive survey of all existing social security schemes. Greenwood wanted somebody not in the Labour Party but who could be reasonably depended upon to come up with liberal recommendations. Although the report bore his name it was not all the work of Beveridge. He had members of the Labour Party helping him to compile it. Among them was Frank Pakenham, later Lord Longford, who as a young man had been a Conservative, working in the Conservative Research Department for Neville Chamberlain and being converted to Socialism through being roughed up by Oswald Mosley's Fascists at a mass meeting in Oxford Town Hall. One of Beveridge's Liberal protégés, a former treasurer of Oxford Liberal Club, who did some of the calculations was a bright Government statistician in his mid-twenties, Harold Wilson. It was during this period that he moved to the Left. A year after the publication of the report he applied to Transport House to be put on the list of Parliamentary Labour candidates. He was adopted for Ormskirk.

The 300-page report, costing two shillings (10p), outlined a social security system covering people from the cradle to the grave and recommended establishing a basic level of subsistence below which nobody should fall. Beveridge explained the aim of his scheme in a broadcast: 'The Atlantic Charter, among other aims, speaks of securing for all "improved labour standards, economic advancement and social security". The security plan in my report is a plan for turning the last two words, "social security", from words into deeds, for securing that no one in Britain willing to work, while he can, is without income sufficient to meet at all times the essential needs of himself and his family.' He envisaged family allowances for all children, maternity benefits, the provision of a National Health Service and assumed that mass unemployment could be avoided: 'A revolutionary moment in the world's history is a time for revolution – not for patching.'

Seldom has a government report caught the public imagination so strongly. Its fame spread like scandal. It was widely reviewed in the Press. It was referred to in the popular radio comedy programme *ITMA*. There were queues outside His Majesty's Stationery Office shops to buy it. It quickly became a best-seller, not just as a Blue Book. Sales of the report and its summary together reached some two-thirds of a million copies. At the turning point in the war it was something practical to discuss as an important part of a better life. After all the ill-fortunes of the war and pre-war this was a glimpse of a new world.

In 1939 several small firms took the opportunity of the war to close down and sack their whole staff. A designer of fonts and pulpits, for which there was suddenly no demand, saw others in a similar plight: 'Many of their employees had been with the firm thirty and forty years and finished with a week's notice. That was not uncommon in 1939 and '40. Very few private firms, unless they were large organisations, had pension schemes. People would have left without pensions anyway.'

Before the war millions of working class housewives had succumbed to the arguments of door-to-door insurance agents and taken out burial policies to avoid the indignity of a pauper's funeral for their loved ones. They paid as little as one penny (less than ½p) a week and if they were able to carry on paying eventually received a few pounds, generally less than they had paid in. If they could not continue to pay then they were badgered by the agents, who got a hefty chunk of the thirty-five per cent 'management expenses' in commission, to take out fresh 'free policies' on apparently the same, but actually poorer, terms. The same people were the customers for Woolworth's spectacles. There were many more examples of 'to him that hath . . .' The report divided the nation. You were either for or against Beveridge; there was no half way.

This was made clear when the House began to debate an all-party resolution on the report in February 1943. By then Arthur

Greenwood, who had been thrown out of the Government by Churchill because he was supposed to be an alcoholic, was free to declare: 'The people of this country have made up their minds to see the plan in its broad outlines carried into effect, and nothing will shift them.' Ministers, however, did not appreciate the strength of public opinion. Sir John Anderson, a wing-collared administrator who counted every penny twice, made a speech that was just one long succession of 'ifs' and 'buts'. Another civil servant turned Minister, Sir James Grigg, a very tough man but a poor performer in the House of Commons, refused to allow a pamphlet on the report to be distributed among the Forces because it would have 'conveyed the impression that the scheme was settled Government policy, whereas in fact no decision of any kind had been taken'. In spite of his censorship, which the popular Press condemned, the pamphlet did get to the Air Force and to the Royal Artillery out in Burma.

These two knights alone were enough to convince Labour Members that the reactionaries in the Government had won the day. The Germans, who feared Beveridge as a powerful weapon in the war of ideas, realized it too. After the first day's debate the German News Service announced:

> The Beveridge Plan was given so much publicity for the sole purpose of demonstrating to the world Great Britain's claim to leadership in the social sphere. In Europe . . . there has been nothing but laughter at this attempt . . . It now transpires that the whole Beveridge humbug has feet of clay . . . The wine of enthusiasm of the British Leftists has been watered down by insurance experts, doctors, pensioned officers, and big business men . . . Nothing will remain of the comprehensive social scheme but the ensuring of a State grant for the veterinary treatment of cats and dogs.

Labour Members, who had always understood that they would not and could not be committed to future policy laid down by the wartime Coalition, reacted quickly. On the second day of the debate they held a special meeting with representatives of the Trades Union Congress and the Co-operative Congress, bodies that had acclaimed the report on publication and had called for its early implementation. Two Labour leaders who saw their first duty to the Coalition, Ernest Bevin and Herbert Morrison, pleaded with the rank and file not to go ahead. In vain. Jim Griffiths, the Minister of National

Insurance in the future Labour Government, moved a dissenting resolution and Arthur Greenwood led 119 rebels, ninety-seven of them Labour MPs, into the lobby against the Government. It was the major revolt of the Parliamentary Labour Party during the Coalition. The long term effects were important. At the end of the debate Jim Griffiths said to Sir William Beveridge: 'This debate, and the division, makes the return of a Labour Government to power at the next election a certainty.'

The hard-line Conservatives had revealed their lack of enthusiasm only too well. 'Can we afford it?' was their basic question. Was it going to cost so much that it would add to the wage burden of our export industries and cripple them in post-war competitive markets? 'The Beveridge Report proposed to fasten on the people a burden of taxation which will render inevitable a catastrophe even worse than that of 1931' said Sir Herbert Williams, one of the members for Croydon. He was not alone. Churchill, who had himself signed the Atlantic Charter with Roosevelt, was noticeably slow in coming forward to help implement a practical piece of it: freedom from want. No wonder many people had their suspicions that the report was just a piece of window dressing for a structure that would never be built.

They did not want a return to 1939. By 1945 the dominant feeling was that it must not happen again, that the same old mistakes were not going to be made. People were not going to be cheated as they had been in 1918. They were now living in a country where the necessities of life were rationed and the shops could only offer them drab Utility goods, but it was a fairer world and unfairness was not going to be welcomed back. Sacrifices had been made and were still being called for. Housewives had to accept a cut in rations to help feed liberated Europe. Some complained, as they did about 'overfeeding' of German prisoners of war. But these 'Hate the Germans' campaigns attracted little support. What concerned people more was that their sacrifices should not be in vain. There had to be some point to all they had gone through. They wanted to wave goodbye to the harsh inequalities of the capitalist system.

From Lord Woolton, Minister of Food until the end of 1943 and by far the most popular member of Churchill's Government, they had learned words like 'subsidies', 'controls', 'priority consumers' and above all 'fair shares'. One of the warnings his Ministry had issued to fighters on the Kitchen Front was: 'It's not clever to get more than your share.' This was the language of Socialism. Fred Woolton knew what he was talking about. In his formative years he had been a social worker in the Liverpool slums. Now people could see the effects of his policy for themselves: bonnier babies, better fed mothers and fitter children. The infant and maternal mortality statistics proved it. Some people were worse off, there was not the variety of food available, diets were monotonous, some argued that they were underfed. But those with the greatest need had been looked after and were better for it.

This feeling had been well expressed by a *Times* leader writer as far back as 1940 in the post-Dunkirk disillusionment. The leader, published on 1 July, was to be remembered:

> If we speak of democracy, we do not mean a democracy which maintains the right to vote but forgets the right to work and the right to live. If we speak of freedom, we do not mean a rugged individualism which excludes social organization and economic planning. If we speak of equality, we do not mean a political equality nullified by social and economic privilege. If we speak of economic reconstruction, we think less of maximum production (though this too will be required) than of equitable distribution . . . The new order cannot be based on the preservation of privilege, whether the privilege be that of a country, of a class, or of an individual.

The Times continued with this theme. From 1941, when its appeasing editor Geoffrey Dawson retired, the paper's leaders on home affairs became the responsibility of the Left-wing historian E. H. Carr, who consistently put forward the idea that the Government must promise to create social justice as soon as possible after the war. For a few years *The Times* was known as 'the threepenny edition of the *Daily Worker*'.

The legacy of the war was one of collectivism. It had been a people's war. 'Post-war reconstruction' was the phrase used to describe the task ahead. People were aware that there was a tremendous and urgent job to be done. They had greater expectations. A world different from the twenties and thirties had to be created, a world in which there would be greater opportunities for all, where inherited wealth and privilege would count for less, where there was greater social justice. As a Welsh conscript put it: 'The Army consisted of blokes who'd been half starved in 1939. What sort of world were they fighting for?' Or as one of the lads setting off for Normandy called out to Ernest Bevin, the Minister of Labour: 'Ernie, when we've done this job for you, are we coming back to the dole?'

Donald Soper, the Methodist preacher who had maintained his pacifist witness throughout the war at his lunchtime meeting on Tower Hill every Wednesday, felt the mood of his audience:

> Among members of the fighting services who'd been abroad I found an awareness about a world that had largely not been appreciated, its many complexities . . . All this created a ferment . . . Whether people realized it or not, there was a groundswell of Socialist thinking, in an inchoate way the idea that we'd got to make a new beginning and start at a different place and pursue a new course . . . People were ripe for new ideas, partly because they'd been starved of them for five years and partly because they'd been preoccupied with the ideas that were necessary for winning the war.

Fundamental changes were needed if Britain was to go forward and not back to the bad old days. The peace had to be won, a permanent peace, a people's peace. The slogan for the fight was 'Never again'. In his pamphlet *How To Win The Peace*, the Communist Party secretary Harry Pollitt declared: 'For if ever there was a time to remember "We are many, they are few" it is now . . . We, the people of Britain need not be afraid of the future. We are the future.' An ex-boilermaker who heard best when surrounded by noise, he too had picked up the groundswell.

These were infectious, heady feelings. They did not suddenly erupt in the summer of 1945. They had been a long time in the making and there was hardly a person in the country who at some point had not found himself caught up and involved. In many ways the revolution had already taken place and the election was to make it official.

2

There's A War On

In September 1939, in the Oxfordshire village of Wheatley, when the billeting officer had found homes for all the children, one unwanted three-year old girl from the slums of London was found asleep and dirty in the corner of the 'Merry Bells' village hall. Though the billeting officer did not really have room for her in her own home she took her in. The girl's hair and clothes were lousy. For the winter she had been sewn into a cut-down adult vest, which had to be snipped off and burned with her few stitches of clothing. The child was terrified of a bath and fought and screamed, made worse when the soles of her feet had to be scrubbed. They were ingrained black. She was not toilet trained nor was she used to sleeping in a bed. Seeing a bowl of custard on the table, she would wolf it as soon as her new guardian's back was turned and before the two daughters of the house could stop her. She ate the custard with her fingers, as she did most of her food.

The child was one of a million, of whom stories were to spread rapidly: that they thought milk came from cans not cows; that they ate bread – always white – margarine and cheap jam on the doorstep or in the street; that their other foods were fish and chips out of newspaper, pickles, ice cream, biscuits and sweets, washed down with strong tea or even beer; that they relieved themselves in the corner of the room, which to them was better than on the carpet; that they went to bed at all sorts of hours and then they slept on the floor; that they were destructive and defiant, foul mouthed, liars and pilferers. Of course it was supposed to be the fault of their parents, who had only sent their children away ill-clad to get free clothing anyway. Improvident and extravagant, they did not know how to use a needle, how to keep their children clean and decent, how to provide them with good wholesome food. How could they when they spent so much time in the pub? Some did not bother to fork out the small return fare to see their children on the occasional

weekend. Indeed there were those to whom evacuation came as a
God-sent opportunity for 'good riddance'.

It was a major invasion of the country by the town, the first
impact of the war upon most people and an eye-opener for the
middle class. This was a new social experience brought directly
into their homes. It was something different from talking loftily
and unknowingly about council house tenants chopping down the
banisters for firewood and keeping coal in the bath. Harold
Nicolson understated it when he said, two weeks after the first
wave of evacuation: 'This is a perplexing social event'. But he was
right when he went on to say 'the effect will be to demonstrate to
people how deplorable is the standard of life and civilization among
the urban proletariat'. The Government carried out its own survey
through the Shakespeare Committee but, to avoid the heartache and
the thousand natural shocks, did not publish it.

The Fabians, earnest as ever in the quest for social truth, felt that
people ought to know what they were heir to, so they made their
own survey, using the unpaid labour of hundreds of qualified volunteers. They worked extremely quickly and a detailed report based
on country-wide evidence was published by April 1940. That was
not the end of it.

The National Federation of Women's Institutes made represen-
tations to the Women's Group on Public Welfare, which made its
own study between 1939 and 1942. Because of its contents and the
extremely scruffy flimsy copy paper on which it was produced the
Fabians dubbed it the 'Louse Report'. Published as *Our Towns*, it
ran through three impressions in March, May and July 1943,
exhibiting the British genius for self-criticism even in wartime. The
authors, a small group of working professional women, pointed out
that no social survey of England as a whole existed. Evacuation had
merely opened a window, through which English town life was
suddenly and vividly seen from a new angle.

Two things stood out about the complaints investigated – they
related to only a small proportion of the evacuees: and the complaints were nation-wide and concerned some of those from every
area evacuated. The effect of evacuation was to flood the dark
places with light and bring home to the national consciousness that
the 'submerged tenth' described by the sociologist Charles Booth
in his late nineteenth century work still existed in our towns like a
hidden sore, poor, dirty, and crude in its habits, an intolerable and

degrading burden to decent people forced by poverty to neighbour with it. The big towns had a formidable and sinister number of overcrowded families and in these towns the children with the lousiest heads were those under five years of age. Yet it was this 'submerged tenth' that escaped most social effort; its members seldom joined trade unions, friendly societies, classes or clubs; they seldom attended places of worship. Their importance as a social factor had received inadequate attention.

The authors of the report came up with recommendations on reconstruction but their real achievement was in shaking people out of their complacency. They asked and answered their own question:

> Why did the disclosures of evacuation produce such a degree of shock and scandal? The answer is probably that, with the increasing stream of social legislation passed in the last thirty years, and the visible improvement in the condition of the poor, the ordinary citizen had come to believe that all was well with our society. This was perhaps a natural belief, for the progress made has been great and the powers conferred by legislation sufficiently far-reaching to ensure even greater changes had they been fully used. But those who have done personal investigation know the extraordinary difference between looking at schemes from above downwards and from below upwards.

The personal experiences of people in wartime gave them a new perspective on society. War brought them closer together. In the face of a common enemy people who would normally have had nothing to do with one another were thrown together, had to work together. Barbara Wootton was on the academic staff at the Institute of International Affairs, working among other things on post-war reconstruction: 'At the height of the bombing it was pointed out that everybody at Chatham House would have to take part in firewatching. It was explicitly put to us by the then director of the Institute that for this purpose there would be none of the usual distinctions of status and that we might very well find one of the porters was in charge of our unit and we must regard everybody in this context as equal. We might even have to be under the direction of a porter.' Appropriately, in 1941 Barbara Wootton published *End Social Inequality*.

Forced to stay alert during the long nights, people found various ways to relieve their boredom, playing cards and other games, reading, talking. While a few were astutely firewatching with eyes on future property development many were enlarging their horizons in discussing subjects they would never have contemplated, including the kind of world they wanted when this lot was over. In schools, aspiring intellectuals looked forward to promotion into the Sixth Form, which brought with it the privilege of firewatching and the opportunity of philosophizing into the night.

Civilians were involved in several ways. Reg Underhill, secretary of West Leyton Labour Party, joined his local Fire Service a few months after the outbreak of war: 'All sorts of people had come into the Service, clerical workers, travellers . . . It was a remarkable organization. Truly and practically democratic. Each station had its own catering committee which appointed a catering officer who would have time off to go and purchase stuff. I suppose there were about fifty men at my station and when you're with them all the while it's not necessary to go out of your way very much to influence them.'

The blitz created as well as destroyed communities. From September 1940, after the Battle of Britain, the raids became heavy and continuous. In London an obvious place of deep shelter was the Underground, obvious to the common people but not to the Government, which at first tried to stop people going down. Not for long. The public quickly made its opinion felt by buying 1½d (just over ½p) platform tickets and tens of thousands of Londoners made tube station platforms and other tunnels their nightly home, far from the sound of bombs and ack-ack fire. Not that all was peaceful down below. Often people couldn't or didn't want to sleep and amidst the stench of humanity a community life developed. People swapped experiences with those on neighbouring 'pitches' and groups enjoyed the singing and dancing and concerts that helped to while away the long hours and keep their spirits up. A similar spirit pervaded communal shelters everywhere.

Above ground, humanity was laid bare. Not merely the window was opened on other people's lives. 'I used to work in Shoreditch and I visited the area after the bombing,' said one middle class observer. 'For the first time I saw the appalling conditions, how people lived in these slums.' His wife was one of the women in green, active in Bomb Alley, the south-east of London:

I joined the WVS at the beginning of the war. It did a lot of oddjobbery. So there was a tremendous mixing of the classes. One of my jobs was to help people write letters. We thought possibly the first thing those bombed out should do was to write to their husbands overseas or in the country to let them know they were all right. Absent husbands might wonder after reading reports of air raids in the papers. Also it's a steadying thing to sit down and write a letter. I discovered for the first time how difficult it was for people who were fairly articulate to write even a few words. We helped them to express themselves.

This was not a patronizing statement. Seeing how the other half lived gave people a greater understanding of their fellow men. The class barriers were breaking down just as the railings round the parks and gardens and in front of people's houses were being democratically burned off and taken away as scrap metal. People were meeting through allotment and horticultural societies digging for victory in the Grow More Food campaign; through pig and poultry clubs, through farm camps ('Lend a hand on the land'); through knitting circles turning out seamen's stockings, balaclava helmets and other warm woollens for the Services; through National Savings groups; on crowded trains, in British Restaurants. In November 1942 the publicity director of the Ministry of Fuel, Stephen King-Hall (who was unsuccessfully to oppose another fuel expert, Harold Wilson, at Ormskirk) issued a notice 'Share Your Fires', calling on people to 'get together with your friends and neighbours now and work out a scheme for sharing firesides this winter'. The Ministry of Food advised people to cook together to conserve fuel, though this was never so short, and morality was so strict, that there was no campaign for 'Bath with a friend'. Servicemen and workers away from home found themselves invited to other people's homes. Well-to-do women were even known to cultivate the friendship of shop assistants, inviting them to tea in the hope of getting a bit extra or priority for something in short supply.

In speaking to one another people were acting out of national character. The traditional British reserve was breaking down. It had started before the war and grown during the 'phoney war', when neighbours had co-operated in digging simple communal shelters in parks and other public places and there were strange things to talk about: gas masks, the blackout, air raid alerts, the start of rationing. The Second World War was a great leveller, shaking the foundations of British society much more than the

First. It was 'a total war'. All classes, rich and poor, both sexes, all ages were drawn much more completely into the struggle. There was much greater social upheaval and much greater social change. As a railway worker put it: 'We got the closest we've ever been to the classless society, not in the sense of distribution of wealth but in the attitudes of people'.

This did not always happen in other countries levelled by war, like France and Holland. Those who could, which often meant those who could afford to, fled. The effect of occupation was to emphasise class differences, whereas the threat of invasion narrowed them. In occupied countries the collaborators tended to come from the upper classes loyal to the old ways. A notable exception was Denmark, where the King and Royal Family set a splendid example of resistance that so embarrassed the Nazis they could do nothing about it. Elsewhere royalty fled, government was carried on by well-heeled quislings and resistance seemed the prerogative of the poor, who did not have so much to lose materially. It was not a simple two-sided conflict. The resistance itself was divided. There were the patriots who were fighting for the countries and regimes they had known. On the other side were the partisans campaigning against the occupying Germans and the old regimes. Their aim was a Left-wing government and an entirely new kind of society when peace came.

We really cannot know what the pattern would have been in England had invasion come. Many people expected and were resigned to Churchill and the Royal Family going to Canada and directing operations from there. On the other hand lesser aristocrats like Harold Nicolson and his wife had their suicide pills ready. How soon would they have taken them? After resistance or after collaboration? Impossible to say. What did happen was that the poised threat united everyone marvellously, producing a sense of common purpose like the concentration in the mind of Dr Johnson's man about to be hanged.

To one mother there was a security in 'the feeling of working together. After working late I felt absolutely safe walking home over Putney Heath. Not a tremor of anything except a bomb. You didn't hear of assaults and murders. We all felt completely comradely with one another. The two younger children could bicycle on Wimbledon Common in the holidays and I didn't have the slightest feeling of danger.'

Working together was a new wartime experience. Indeed, working at all was a new experience for some. Before the war Bob Walsh opened and ran with his wife, Molly, the House of Hospitality for the unemployed in Wigan. About a third of the working population there was unemployed. 'We helped in family welfare and with advice. In this we had the services of trade union officials who were Catholics. We also ran discussion groups. One of the subjects that always came up was the waste during the building of the giant Euxton munitions factory near Chorley just before the war. There were lots of stories about theft and concrete mixers just being buried in the ground. People who had known the hard times of the Depression were cynical about how government money could be found when we were really up against it.' The war brought prosperity to depressed areas like this. The new Euxton munitions works drew its employees from twenty miles around. They travelled what for most of them was a previously unknown distance to work, soon getting used to the long hours. Mobility brought good wages and security. After Dunkirk there was full employment in the country, with people working more than plain time for rising wages. Many working class families now had two or three incomes instead of one or none.

Thousands of craftsmen, divorced from their trades by the Depression, were redrafted back into them and found themselves in factories alongside administrative and clerical workers who had known nothing but office life. This led to the growth of trade unions as John Boyd, a future general secretary of the Amalgamated Union of Engineering Workers, saw from the engineering shop in Motherwell, Lanarkshire, where he was helping to turn out armour plating for battleships and steel sections for tanks:

Both groups became very well organized because the need was there to be organized. So much discussion had to take place about changes that had to be made quickly and smoothly. They all began to realize the value of trade unionism and trade unionism thus grew phenomenally. There were great restraints on wages in Scotland. No employer was throwing his money around even though he was on cost plus. Most workers had to earn what they got. Trade union branches were fairly well attended. Lots of debates took place there. Members were interested. That was matched with the new found importance that workers in factories and mines realized they had. They saw administrators being taken away from their so-called key and highly paid jobs and drafted into factories and pits. Workers realized how important they were when it came to the crunch. All these other jobs, lucrative and interesting and satisfying, didn't really matter. What really mattered was growing food and making things. All sorts of people realized how important people in factories were.

Factories themselves were changing, becoming a bit more human. Gone were the notices 'No Hands Wanted'. Workers were being wooed with crèches and canteens. The canteen was often more than just a place to eat. It was a concert hall where amateur and professional performers made lunchtime a workers' playtime. Life at work was more fun; it was also more earnest, more than just earning a living. The shop floor was beginning to get involved. The aim of Joint Production Committees was to get management and workers co-operating to increase output. Companies – with the notable exception of Ford – were recognizing trade unions. In their turn they were able to bargain from a position of greater strength. The pre-war struggle of those in work had been to preserve the level of wages and prevent cuts. Now they could improve their lot.

Not just in factories were unions showing their strength. Reg Underhill in the Fire Service:

People who probably had never before had experience of a trade union now began to appreciate its uses. At one stage the Union arranged for us to do part time evening work at factories in addition to our fire duties. This was paid for at the regular factory rate. I also acted as what was called 'fireman's friend'. There was a very strong disciplinary code in the Service. Quite as strong as the Army, possibly stronger. If a fireman was on a charge he had the right to be represented by an outside individual, often a lawyer or somebody like myself. It was extraordinary really. On the one hand this strong discipline yet the men had a trade union to represent them. Something the Army didn't have.

Union influence broadened. A Birmingham trade unionist:

There were all these things like Navy Day and Spitfire Week. We adopted a different Service each year. There used to be plaques in the Council Chamber saying how much we'd managed to collect. And then there were National Savings Committees run by the unions in the factories. I was the factory group representative of our National Savings Committee. Holidays At Home: I arranged a baseball demonstration and match with some Americans posted nearby. The unions built up influence and

B

strength in social areas. The mere fact that Ernest Bevin was a member of the Coalition Government, head of the largest union, was enough to ensure co-operation. The Government knew this. We had reports of enemy damage, damage done to the enemy and by the enemy. It was all under the Ministry of Information, who passed this on to each Area Information Committee, on which the unions were represented. This all increased our prestige and influence.

One piece of enforced employment was probably of greater social significance than economic value: the Bevin Boy scheme. From December 1943, to get men down the pits and keep up coal production, one in ten conscripts was drafted to the mines, irrespective of social background. Among them were future comedians Stanley Baxter and Eric Morecambe, but the experience was no joke. Eric Morecambe was soon invalided out with heart trouble. There were some who chose prison rather than the pits. Most of the 45,000 lads were aged about seventeen at the time so they were not voters by 1945 but they were in a position to bring home to the public what the job was like and why it was unpopular. A blue scar became a badge of toughness, especially for a suburban lad in a primitive Northumberland pit:

> It was an eye-opener to my family that I didn't find it more disagreeable mixing with totally different people and doing manual work. I got on well with the miners and used to come home on holiday and tell my family in Barnes about my experiences. They came to understand a lot more about the miners' way of life, especially after my lifelong friend was killed in a shaft only six months after joining. My family knew him. His own family got no compensation at all from the authorities. We could all understand the attitude of the miners against the mine owners. They didn't strike me as militant. They weren't an aggressive, rabid people.

The biggest change in employment was among women. As in the First World War – the major event in their emancipation – they were brought into factories to ease the manpower shortage, doing mainly unskilled and semi-skilled jobs. Their nimble fingers and patience made them ideal for dexterous and monotonous jobs, from machining small components to handling explosives. Indeed, not enough women volunteered and, with certain exceptions, they had to be called up for industrial service. By the middle of the war even grandmothers were being compelled to work and about half the women of working age were employed in some way. Doing a job and keeping a home often involved problems of travelling, finding time to queue at the shops and somebody to mind children. This led to some improvements in social services, for if women were going to give more then they expected more.

In factories they were getting an income, an independence, an industrial and political education they would not have got at home. They were becoming a power within the trade union movement. In 1943 the anti-feminist AEU was the last of the five main unions in the engineering industry to admit women to membership. Not that working class women were completely emancipated. When it came to the election it was still in many places a man's world. Canvassers who asked voting intentions were often told: 'I shall have to ask my husband'. Women also served in the Timber Corps and the Women's Land Army, which was thought to be different from factory work in being uniformed and away from home. They knew, however, that they had been led up the garden path when in the spring of 1945 the Government refused them a gratuity. Challenged in the House, Churchill 'would not attempt to argue the complicated provisions of his statement'.

The war accelerated the decline of domestic service. Fewer servants were available and fewer people could afford them. 'Treasures' who had lived in became 'dailies' coming in two or three times a week, to be treated to an embittered nostalgia and a diatribe on the iniquities of taxation. The middle class woman was also going out to war. Before the war she had either never worked or had often been forced to resign her job on marriage. This was the rule in most white collar occupations. Now the middle class woman was being used in an official capacity that would not have existed in peacetime: helping to administer rationing and welfare schemes, in collecting social information for the Government (Margaret Cole, the Fabian, worked on the enquiry into manpower and war material production), on industrial organization (Jennie Lee was an inspector for the Ministry of Aircraft Production). Investigating for the Public Assistance Board or collecting insurance, they found themselves dealing face to face with people they would not previously have met. One thing most of them would not previously have done was to support the Soviet Union, yet many middle class women cheerfully shook charity tins for Russian horses, Soviet medical aid or a Joe Stalin bed in the cottage hospital.

Russia was the great pseudo-experience. Distance lent enchantment to the heroism of the Red Army, to the sacrifice of her people carrying out their scorched earth policy, to the magnificent stand at Stalingrad where they were fighting in one part of a factory and making weapons in the other. Douglas Long, an avowed Communist who remained an Able Seaman throughout the war, was stationed at Chatham in 1944 when five Russian submarines put in for a refit:

> There was an enormous bar at the Dockyard, must have been 100 yards long, and all they served was pints of mild ale. Somehow our chaps never gelled with the Americans and one section of the bar was the Yank section. Our boys did gel with the Russians, who came in despite the language difficulties, and so there was a sort of Russo-British bit of bar. There was a group of Russian matelots and British in there one day talking to each other in pidgin English, pidgin French, pidgin German, whatever they could manage. One Russian, a boy, didn't look older than sixteen, hung back as though a little shy about joining these men, big beefy chaps all of them. They were slapping each other on the back and saying where they came from: 'Me . . . Sheffield', 'Me . . . Manchester'. And the Russians: 'He . . . Moscow', 'Him . . . Kharkov'. Then one of them remembered this boy and touching his shoulder said: 'Ah . . . him Stalingrad'. Suddenly there was complete silence. It was as though they'd all heard the distant rumble of the guns. And then these big beefy British sailors without a word embraced this boy.

Those closer to the Russians at war were less enchanted, however. Many sailors on the Murmansk convoys, after braving the Arctic seas to get supplies through, found the reception less than grateful. Some individuals got on with one another but there was a general policy of non-fraternization. 'They took everything and gave nothing' was a common verdict. They were also quick to take from the British prisoners of war they liberated in Eastern Europe the watches they had preserved throughout their captivity. Intent on reaching Berlin, the Russians decided the easiest way of coping with these ex-POWs was to put them into camps not unlike those from which they had been freed. On repatriation they were specifically briefed by British officers not to give interviews to the Press and at all costs not to mention the treatment meted out by the Russians, who were often seen to be as harsh to their own people as to the enemy. Thus the heroic impression was largely preserved until well after the election.

In the Services people were brought close together. Living together, they could not help seeing other ways of life, being presented with different points of view. In the boring periods of inactivity they talked to one another, read, exchanged ideas, wrote letters home expressing, among other things, their hopes for a better world. Their words fell on willing ears. Life was hard for the wives of servicemen in the lowest ranks, especially in the early years of the war and if they had young children. If the meagre official allowance and the compulsory allotment from the husband's pay were not enough they either had to fall back on sweated 'out work' or seek a supplementary allowance, which involved the inquisition and the indignities of the hated pre-war means test.

While they were suffering their sisters in the Services were discovering the suffrage. Many of them, also illiterate, did not know they were eligible to vote. In the Services they learned to express themselves and like the Land Army girls early in 1945 they had something to be vocal about. Sir James Grigg, the unpopular Minister of War, decreed that single girls in the Auxiliary Territorial Service should be posted abroad wherever the Government thought fit. This was opposed by the leader of the Left, Aneurin Bevan. Correspondence about it soon broke out in his weekly paper *Tribune* with a letter from 'ATS Sergeant' rebuking women MPs, who appeared mostly to have voted for it. She argued that they were quite wrong, as many girls did not want to be sent abroad. Their menfolk strongly opposed the idea and they had not been consulted. Doris W. Mobbs in the same issue was baffled that the normally sensible Bevan should be so unbalanced over this and said conscription of women was 'a great step forward in the ever growing recognition that the responsibilities of running the community should be shared more equally between men and women'. She rebuked Bevan for 'trying to put the clock back'. In a later issue Francis M. Shattock wrote to say it was ridiculous that they should be consulted and what would have happened if the men had been consulted as to where they would like to be posted before D-Day, stressing the point of equality. The Left-wingers on this occasion seem to have been on the side of the male chauvinists.

All was not community in the Services. As one girl in the ATS put it: 'In Civvy Street you accepted people for what they were. In uniform though there was still this thing of "He or she's an officer". So he got and demanded respect.' The distinction between officers and other ranks was good raw material for camp concerts and when it came to the election part of the feeling behind the Service vote. Anthony Sampson, who as an author was to dissect the anatomy of Britain, was serving as a naval officer on a launch off the German coast when the results were declared: 'There was jubilation below decks, which I didn't immediately understand. We had been cut off from political debate during the war.'

Those most out of touch were titled women like Lady Cunard, who privately complained in the middle of the war that she never had enough to eat in England and 'What are the Merchant Navy doing?' Similarly Lady Astor flew into a temper because her husband, then Lord Mayor of Plymouth, would not let her have any of the large consignment of chocolates and sweets sent from America as a gift to the people of the city. Like the Bourbons, these ladies seem to have learned nothing and forgotten nothing. Nor did they keep their opinions to private dining tables. At an election meeting specially held for women in Horsham town hall Lady Winterton declared: 'The war casualties among the sons of the capitalist class are always higher than in any other class, because they are immediately flung into the war while the rest of the population is getting ready and they are the ones who are always killed first. I am very annoyed when I hear it said that the capitalist class wants war and that wars pay them. Indeed during war industries come under a good deal of control. It is a very silly lie and I can never understand it.'

These attitudes might have been amusing in the pre-war pages of Evelyn Waugh but such selfishness, condescension and arrogance were, like their perpetrators, to have a smaller place in the post-war world. Wartime events and experience had created the spirit of a new age. It was very much public opinion, coming up from below. The politicians were much too busy running the war to lead opinion and what had been the ruling classes were out of touch with it. The common man had got used to seeing himself in a new light.

3

To See Ourselves

Harry Watt, documentary film maker, was on location for *The Overlanders* in the Australian desert when he heard the 1945 general election results. He lost no time in despatching a messenger to Alice Springs, 150 miles away, with the order to send a cable to his chief, Michael Balcon, at Ealing studios in England. It requested a day off for the unit 'to celebrate the birth of a new world'. Balcon's reply was characteristic and terse: 'Are you kidding?'

Yet Harry Watt together with Robert Hamer, Charles Frend, the brilliant Brazilian Cavalcanti, and all those who were part of what scriptwriter T. E. B. Clarke has called 'Mr Balcon's Academy for Young Gentlemen', had throughout the war years already achieved a new world. It existed on film. By the outbreak of war the picture palaces selling sixpenn'orth o' dark and a world of dreams were well established. Here the patrons could for three hours or so escape from the world of dole queues, hunger marches and means tests. The dream world was essentially an unobtainable one of silken boudoirs and ritzy nightclubs. It was also an American one. Most films were imported from Hollywood and English films, with a few notable exceptions, were thought best avoided. Americans remained a dream race. Very few English people before the war had actually met an American.

Realistic contemplation of the world about us in cinematic terms was almost totally confined to the documentary film, which was not encountered by patrons of the commercial cinema ensconced in their velveteen seats and overawed by the Odeon baroque when the lights went up and the mighty Wurlitzer played. Documentary was about a different world and it was shown in a different world. The reputation of British documentary was established early under John Grierson but 'the Trade' for years resisted the very idea of it in the cinema.

Documentary began in schools, village halls and Women's Institutes and for long bore an aura of education rather than of entertainment. Such organizations as Kino, working with the Left Book Club, showed films about the Spanish Civil War and the Sino-Japanese conflict. Audiences were ready and willing to pay good money to see such full length films as *The Defence Of Madrid* and, no doubt mindful of this, Harry Watt, Grierson's fellow Scot, was haunted by the twenty or thirty million people who did not go to the commercial cinema. He dreamed of making the sort of documentary such people would cheerfully pay to see. Grierson himself seems to have been impatient of this point of view, though Watt went some way to achieving his end in 1939 with a commercial showing of his *North Sea*. Previously, despite critical plaudits for such documentaries as *Housing Problems* and *Enough To Eat*, 'the Trade' had despised the documentarists as so many dangerous Leftish intellectuals. Their real bonus, however, came with the outbreak of war, not that any of them could have realized it in that fateful September.

Like theatres, all cinemas closed down. The studios themselves came to a halt. Work continued only on Bernard Shaw's *Major Barbara*, as it was to do for many more months. Quick, slick productions were never the hallmark of its Hungarian creator, Gabriel Pascal. Yet within weeks organizations up and down the country suddenly wanted films of an instructional and severely practical kind. *How To Deal With An Incendiary Bomb*, *How To Make The Best Of Living In An Anderson Air Raid Shelter* as well as appeals to grow more food, knit comforts for the troops and put money into National Savings were the sort of subjects the authorities decided could be presented in cinematic terms. Harry Watt worked on the first of these, made in the last weeks of peace and called *If War Should Come*. Going to the air raid shelter, checking gas masks and obeying the air raid warden were its themes and it emerged as 'factual but phoney'. The Government never dared show it.

The first weeks of war in the film world were chaotic, with not enough film makers to meet the official demands. Small maverick units mushroomed, fortunes were made – as well as some very inept propaganda films. Gradually, however, something resembling a system was introduced. The Ministry of Information, which had not come into being till after the declaration of war, decreed that all film must be bought from them at £1 a foot. The GPO Film

Unit, famed for pre-war documentary films, was taken over by the Government and became the Crown Film Unit. Such experienced film men as Sidney Bernstein were placed in key positions where they could pursue enlightened policies and set to work for them such promising young artists as John Piper and Henry Moore. On the lower rungs of the hierarchy, working from a tiny office, John Betjeman, later to become film critic of the *Daily Herald*, might be discovered. None of them earned more than £10 a week and the Ministry of Information at first appointed Kenneth Clark, director of the National Gallery, to supervise them as he was thought to know 'all about pictures'.

Probably the most important appointment was that of Cavalcanti, the Brazilian film director who had worked for many years in France. He always had trouble with the English language and when he erupted into a rare Latin rage his French and Portuguese epithets would become inextricably mixed with his limited English and reduce those he upbraided to helpless laughter, secure in their knowledge that basically he was the kindest of individuals. Affectionately dubbed 'Cav' by all and sundry, his technical skill was beyond question. Typically, the authorities at the beginning of the war regarded him with a good deal of suspicion as 'an undesirable alien'. This was the man who, aware that history was happening all around in the first weeks of war, sent out on his own authority six small film units to record what was happening, having waited in vain for an order from the Ministry. When the resulting film was presented to the Ministry they seemed horrified and refused to take responsibility for it. Called *The First Days*, it now ranks among the classics of documentary. The film makers had realized before the authorities the necessity of presenting the public with hard facts, an attitude that did not come into its own until after Dunkirk.

It was then that the early crude propaganda shorts were increasingly replaced by the work of such directors as Humphrey Jennings in films like *Listen To Britain*. Here and there it may seem now naïve, but its subtle, even beautiful evocation of England and the English remains undeniable. As the Battle of Britain raged overhead the physical demands on the documentary film makers had become enormous. Like other sections of the community they laboured harder than ever before. They worked through every daylight hour, usually rising at five am to do so and often falling asleep

B*

wherever they happened to be. If they found themselves near Soho
Square they sheltered from the night time bombing raids beneath
their Headquarters at No 21, which provided the shelter scenes for
London Can Take It. Films were often made in as little as two
weeks from first conception to married print.

Meanwhile, once the cinemas had re-opened, the purely commercial entertainment film had found itself with problems of its
own. Clearly, with shipping space limited, the possibility of cuts
in American products had to be faced. Yet half the British studio
stages were almost immediately requisitioned for war work. It was
made clear that only about one third of the artists and technicians
would be spared from conscription. Soon films were being made in
an atmosphere of strenuous but comradely hard work in which
the old pre-war extravagance had no place. Film units found themselves pushed out into the streets and factories, where they found
new faces and new sorts of stories. This shows clearly in *Major
Barbara.* The beginning is as studio bound as Pascal's other productions but halfway through occurs a Salvation Army meeting and
a fight shot by the river at Tower Bridge. The climactic visit to
Undershaft's munitions plant includes documentary style shots of a
real factory with real workers sweating over molten metal. To
cap it, the final shot is of the three stars of the film arm in arm and
shoulder to shoulder with the munitions workers, an image that
presumably had Shaw's approval since he wrote all the material
not in the original stage play. Much of the film was made in the
worst possible conditions during the London blitz. At the approach
of enemy aircraft, spotters on the studio roof would sound an alarm
and cast and technicians would shelter in storage spaces below the
concrete floor of the sound stage.

None of the films conceived after the outbreak of war had a
showing till 1941. The adaptation of A. J. Cronin's *The Stars Look
Down,* with its blistering criticism of pre-war life in the South
Wales mining valleys, was fortunate in anticipating the self-ques-
tioning and realistic treatment soon to become so popular. More
stagey was the adaptation of Walter Greenwood's *Love On The
Dole,* which had been held up by censorship troubles and suffered
from melodramatic flaws in its plot, though it proved popular. The
fictional propaganda film of the early war years suffered from the
same sort of blatant crudity that had so fatally flawed the more
inept documentaries. The breakthrough to reality came with *Next*

Of Kin, an Army instructional film on security made by the Ministry of Information. This was never intended for commercial showing although it used a fictional story to get its message across. Directed by Thorold Dickinson at Ealing, it used a professional cast, many of whom were excused their normal service duties to make it.

One of these was Jack Hawkins, who has told how disgusted he was to hear that while working on the film he would earn no more than his officer's pay of eleven shillings (55p) a day. With fellow actor David Hutcheson he sought out Michael Balcon to protest. Hutcheson held open the pocket of his British Warm and invited Balcon to slip in an extra £20. Balcon was adamant, saying he had made a solemn promise to the Minister that *all* participants would receive no more than their Army pay. Stephen Murray, playing a more important part than Hawkins in the film, fared worse. He was a drill instructor and received only a lance-corporal's pay for his participation. Insult was added to injury when for his edification he was marched to see the completed film on six different occasions. He is unlikely to have been among those who were still cheerfully paying to see it several years after the end of the war. Harry Watt's most famous documentary, *Target For Tonight*, used not actors but real airmen to play the fliers, though not necessarily in their real ranks. Even in the least class-conscious of the Services, while a flying officer might deign to act the part of a flight sergeant, on no account might an NCO assume the rank of officer – not even for a film.

Clearly the documentary and the feature film were moving closer together. Audiences might still want to escape but the war effort demanded that at least some entertainment films should be drawn from the ever present reality. The Ministry of Information had as a main aim the influencing of subjects for commercial studio production. Feature film technicians too were aware that they were working under terms of temporary deferment from military service as much as the documentarists and that their films should therefore be an equal contribution to the war effort. Slowly British film audiences became aware they were no longer seeing dream people in unobtainable settings. Hollywood, remote from the battle zones and the man in the street, was even more out of touch. It had not grasped the immensity of the conflict or the deep psychological changes occurring in people. In Britain they were now seeing themselves, at home, at war and at work. And they were the heroes. If they were the heroes on the screen might it not be that they were heroes in real life and deserving of a hero's happy ending?

Harry Watt, remembering Orwell's dictum that 'the working man is invisible and the more important his job the more invisible he is', maintains the great and unacknowledged revolutionary achievement of film documentary was to make the invisible visible. Ealing Studios presided over the new sort of film that soon became known as feature-documentary. The first of these was *The Foreman Went To France*. The realistic documentary touch was at once obvious in the casting of two of the principals. Gordon Jackson was at the time an engineer working for Rolls-Royce, with little or no acting experience but for a poetry reading or two on Scottish radio. Tommy Trinder was cast as a wisecracking Cockney soldier on the insistence of Cavalcanti, by now chief editor at Ealing, who had been known to stand in labour exchanges for hours on end, swooping with a whooping cry whenever he spotted someone in the queues who was 'the type' he was currently looking for. Though much of Trinder's verbal humour must have eluded the Brazilian, his choice effected a small revolution in itself. Previously the working man had always been depicted as a comical fellow, not to be taken seriously and to whom none of the other characters owed anything but condescension. Trinder was funny but he was also real. This performance he was to equal later in *The Bells Go Down*, an adaptation of a popular novel about the Auxiliary Fire Service. *The Foreman Went To France* was something new for cinemagoers and was a considerable financial success.

Ealing followed it up with *Nine Men* directed by Harry Watt, who also used Gordon Jackson as one of the group of raw conscripts who have their first taste of battle in the Western Desert. Gordon Jackson endured some aspects of Watt's documentary realism with chagrin. He was expected to take his share of abuse from sergeant-majors while square bashing like any raw recruit, although there is not a single sequence in the film where he drills. Watt stayed unrepentant: 'The whole point was to make Gordon pick up a .303 rifle like a trained soldier – at the point of balance. That's what documentary is all about.' The film cost about £20,000 to make and grossed a fortune. Nor did it meet with success only in England. It was much admired in the USSR and on the strength of it Gordon Jackson after the war found himself on a goodwill mission to Russia, where he was regarded as a typical young British worker-actor alongside typical young British MP James Callaghan.

Before that, however, Jackson played in Launder and Gilliatt's *Millions Like Us*, the first and only feature film to deal with the subject of women at war work in factories. Looking back on it Jackson says: 'I suppose that film must have reflected many people's lives at that time. The young factory girl in love with the boy in the RAF who's reported missing. Mind you, there still remained a little of the old condescension. The factory floor stuff has the right realism.' The role of women in the Services was examined in Leslie Howard's film about the ATS, *The Gentle Sex*. While researching the script for this Bridget Boland decided she had no right to write about women in the Services without joining them, and threw up a comfortable screen-writing job to enrol in the ATS, so taking the first step towards a very special role she was to play in the Army Bureau of Current Affairs.

By degrees, going to the cinema assumed an importance in most people's lives that it had never held before. Harry Watt was moved and comforted by the remark of a tough Sheffield steel worker who came on a publicity visit to Ealing: 'You know, guv, if it wasn't for people like you making films that me and my mates can go and enjoy there are times when we just wouldn't be able to carry on.' There is no reason to suppose that this was any sort of sentimental exaggeration. During the war cinema attendance rose from a weekly average of nineteen million to thirty million. The adolescent could buy little but a visit to the pictures.

From about 1942 British films developed a freshness and an integrity that may, in large part, have derived from their being made from original screenplays rather than being adapted from something that had first appeared in another medium. Michael Balcon at Ealing was sometimes content to give the go ahead for an idea that existed in no other form than half a foolscap page of typed notes. Balcon was generally prepared to let his bright young men have their head and though most of them quarrelled with him at some time or other they later admitted that much of the credit for the new look in British films during the war years must go to him. Gordon Jackson: 'He was a very shrewd businessman who grew rich by having the sound sense to sit back and let the intelligentsia at Ealing get on with the job. Under him Ealing went from dreadful propaganda stuff like *Convoy* to a wonderful realism.'

It would, of course, be quite wrong to suppose that the wartime audience met with nothing but an unremitting diet of realism. The film of pure escapism, usually comedy, prospered. The documentary feature also prospered in direct competition with these products. Noel Coward's career in the theatre had thrived on escapism. In his film script for *In Which We Serve*, the story of a naval destroyer and its crew, he tried for realism, based upon Mountbatten's ship *Kelly*. It was David Lean's first big directing job. After an impressive opening depicting the building of *HMS Torrin* in a documentary style that might have been taken from a Crown Film Unit film, it collapses into stiff upper lip theatricality markedly absent from most of Ealing's output at this time. There was also more than a hint of the old style condescension to the other ranks. Yet the film made more money than any other wartime picture. Coward and Lean failed once more to subdue a basically patronizing attitude in the filmed version of Coward's play *This Happy Breed*, which was released in the first half of 1945. Indeed, parts of the film were remarkably insensitive and Left-wing reviewers gave the thumbs down to its content.

Just as theatre during the war years was so much more than what happened in London's West End, so films, to a lesser extent, were more than just 'this week's attraction' at the palace on the corner. The schools and village halls and Women's Institutes where documentary had found its first home were still there. Now they burgeoned into new life, giving free film shows in which the booming sound never quite seemed to marry up to the often blurred picture on the spotty screen. The programmes were usually made up of documentary propaganda shorts. With luck one of them might be a Humphrey Jennings such as *Fires Were Started*. Sometimes there might be a full length feature with long breaks when they changed the reels. *Next Of Kin* first made itself known to a wider audience in this fashion.

Mobile cinemas followed the troops, and the Army Kinema Corps was responsible for the projection of these films both to soldiers in their bleak Nissen huts and to rural civilian populations that in pre-war days had perhaps never had an opportunity to see films. A soldier could find himself in the Army Kinema Corps for no better reason than that his father was a cinema manager. In military terms, this qualified him to do anything from driving the lorry carrying the projection equipment to directing an army training short. Fortunately most training films were the province of the Army Film Unit. Thriller writer Eric Ambler found himself ordered to write one along with Peter Ustinov, already beginning to be looked on as the boy wonder of the British stage. Eventually their project became *The Way Ahead*, a film for the commercial cinema that once again blended documentary realism with a strong fictional story and implicitly, as the title conveys, asked what Britain was fighting for.

Once the Ministry of Information had realised what an immensely powerful propaganda weapon the film was the concept was widely disseminated. Nor was this understanding limited to government agencies. The British Council made a documentary short called *Each For All*, explaining the structure and work of British trade unions and examining negotiating methods. From here was but a short step for a union to make a film about itself. The first to do so was the Amalgamated Engineering Union. In *Unity Is Strength* the history of engineers and their fight for reasonable conditions was told in a script by Ted Willis and by professional actors seen shoulder to shoulder with real AEU members. It received no showing on commercial circuits. The intractable problem that had so frustrated Cavalcanti and Harry Watt in pre-war days still remained. 'The Trade' had very definite ideas about what it would and would not show.

The Co-operative Movement was to learn this lesson in 1945. They too had become aware of the persuasive power of film and to mark their centenary year, 1944, had made a film called *Men Of Rochdale* that told the story of the twenty men who had started the first Co-operative store in Rochdale. This achieved some commercial distribution, possibly because Sydney Box, then emerging as a key figure in the commercial film world, was one of its producers. Thus encouraged, the Co-op went on to make a more ambitious film called *Song Of The People*, a three reel 'musical', a sort of social history of England from the Peasants' Revolt down to the outbreak of war. The music was played by the London Symphony Orchestra and composed by Mischa Spolianski, who went on to have a long and distinguished career in Hollywood. The script was written by Paul Potts and part of it was published in pamphlet form costing one shilling (5p). Rank and other film companies were alarmed at the idea of the Co-op possibly challenging them on their own ground. *Song Of The People* had few commercial bookings, but the Labour Party and the Co-operative Movement did arrange screenings as soon as it was first shown to critics in May 1945, scarcely two months before the general election.

About the same time Ealing Studios ran into distribution problems with their filmed version of J. B. Priestley's play *They Came To A City*, directed by Basil Dearden. Managers of West End cinemas refused to show it, saying that they felt a film without a plot taking place in the confines of one set would have no appeal. They insisted that Priestley's arguments as expounded in the film had nothing to do with their decision. So, despite the fact that the film had exactly the same cast as the West End show notching up one of the longest-running productions of a serious work during the whole war, and that the same jeremiad forecasts had been levelled at the play as were now levelled at the film, its distribution was severely limited. It did, however, play in many suburban and provincial cinemas in the weeks immediately before the general election, where it was advertised in terms usually associated with a different sort of film: 'It's daring! It's exciting!' the posters proclaimed.

It was, by the end of the war, generally accepted that films could be daring and exciting as well as influential. Wanting to tap this influence but with no idea how, leading politicians from all parties made their campaign speeches at the end of newsreels. Remote behind their desks and dwarfed by office furniture, they declaimed unconvincingly in the most inept pieces of filming that had been seen for many years. Yet as the country prepared to go to the polls the exciting developments in the world of film seemed to come into sharp focus. They seemed to illuminate a different and a better world ahead, where to control one's destiny might be something more than a dream that flitted for an hour or so on the silver screen. The common man was about to step into the limelight.

4

Behold The Swelling Scene

Major Michael Mac Owan looked at his watch. 'Thirty seconds to go,' he murmured. The tense faces of his men told their own story. The noise outside was intimidating, getting louder every moment.

'Right, lads. It's over the top and make sure you shut that lot up.'

As the men took their places there was suddenly total darkness – and with it total silence. A sharp narrow spotlight picked out an acting area. For Mac Owan's men were all actors and this a play. A play in which anything might happen. Actors in uniform, like the rest of the audience, rose in their seats and protested at the events on stage. Nazi stormtroopers, also actors, would march in, declare that everyone was locked inside the theatre, and march out the protestors to be 'shot'.

For tough audiences of conscript soldiers from the Glasgow slums or the Welsh mines, for those who had grown up as Geordies on the dole, theatre had always been something that the rich amused themselves with, something they dressed up for, as much to be seen as to see. Usually when told that the Army Bureau of Current Affairs had devised 'a play' for them to see their response was surly and derisive. Crowded into tiny Nissen huts, never constructed for a theatrical performance, they were noisy and raucous before the show began. But the ABCA Play Unit's techniques were irresistible and the toughest audience usually got to its feet at the end of the show to cheer with enthusiasm. 'Was this then theatre? Was this what the West End audiences had treated themselves to for years in London?' they must have wondered.

Of course it was not, though this was where Michael Mac Owan and many of his actors had had their training. Plays with any kind of social theme were rare in pre-war years. Theatre audiences wanted to be entertained. This was well understood by Bernard Shaw, who used to complain that because his plays revealed him as such a fine jester nobody would take him seriously when he discarded cap and bells. In the inter-war years his plays were seen mainly at Barry Jackson's Birmingham Repertory Theatre and the Malvern Festival, where the audiences were necessarily limited. Their themes in any case were more philosophical than social. *Geneva*, seen in 1938 for seven months at the Saville and the St James's theatres, confined itself to international politics and lampooned the League of Nations. J. B. Priestley, too, starting with his first play *Dangerous Corner*, combined entertainment and philosophical reflection. Shortly before the war he entered theatre management with the London Mask Theatre Company, a joint venture with Ronald Jeans and Michael Mac Owan. The company existed to put on both new plays and established successes, including some by Priestley himself.

But the Westminster, the London Mask Company's home, in common with all playhouses, closed on the declaration of war. The air raid scenes in the early sequences of the film version of H. G. Wells's *Things To Come* had impressed many people, including most members of the Government, as typical of the instant and confused carnage to be expected. The Minister of Health expected that possibly a quarter of a million casualties would have to be dealt with in England within three weeks of the outbreak of a war. To herd people together in public buildings like theatres and cinemas did not seem wise. When it became obvious the apocalypse was to be delayed a little the Government had second thoughts, especially when they realized that the entertainment business would be a vital morale builder. One by one the theatres re-opened. The first was the Intimate at Palmers Green, a repertory run at that time by John Clements. Terence Rattigan's *French Without Tears*, a proven success that had already run for years in the West End, was chosen as the first play. Clements no doubt reasoned that people would be in need of laughter during wartime. If so, his judgement was borne out by the fact that the four longest running plays in the West End throughout the war were all comedies.

Serious plays about serious themes, including political and social ones, were by no means absent, however, and the most successful ones ran almost as long as the comedies. The urge to listen to new ideas, the willingness to be stimulated into discussion, so prevalent in the new world coming to birth outside, was soon just as evident behind the proscenium arch. *Watch On The Rhine*, an American import involving a serious discussion of what Nazism stood for, was avowedly political. Before the war it might have closed. Emlyn Williams's production ran for 673 performances and later, when he took a new production to the troops overseas, it remained extremely successful. The same company toured an almost equally successful piece by Terence Rattigan. This was *Flare Path*, his first serious play.

First produced in 1941, it to some extent echoed the realistic portrayal of the psychological stresses of war then being explored in British films. Set in a hotel near a bomber station during and after a raid over Germany, it follows the fortunes of a bomber crew and their friends and relations who wait. It was a situation many of the audience must have known first hand. Yet servicemen home on leave and searching for relaxation were as willing to come to a play of this sort as to queue up and see the latest Jack Hulbert and Cicely Courtneidge musical or, for the more sophisticated, a revue with Hermione Gingold. Indeed *Flare Path* was extremely popular with aircrew, although RAF brasshats lacked enthusiasm. Air Marshal Sir Arthur Travers Harris, who was at the time earning his nickname 'Bomber' Harris by advocating blanket bombing of Germany and occupied territories, paid a backstage visit to the West End production and deplored the play. He thought that an aircrew member should never be shown as being frightened. Other authorities do not seem to have joined his protest. The Official Censor was much more concerned at the use of the word 'lavatory' than the portrayal of an airman on the verge of breakdown.

The play was very nearly not seen at all, for its author had Act One with him in a flying boat when pursued by a Heinkel over the Mediterranean. With the rest of the crew Rattigan began to throw out all excess weight so that they might show a better turn of speed than their pursuer. The playwright was nerving himself to throw out the unfinished playscript when it was realized that the Heinkel had turned away. Afterwards Rattigan wrote Act Two with the breakdown scene that so distressed Harris and that aircrew understood so well. Another serious play that ran almost as long as *Flare Path* was Emlyn Williams's *The Morning Star*, a study of Londoners under the blitz. There seemed to be no reluctance to attend a theatrical presentation of what all too many Londoners had witnessed and suffered in reality. Indeed theatre-going, though increasingly popular throughout the war, could be a hazardous undertaking.

Although several London theatres were destroyed by enemy action such disasters fortunately never occurred during a performance. Nevertheless, when the alert sounded it was customary to stop the play and for the manager or the leading actor to come forward and make an announcement to this effect. While touring, it was the actors' responsibility to ensure that they knew where the nearest shelters were in each town and to pass this information to the audience, who were given the chance of leaving or remaining for the rest of the performance. Neither Jack Watling, whose first big West End part was in *Flare Path,* nor Rex Harrison can remember that anybody ever left but Harrison considered they might just as well have done for after such interruptions actors became aware that their lines were no longer being listened to. The audience would be silent, listening for planes, so unresponsive that the auditorium seemed empty. One side effect of the blitz – and later of the 'doodlebugs' (flying bombs) – was to disperse London companies, bringing more good theatre to the provinces.

From the beginning of the war elaborate arrangements were made to take entertainment to every kind of serviceman and woman, wherever they might be. For some performers this was not much of a change and perhaps no hardship, since their reputations had been established on tours. For many others it was a different story, a story that resulted in the unkinder soldier critics devising new spell-outs from the letters ENSA, which in fact stood for Entertainments National Service Association. 'Even NAAFI Stands Aghast' and 'Every Night Seems Atrocious' were but two of the variations. As well as its original productions, ENSA was also responsible for the administration of West End successes, which toured service camps for a month when their London run was complete. The administrative headquarters were at the historic Drury Lane Theatre, where actors might sometimes be found debating the latest Ministry ruling as it affected their profession. One such edict decreed that all key actors and entertainers should remain in their jobs and be exempt from conscription.

In the Army there were frequently under-currents of an 'us and them' feeling, a resentment against officers that speedy and regular promotion from the ranks never quite eradicated. It was a feeling that had to be recognized. The troops were even encouraged to express it in their own concerts as a safety valve. Any comedian who guyed the Army system and the officers who ran it was guaranteed wide popularity. It had long been a stock in trade of a touring comic to acquaint himself with local names and it was no different with the Army. So a very young Terry Thomas might elicit a roar of approval at the expense of a disciplinarian Major King with: 'Shall I tell you a story? Well, once upon a time there was a King who loved bullshit – '

The best comedians have always been social commentators and never more so than in Hitler's war. Some of them also functioned as a kind of social worker. Fresh back from a tour of a war zone, they would telephone parents and friends of the soldiers they had met, assuring them that their loved ones were well and cheerful when seen a few days ago, and passing on messages. Trinder also made a point of asking for complaints. The most persistent seem to have been about a brand of cigarette of infamous repute manufactured in India and known somewhat enigmatically as 'Victory V'. Sir James Grigg, the Secretary of War, on at least one occasion during an official tour declined a soldier's invitation to sample one of these awesome confections. After a concert in Taranto, Trinder offered to bring the offending product to the notice of the authorities once and for all and asked if his audience would let him have some to take back to London: 'I think practically everyone in the audience tossed a packet up on to the stage. I ended with a suitcase full. I took them back with me to London to give to Winston Churchill. He wasn't in when I got there so I left a note along with the cigarettes saying "The lads can't smoke these. They hope perhaps you can." Funny thing was very shortly after that the issue of Victory V was stopped though I don't know whether I had anything to do with it.'

Not all troops were so lucky as to have a visit from such topliners. ENSA had many sides and catered for factory and civilian audiences at home, sending out performers of dubious worth as well as stars. Other actors and performers served in a more orthodox military capacity when called up, though they frequently produced and acted in shows of their own devising or even established theatre companies.

In 1942 Michael Mac Owan, then Education Officer for London Anti-Aircraft, found his unit up for inspection by William Emrys Williams, who personified ABCA. 'I remember you,' proclaimed

Williams. 'I used to come and see the plays you produced at the Westminster before the war. Absolutely wonderful. You know, you could help us.' Williams knew he was the man he wanted : 'I had such a high opinion of Mac Owan's work in the theatre. He was the most marvellous producer. I wanted to use him somehow and sure enough he found a way of turning current affairs into theatre.' ABCA had always encouraged discussion and warned its lecturers off lengthy monologues. Theatrical presentation of ideas was but the next logical step. Mac Owan soon received orders to set up a play unit inside ABCA to illustrate some of the ideas they were discussing.

Mac Owan had used Stephen Murray as an actor with the London Mask Company and knew he had fears that the London District Theatre Unit, having no official status, might face disbandment. He approached Murray to write a play for the ABCA Unit and it was agreed that the style might be derived from the American Federal Theatre's *Living Newspaper* productions, which both men had seen, and take a little inspiration, too, from the style of BBC documentary features then being broadcast. Williams rang Mac Owan up every fortnight for the next six months, eagerly wanting to know when the production would be ready. Since everyone concerned had other jobs to do as well, it took six months before Murray's play could be shown. London District Theatre Unit staged it as a curtain raiser to their production of Shaw's *Man Of Destiny*.

Murray had given a brilliant performance as Abraham Lincoln in Drinkwater's play at the Westminster just before the war, and he wrote *United We Stand* around Lincoln. Williams brought the Adjutant-General, Sir Ronald Adam, with him and backstage after the show both men were brimful of enthusiasm, Adam going so far as to recommend that every unit in the army should have such a theatre group. Though Murray and Mac Owan knew this was impossible, they did not argue. Murray's actors gained their official status and the ABCA Play Unit was born, though in a sense their real baptism of fire was yet to come. This happened when the play was taken to a gun site to feature as part of a regular ABCA hour. The men were marched to the performance and seemed bored and restless. Yet as the play ended they stood on their chairs and cheered.

The ABCA Play Unit was launched on its remarkable career. It toured anywhere in England and towards the end of the war in

Europe, taking with it basic sets designed by Stephen Murray consisting of four rotating telescopic towers, curtains and interlocking rostrums. The productions were always played in totally darkened surroundings. This was so important that on one occasion Murray himself painted out with black paint thirty-two skylights. The blackness meant that the audience's total concentration was thrust on to whatever took place within the stage lights. Lighting changes were timed to a split second and every production played at exhilarating speed. 'Everyone took a turn at acting,' says Murray, 'and on the switchboard or carting rostrums or scene shifting. It was understood these jobs were done in rotation.' The plays themselves were not intended to make propaganda for any group but to inform and, as ever with ABCA, to stimulate discussion. They dealt with such topics as what should be done with Germany after the war, Lend-Lease, or the desirability and possibility of full employment and social security.

By the end of the war ABCA had three companies on the road. Stephen Murray saw no loss of enthusiasm: 'Audiences who came to see us were no longer marched in as they often were to begin with. Now they had to pay for their seats but the marvellous thing was they still did come and we were as successful as ever. We were now known as the "Army Topical Theatre" and even survived being billed as the "Army Tropical Cabaret". We always played to capacity houses.'

This success was achieved with no elaborate scenery, staging or expenditure of hundreds of thousands of pounds. As ever, all that was really needed for good theatre was a group of actors on a makeshift stage, armed with a good script and under sure directorial control. It is odd that so skilled a playwright as J. B. Priestley should have missed this. Having seen one of the Unit's early productions, he became fired with enthusiasm and promised 'a real play, something better than this'. Through what no doubt were the worthiest motives, he felt ABCA deserved something more than the then somewhat improvised set-up, and wrote a conventional three-acter called *Desert Highway*. Such a play belonged not in the Nissen huts and bleak halls the ABCA Play Unit usually found itself in but in a theatre, and after a short tour of the bigger Army depots it did in fact have a three-month run at the Playhouse Theatre in 1944.

That Priestley should so have misunderstood the needs and

nature of ABCA's Play Unit is all the more remarkable in that a year before he had already written a play much closer to their discussion style. This was *They Came To A City*, which had opened at Bradford and then in April 1943 moved to the Globe Theatre in London. Nine well contrasted characters arrive, they are not sure how, outside the walls of a strange city that is never described other than by the reactions it provokes in the visitors. At the end of the first act the city gates open and the characters enter. The second act encounters them as, one by one, they return from visiting the city and we hear their reasons for staying and working in the city or returning to their old lives. It is a play of total idealism and just the sort of thing one would expect to fail in the English theatre, but it is extremely skilfully written and was brilliantly played by a cast that included John Clements, Googie Withers, Raymond Huntley and Norman Shelley and which J. B. Priestley rated 'the best I ever had'. It is still doubtful, however, that it would have notched up 278 performances had it not come in the wake of the Beveridge Report, which already had the whole country discussing what kind of future was desirable.

The play seems to have been all things to all men. Priestley himself was told by different people that it was variously a play about life after death, Left-wing propaganda and a discussion about town planning! He also declared that its inspiration was the different attitudes to post-war planning then being so widely discussed. After the West End run the play, with its single simple set and boldly drawn characters, made immediate appeal to repertory companies and to amateurs up and down the country, a popularity that lasted up to and past the general election of 1945. Though it worked within the old convention that the ABCA Play Unit had thrown overboard, *They Came To A City* was the sort of play that made it clear to more and more people that the theatre was an exciting place where ideas could be discussed. In other fields the breaking down of the barrier between performers and audience had made plain that this forum was not something apart, or for one section of society only.

Before the war there had existed small, politically aware theatre groups from which many of the most exciting developments of wartime theatre were derived. Most important in the thirties had been the Left Book Club Theatre Guild. The Unity Theatre in St Pancras offered the Guild much practical help in staging productions, the famous negro singer Paul Robeson consenting to act without a fee. Unity Theatre had been established for the express purpose of giving working people who might have no other drama club the chance to step upon a stage and work shoulder to shoulder with professional actors. There such working class performers as Alfie Bass and Bill Rowbotham, who later changed his professional name to Owen, began what were to become distinguished careers as character actors. The idea of professional and amateur side by side was also borrowed by the ABCA Play Unit, which by no means confined itself to using professionals.

The Unity Theatre Federation originally embraced ten theatres up and down the country, though this number had grown to thirty-six by 1945, the most well known outside London being that at Glasgow. The touring tradition was always strong in Unity and they favoured such productions as Gorki's *Lower Depths* or an adaptation of *The Ragged Trousered Philanthropists*, plays that tried to make some social point in an entertaining manner. Original plays at the parent theatre in London were often by Ted Willis (who originally wrote under the name of John Bishop), and finally in 1945, during his most active period of work for ABCA, he became president of the Unity Theatre Federation. Throughout the war Unity remained dominated by the Communist Party. Many of the actors were active Party members. Some people were convinced that each of the Unity theatres was a Communist cell. Certainly during the London blitz many of the London based Unity actors formed themselves into cells of six and went into the air raid shelters in the Underground to entertain, though mainly with music hall songs and sketches.

By 1945 theatre was generally appreciated as one of the good things of life. After all, if you could go to a show in a crumpled, even bloodstained, battledress after a brush with the enemy, dressing up to see a show no longer seemed quite so important. There was also a Leftward look about the theatre that nobody could quite escape. As the election campaign opened even the Mayor and Mayoress of Croydon, together with their counterparts from Sutton and Cheam, had to sit through a performance of Croydon Unity Theatre's production of *They Came To A City* during an Anglo-Soviet Unity Conference at Croydon Hall. After the campaign Jennie Lee, who twenty years later was to become Britain's first Minister responsible for the Arts, complained that 'Labour

Party headquarters made no effort to play up the array of famous artists, writers and actors who were actively working for a Labour victory'. Nor did the manifesto *Let Us Face The Future* have much to say about Labour's attitude to the arts, a curious oversight and a warning of future philistinism. Transport House was unappreciative, even unaware, of the work that was being done for it.

5

A War Of Words

As the wartime Coalition was crumbling, Tory publicist E. D. O'Brien went home one weekend and settled down to write a book. The invitation to do so had come from Conservative Central Office some time before but he had initially refused. On reading *Can The Tories Win The Peace? And How They Lost The Last One*, published by Gollancz and written by Konni Zilliacus, he had become so incensed at what he saw as 'a work without one single word of truth in it' that he phoned Peter Thorneycroft to tell him he had changed his mind. He would write a book giving reasons why Britain simply could not afford to have anyone but Mr Churchill and Mr Eden in charge of its affairs. It was written between five pm on the Friday and eight am on the Monday of a single weekend. Called *Big 3 Or Big 2½?*, it was published by Hutchinson barely in time for the election. However cogent the reasoning of its author, it scarcely had time to make any converts. This response, too late and too small, was characteristic of the Conservative attitude to the cascade of Socialist advocacy that had been tumbling from the publishing house of Victor Gollancz for years.

As long ago as 1936 Gollancz, Jewish bon vivant of uncertain temper and firm believer in his own idiosyncratic style of Socialism, had joined forces with John Strachey, a Marxist though not a Communist Party member, and with Professor Harold Laski holding a watching brief, to form the Left Book Club. Its declared aim was to avoid war by the creation of a Popular Front, an idea that had support from Robert Boothby for the Conservatives and Sir Richard Acland for the Liberals. Gollancz's idea was to persuade a large number of people to undertake to buy his Club books if they appeared at a reasonably low price. This was propagated at Left Book Club meetings, where books and all aspects of a Popular Front were soon being avidly discussed. Within a year the Club was enormously successful and by 1938 had 57,000 members. Soon alternative choices were introduced followed by a 'Topical' series and an 'Educational' series. John Strachey wrote a number of these, beginning with *The Theory And Practice Of Socialism* in 1936, a book that provided for many the whole political and philosophical ethos of the Labour Party.

Yet the Party was opposed to the Club. Although Clement Attlee's *The Labour Party In Perspective* was the Club's choice for August 1937, and an unpopular one, the Party did not like Aneurin Bevan and Stafford Cripps consorting with Communists like Harry Pollitt. Despairing, as more and more of its members joined the Club, the Party started its own Labour Book Service. It then threatened all its members with possible expulsion if they persisted in buying Left Book Club choices. Not surprisingly, there was a storm of protest, the Labour Book Service died an early death and the Left Book Club continued to flourish with all manner of small groups setting up under the banner. Any one of these groups might include railwaymen and doctors, professional and manual workers. BBC musicians formed a Left Book Club group. There was even one in the offices of the *Manchester Guardian*. The *Left Book News* appeared monthly, with reviews of the books and other articles. The books themselves, printed between orange soft cloth covers, covered every conceivable subject of Socialist concern by every prominent name.

The Conservatives seem to have been at least vaguely aware of the desirability of some sort of riposte to Gollancz, and in 1937 Foyle's, the world's largest book shop, established and administered the Right Book Club. Though this was quite enough for some Left hardliners never to buy a book there again, and although David Low produced a cartoon about the Book Club war depicting embattled Blimps, books in hand, about to engage with Gollancz cohorts, Foyle's challenge was scarcely a polemic. More like our book clubs of today, it offered mainly biographies of Establishment figures interlarded with such titles as *The Foundations Of British Patriotism*. Edith Sitwell, coterie poet and inordinately proud of her Plantagenet profile, wrote a biography of Queen Victoria published by the Right Book Club, while Sir Charles Petrie, Right-wing historian and apologist for Franco and indeed Philip II of Spain for good measure, contributed a life of Neville Chamberlain.

While Foyle's brainchild resolutely avoided meeting Gollancz on his own ground, a third and probably more important development than either took place in the publishing world. This was the birth in 1935 of Penguin Books. In 1927 Victor Gollancz, working for Ernest Benn, had introduced a series of cheap paper-covered books by recognized authorities on a diversity of subjects. The idea was now adopted by Allen Lane, who had once been struck by the tawdry display at a station bookstall while waiting for a train with Agatha Christie. Penguin was no overnight success but, helped by W. E. Williams, its reputation began to build with the Pelican series, the first of which was Shaw's *The Intelligent Woman's Guide To Socialism.*

Later came the Penguin Specials. No reprints these but specially commissioned by the publishers, their great virtue was topicality. The sales of the series were greatly helped by distribution through Woolworth's. Despite the speed of international events throughout the thirties, within weeks Penguin was capable of producing books discussing what had really happened at Munich or what the full implications of Nazi anti-Semitism were or why it was so important not to let Franco have things all his own way in Spain. Much of the ethos of British Socialism derived from what happened in the Spanish Civil War and continued to do so even after Hitler became chief villain. No war, certainly no civil war, had been so much written about. Those that did not go to join the fighting read about it. Penguin were particularly fortunate during the war because paper was allocated on the basis of how much individual publishers had used in peacetime. Since Penguin had then been in first full spate they had used a lot and qualified for ample allocation, which permitted large runs of Penguins, Pelicans and other sub-series.

Although the independent house of Penguin was less doctrinaire than the Left Book Club, Lane and Williams saw its role essentially as an informing one and by 1940 it had published books on every subject imaginable from agriculture to health and from religion to psychology. Many, though not all, of the authors were men of the Left, not least H. G. Wells whose *History Of The World* was published by Penguin, and R. H. Tawney who contributed *Religion And The Rise Of Capitalism.* The war all but closed down the political book clubs, though they continued to exist, nominally at least, till 1948. Gollancz's creation, which had been called into existence to try and avert war, suffered a body blow in September 1939. Though some of the membership came back in the war years

it never really flourished again, for the truth was that Victor
Gollancz, whose personality had meant so much to the Club, had
lost interest.

Oddly enough, the very dispersal that so undermined the functioning of book clubs favoured an increase in reading. On lonely gun
sites or while waiting for air raids during the night hours, when the
BBC transmitters had closed down and talking was done, what
better solace for soldiers, firemen and wardens than to turn to a
book? Suddenly everyone wanted books. The Government besought
the public to send their unwanted ones to men in the Forces, and
books have quite possibly never before or since been so treasured.
New publications had to conform to what were known as 'wartime
economy standards' and production was supervised by the Paper
Controller. This limitation and the convenience of its size favoured
the paperback so easily slipped into a battledress pocket. Gollancz
now produced a series of books to those standards but within board
covers. Their yellow dust jackets and bold black and magenta
lettering were soon to become famous.

One of the first of these, which appeared in 1940 after the fall
of France, was *100,000 Allies – If We Choose*. It argued that Britain
did not stand alone but that throughout Europe there waited the
Left-wing allies who largely ran the Resistance movements and to
whom the future would surely belong. This was the first time the
idea of a European revolution, of which Britain would be part, had
been mooted: it was to be a revolution not only against Hitler but
against all those aspects of political life that had helped him to
thrive.

Destined to become much more famous as one of those books
that give a phrase to the language was *Guilty Men*. Unrelentingly
recriminatory in tone, this dissected the Munich settlement and the
men who made it with the clear implication that nothing of the
sort must ever be allowed to happen again. The book appeared
just after the *débâcle* of Dunkirk, when people were beginning to
grope for explanations as to just how their country had come to
such a pass. Conservatives saw the book as 'wartime sedition', but
it triumphed over censor and Paper Controller alike and went on
to sell a quarter of a million copies. The author's name was given
only as 'Cato' and there was much surmise at the identity behind
the pseudonym. In fact it belonged to three Beaverbrook journalists,
who had worked on the book together. They were Peter Howard,

who later succumbed to the embrace of the Moral Rearmament Movement; Frank Owen, then editing the *Evening Standard*; and Michael Foot, a brilliant young journalist who was to succeed him in that post.

Their book set a new fashion. Throughout the war years a series of slim volumes in yellow jackets came from Gollancz, all written under such assumed names as 'Cassius', 'Gracchus' and 'Celticus', which suggested Roman tribunes of the people while barely disguising the assorted talents of Michael Foot (again), Tom Wintringham and Aneurin Bevan. The steady stream of books in this series became a torrent in the months immediately before the 1945 election, all selling at half-a-crown ($12\frac{1}{2}$p). Most influential of these perhaps was Tom Wintringham's *Your MP*, written in 1943 but re-issued by Gollancz in time for the general election and available from newsagents. Wilfred Brown, a socially conscious industrialist, was helping a new radical party, Common Wealth, with its administration: 'The Party put some girls on to researching the records in the British Museum. They dug up so much dirt about people backing Hitler out of fear of Communism that the leader, Sir Richard Acland, felt he had to use his authority to say "We're not going to use this stuff to destroy people. We must confine ourselves to making our point." '

Wintringham, a veteran of Spain, was asked to write the book but by the time it was completed Common Wealth found that their paper allowance was insufficient for them to publish. Instead it was passed to Gollancz. It carried an index giving a detailed voting record of many MPs, not on Munich, but on the Hoare-Laval plan that acknowledged Italian rights in Abyssinia; on the state of air defences in 1938; on the defeated proposal to increase Old Age Pensions in 1939; on the Chamberlain vote of confidence in May 1940 and on the much discussed Beveridge Report. People now could look up the facts on just where their elected representatives had stood.

On the first appearance of the book the *Daily Mirror* had proclaimed it 'can win a general election', an assertion that Gollancz reproduced on the book's cover when it was re-issued in 1945. It was a claim endorsed by Margaret Cole in a Fabian pamphlet that appeared a few months after the election: 'In the realm of ammunition for speakers, the polemical books, such as *Your MP, Can The Tories Win The Peace?*, and *The Trial of Mussolini*, prepared and in some cases issued in advance by Victor Gollancz, provided endless and effective stores. The curious may be interested to know that of the 300 odd MPs pilloried in the first of these . . . 111, over half of those who stood for re-election, lost their seats.'

Yet, contentious though these books may have been, they really sold so well because those who bought them sought facts. Another aspect of this thirst for knowledge is revealed in the success of a different sort of book, also published by Gollancz. Hewlett Johnson, the 'Red Dean' of Canterbury, conceived the idea of a book about the USSR after making a pre-war visit there. Gollancz had been very enthusiastic about the idea. The Dean's associate, A. T. D'Eye, helped with the book:

I stayed at the Deanery and worked on *The Socialist Sixth Of The World*, appropriately in the Red Room. All the walls were scarlet and the ceiling was deep blue with golden stars. It had a lovely view over the Deanery garden. The Dean chained me down. That was the only way we were going to get the book finished. He was much more disciplined in his writing habits than I am, going to bed at ten and getting up early in the morning. We had a lot of discussion about publishing it under our joint names but I thought it would go much better under the Dean's name. Gollancz was of that opinion, too. The book was ready for the printer and the final proofs corrected just before the outbreak of war. Then Gollancz got cold feet because of the Soviet-German non-aggression pact of August 1939 and didn't want to publish. We made him stick to the agreement and the first edition appeared in December 1939. It went to well over twenty impressions and must have been one of Gollancz's most successful books. In America the paperback sold over a million copies.

The ninth impression came out in July 1941 just after Hitler had attacked Russia and, on its way to becoming the most widely read book on the Soviet Union, was quoted in many a barrack room argument. It was certainly the source for so many stories of planned Socialist efficiency as opposed to capitalist muddle.

Not unnaturally, a great deal of wartime reading was purely of the escapist kind but much fiction began to reflect contemporary life under arms in a realistic and thoughtful way. A lot of this appeared in little magazines that then flourished. In times of danger arts and education flourish on personal and national levels since people feel constrained to savour them while they can. The war years demonstrated this in many ways.

Poetry, for instance, was taken seriously. Men in uniform not only read it but wrote it. Earl Wavell edited a collection of such verse and called it *Other Men's Flowers*. Another anthology called *Poems From The Forces* was a best-seller. Some of the poetry that was read was war poetry dating from the Spanish Civil War, written by men who had died in that conflict. These poets had made a political commitment and, mindful of the barren soil they had tilled, the new men seemed hesitant. No poem of the Second World War gained the immediate wide currency that Rupert Brooke's had enjoyed in an earlier conflict unless it be *To Johnny* by John Pudney (who was to be a 1945 Labour candidate) by the accident of it being exquisitely spoken by Michael Redgrave in the film *The Way To The Stars*. Poetry, fiction and factual writing were in great part contemplative and forward looking. Whole sections of the population that had never been affected by Socialist propaganda found themselves guided gently to the Left by their daily reading. Nor, indeed, was this confined to books.

In the summer of 1940, as Britain stood alone and it was necessary for barriers to go down if all were to stand together, a change came over Fleet Street. A number of young and able journalists who believed that the war had to be fought and controlled by the people, if Hitler and the Nazism they hated were to be defeated, found themselves in editorial positions. Besides Frank Owen and Michael Foot at the *Evening Standard* there was Hugh Cudlipp editing the *Sunday Pictorial* and William Connor writing under the name 'Cassandra' in the *Daily Mirror*.

One commentator writing in 1945 observed of these young journalists: 'They were no saints; nor Lenins. They were not revolutionaries but sincere radicals whose ire was up. They had their chance; they took it.' In the darkest days of 1940, while these young talents were coming to the fore, there was little interference by the Press lords or the Government. The military situation was so alarming to them that they grasped at any radical straw. They needed the people on their side and these young men seemed to know the language. This was quite enough for the Independent Labour Party and the Communists to consider these same young men as editorial stooges, part of an imperialist trick to make the workers fight Germans. So the Fleet Street revolution attained a spontaneity and

C

authenticity that to some extent it lost after Russia entered the war and the Communists tainted it with their circus of pre-arranged demonstrations.

In other circles as the Nazi danger receded so the new radical Fleet Street was seen as the real danger. Herbert Morrison, having closed the *Daily Worker*, threatened the *Daily Mirror* too. Editorials were attacked in Parliament, dubbed as treason, and Sir James Grigg was soon being egged on to pluck their authors from the popular arena. 'Cassandra', Hugh Cudlipp and Frank Owen were all drafted into the armed forces. Only Michael Foot, whose health precluded him from call-up, remained. Contrary to popular supposition at the time, Beaverbrook did not dismiss Foot in 1945. In fact Foot resigned and his resignation letter shows signs of real regret. He had come to feel a warm affection for the man about whose political philosophies he could be so vitriolic. It seems that only the approach of the general election made Foot feel his position had become invidious and that new circumstances demanded his departure.

Despite these removals and Fleet Street's edging back to a more predictable stance, the radical attitudes were remembered and nurtured fondly elsewhere. The weekly picture magazine *Picture Post*, for instance, under Tom Hopkinson played the sort of role today assumed by television. Articles with photos about what the post-war world should be like were plentiful. They were originally presented from a reforming viewpoint though as the general election approached there was an attempt at more objectivity. Even *The Economist*, under a temporary editor, and *The Times* gave themselves a radical air from time to time, the latter's editorial attack on Churchill's clumsy intervention in Greece being much resented in Conservative quarters.

Tribune had been founded in 1937, when Victor Gollancz had wanted to make his Left Book News a weekly. He had abandoned the idea and joined the *Tribune* board along with Aneurin Bevan, Harold Laski and Stafford Cripps, after negotiating an agreement whereby a number of pages each week would be devoted to the Club. The paper began to make a name for itself in the early war years under Raymond Postgate's editorship and later under Aneurin Bevan. Frederic Mullally was working on the paper in 1945:

Nye was effective editor. We had a pretty free hand but nothing really went in without Nye's say-so. George Orwell was literary editor and came in once a week to write his weekly column *As I See It*. He got £5 a week for that and £5 a week for the literary editorship. I got £12 a week. All the inside political stuff that we printed mainly came from Nye and Michael Foot, who increasingly wrote the leaders after Nye became a Minister. He was the fastest leader writer in Fleet Street. The only man who could write a complete leader from start to finish in twenty minutes. There was always a Monday morning conference, which could be pretty lively with Nye sometimes launching into an impromptu, impassioned speech. Spectacular!

This was the team that built up a relationship between the magazine and servicemen readers that was matched only by the far greater resources of the *Daily Mirror*. The *New Statesman* continued to be its quirky self and lay bare its Socialist conscience week by week while lambasting Conservatism in a manner that more and more people were finding readable, if not downright irresistible. Only the *Daily Herald*, official organ of the Labour Party, was so dull that Left stalwarts must have bought it from a sense of duty rather than an expectation of pleasure. Those who despaired of the barren, unimaginative attitudes of Transport House felt at least justified in hoping that so much social comment from books, magazines and newspapers might be regarded as seeds that would bear bountiful fruit as soon as a general election dawned.

In the face of so much radical editorialising and the onrush of Gollancz political books, what was the Conservative response? Almost complete paralysis. It is true that from late 1943 the Conservative Party did issue a series of *Signpost* pamphlets. Contributors included such university men as Kenneth Pickthorn and G. M. Young, who were apt to ponder the nature of Conservatism in rather academic, not to say slightly ridiculous terms. Pickthorn, for instance, could write in all seriousness:

A Conservative is a man who believes that in politics the onus of proof is on the proposer of change, that the umpire when in doubt should give it to the batsman. There will be few to go as far as the Duke of Cambridge who is supposed to have said that 'any change at any time for any purpose is highly to be deprecated' . . . but there will be many who do not doubt that always in politics Change must make her case before receiving a welcome.

And G. M. Young could see no incongruity in the following:

> The old individualist creed really came to this: remove obstruc-
> tions, let the water flow freely and then as the stream rises every
> bucket will come up full . . . if you asked why some men had
> bigger buckets than others they would have said 'Because they
> or their families before them have done something which their
> neighbours were prepared to pay for more handsomely; they
> have discovered things or watched the markets carefully; they
> have ventured to send cargoes to distant shores and brought back
> sugar and tea . . .'

The *Signpost* was supposed to point to the future. In fact it
pointed only to convoluted donnish musings on the nature of Conservatism and out of date, out of touch moralizings. These and
many more of the pamphlets reveal a strong prejudice against any
kind of planning. To be fair, those written by Conservatives serving
with the Forces do reveal more knowledge of the world. Hugh
Molson, in a very well argued tract on economics, must have been
the first Tory to quote Keynes with approval. Aubrey Jones's contribution to the series was well argued although written not far
from the heat of battle: 'I began writing this pamphlet in the few
brief moments I could spare from the Sicilian campaign.' The Tory
Reform Committee, with a research organization backing it from
the summer of 1943, produced tracts on coal, employment, finance
and social insurance. These did not bear their authors' names but
Hugh Molson and Quintin Hogg were almost certainly among
them, and in 1944 Hurst and Blackett published Hogg's summary
of the Tory Reform Committee's work called *One Year's Work*.
Hogg was the only real writer among them as he was amply to
demonstrate in his *The Left Was Never Right*, put out by Faber
and Faber. This remained the only polemic refutation of the Left's
case argued at length and distributed by a commercial publisher.

The point about the Conservative pamphlets is not that they
were dull to look at, or slim, or badly written. After all, not all of
Gollancz's products had the sparkle of a Bevan or a Foot. The fact
is that their distribution, despite hopeful reminders to the readers
to circulate them among their servicemen friends, was necessarily
narrow and almost entirely confined to Conservative Associations.
In fact they were preaching to the faithful while the evangelism of
the Left books was making converts. Only when the general elec-

tion loomed was there a stirring and a realization of danger. Hutchinson, in particular, brought out a series of slim volumes modelled on Gollancz's. Many of them were written under Roman pseudonyms, their authors apparently not having noticed that this was a device Gollancz had now abandoned. E. D. O'Brien was an exception here and though his book was written in one weekend, its author fortifying himself for the stint 'in the manner of Balzac', his response in common with the other Right-wing authors was too late.

Despite such resounding titles as *The Party That Runs Away* and *Will You Be Left?* they did not in most cases appear till a few weeks before the election and many were not reviewed till after polling day. This simply was not long enough to stem the radical tide in reading that had been running for years. O'Brien considers this had come about not because of a lack of talent but because of stubborn reluctance in the Conservative Party to recognize the value of propaganda by the written word.

The Liberals had staked out a corner of this battlefield, but the colours of Beveridge were carried off by others and their dwindling resources seemed incapable of mounting a really brave show. Ramsay Muir, most authoritative of the Liberal writers and thinkers, died in 1941 leaving no obvious successor able to match either his prolific output or stimulating style. Able though they were, neither Roger Fulford nor Ivor Brown found the mantle quite fitted. The money from the Lloyd George Fund dried up by about 1931 and the Party was increasingly unable to finance social research. *Britain's Industrial Future*, which they published in 1928 and which came to be known as the Liberal Yellow Book, remained a seminal source. It first projected ideas about worker participation and works councils.

In the middle of the most literate election ever the Conservatives also faced up to the role of being a 'one book party'. Lord Beaverbrook, at a meeting of the North Paddington Conservative Association at the end of April 1945, made a remarkable statement, the more remarkable in that he had for years employed on his papers a Left-wing and a Right-wing journalist in the shapes of Michael Foot and Beverley Baxter, a Conservative MP known disrespectfully in some quarters as 'Cleverly Backstairs'. Beaverbrook stated: 'It is no use supposing the electorate after ten years of political truce is informed on political issues.'

In fact there had only been five years of truce and these were years in which many members of the public had come to regard themselves as never so well informed politically. Clive Jenkins was a young man eager to learn: 'There were lots of private libraries in Wales and the manager of our local Co-op Insurance lent me books. He gave me an *Introduction To Marx*. The full time secretary of the Band of Hope and Temperance Union was a social democrat and lent me Book Club choices like Attlee's *The Labour Party in Perspective*, which was really a pretty boring old book. And then I got introduced to things like *Guilty Men* and *The Trial Of Mussolini*. I remember you had to put your name down on the waiting list for your copy of *Guilty Men*.'

No such waiting list was available to the angry reader who wrote to the *Ilford Recorder* in March 1945, having ordered a copy of *Why Not Trust The Tories?* from his local library only to receive a card telling him the library intended taking 'no action' about his request. Certainly the yellow jacketed books were unpopular with the Right, where *Guilty Men* had not yet lived down its 'seditious' label. At one of his election meetings in Croydon, old-style Tory Sir Herbert Williams, soon to be resoundingly defeated, insisted the book 'contained slanderous and lying statements'. Significantly, he never felt disposed to assert this claim in a court of law. In Horsham, Conservative customers went to a bookshop and threatened to withdraw their custom unless the Gollancz yellow peril was removed from the window in which it was so prominently displayed.

It was all to no avail. Nothing seemed able to assuage the thirst for political books. Richard Crossman, fighting his first campaign at Coventry, reported that his local organization had found itself in difficulty because of a 'serious and absurd underestimate of the Print Order from Transport House for reading material. Every twopenny or threepenny pamphlet at open air meetings is immediately snapped up,' he wrote, 'and usually paid for with silver, for which no change is asked. I believe if we had in stock 40,000 Penguins we could have sold them easily. The free literature is glanced through and tossed away. What we sell is taken home and thrown back at us at the next open air meeting in the form of precise and thoughtful questions.'

The Gollancz series were frequently carried to Conservative meetings during the general election campaign and quoted at candidates. Questions like 'Do you know what Churchill said in 1926?'

often raised the temperature of debate, but in the main the habit of reading political theory had created the thoughtful electorate that Crossman had observed. When the election was called the Italian writer Ignazio Silone, hounded from Italy by Mussolini in the thirties and whose anti-Fascist novel *Fontamara* had been published in Penguin before the war, was able to observe: 'Now Britain has the chance of leading the democratic revolution.' Like many others in European resistance movements he had been listening to the BBC.

6

Starting Them Talking

In December 1942 the *Radio Times* published a picture of a ten-year-old girl who a few months before had broadcast a message to her soldier uncle stationed in Iraq and then sung *Mighty Lak' A Rose* for him with a relaxed confidence that left the studio staff gasping. She was soon heard again in a talent discovery programme called *It's All Yours*. The *Radio Times* expressed its good wishes with 'May she sing as charmingly at twenty and thereafter as now she does at ten!' Her name was Petula Clark.

This broadcasting of messages to families split up and perhaps half a globe away was one of radio's wartime services that helped foster a fondness for the 'wireless' as families and firewatchers alike crouched around it in the pervading gloom. As early as 1939 the microphone had visited a Somerset farm and heard evacuee children say how happy they were there, and over the Christmas holiday period in 1940 there had been three broadcasts of messages home from evacuees in Great Britain and the USA. No doubt officialdom thought it desirable that Britain should think of itself as one family, however distant some of its members, united against a common foe.

The BBC seemed to have a particular understanding of the British family's wartime problems, not least because it had itself been both bombed and evacuated. Plans for its evacuation had existed since before the war, when BBC Staff had been instructed to make their way to their evacuation area on hearing the news announcer say 'This is London' instead of the usual 'This is the National Programme'. In the event some departments moved in 1940 from London to Bristol, others to Woodnorton near Evesham, 'the appropriate setting for a nightmare'. Nightmare came in fact to Broadcasting House in Portland Place on 15 October, 1940, when a German bomb scored a direct hit, killing seven of the staff. Bruce Belfrage, who was reading the nine o'clock news, paused imperceptibly after the audible crash and then continued coolly and without comment. A few weeks later a land mine set fire to the building. Once again there was no panic.

For a while newsreaders, who had cast aside their peacetime anonymity for 'security' reasons, enjoyed the kind of adulation later lavished on pop singers. A letter written to the *Radio Times* in March 1940 by Iris Humphries of Bristol was typical of many: 'Since the war has started I think the announcers have helped us quite a lot with the cheerful way in which they have carried on despite the fact they had terrible colds.' When the *Radio Times* was asked for photos of the owners of these voices that carried on, come bombs or colds, it obliged with a two page spread of the whole newsreading staff. Lord Reith, BBC Director General till two years before, had always favoured an impersonal voice whose owner was clad in a dinner jacket to give the news to his unseen audience. This was the first Reithian rule to be abandoned. There were to be others.

Though broadcasting to foreign, and especially occupied, territories played an important part throughout the war, at home the notion of what broadcasting should be about proved less a question of 'Nation broadcasting unto Nation', so much as a nation broadcasting unto itself. The informative, educative aspect of peacetime broadcasting was still maintained but the education was soon to embrace new themes and new voices. The BBC was going to be loved as well as respected. True, there was a bad start when, following Chamberlain's broadcast declaration of war, several days of organ music were interspersed with little but news bulletins. This was part of the general paralytic malaise that the authorities seemed to have deemed obligatory for all kinds of entertainment. Broadcasting, however, seems to have started questing for a new role and a new responsibility sooner than theatre or films.

Before Dunkirk, which shook the nation into a mood of self-criticism, the BBC was already moving towards the new mood. On 15 April, 1940 William Gallacher, Communist MP for West Fife, gave a talk on *The Co-operative Movement And The War* after the nine o'clock news, the top talk 'spot' used so influentially by J. B. Priestley. Nobody objected to a Communist being able to air his views, though there was some grumbling about free advertising for the Co-op. A month later there was a discussion on Family Allowances. These were already received by serving men, ran the argument. Why not, therefore, extend the idea to every family?

c*

L. S. Amery spoke in favour of the idea and Herbert S. Elvin opposed it; they were joined by 'a mother of six' and 'a skilled craftsman'. Though this anonymity for the less exalted members of a discussion group has overtones of Reithian patronizing it may well have helped the equally anonymous listener to identify, and this was by no means the last time the device was used.

This chance for a new adventurousness in subjects and styles was no doubt more easily grasped once the evacuation of BBC units had taken place. The broadcasters and makers of programmes were removed for a while from the physical presence and restrictions of 'Administration' and once out among the people were able to reflect reality and opinion in a way that was matched perhaps only by the documentary film makers, some of whom admit to having been inspired by the wireless. Beset by bombings and shortages and censorship, 'Administration' were no doubt very soon happy to know that something was going out on the air and only rarely ready to dig in their heels over its content.

The Forces Programme first went out in February of 1940 primarily aimed at the British Expeditionary Force in France, but after Dunkirk, though the name remained, such artificial differentiation was no longer tenable. In a backs-to-the-wall situation citizens were soldiers too, while soldiers were increasingly determined to be citizens. The BBC soon accepted that radio, by its very nature, brought people together and was therefore possibly the greatest single morale builder. Hence the evacuee message programmes and others such as *Parish Magazine*.

This latter first went out on 17 May 1940 and was produced by John Pudney, the poet and author who had in the previous autumn written a series for the *News Chronicle* called *Keep The Home Fires Burning* designed to tell troops what was happening back home. The radio programme, which spent twenty minutes in a different market town each week, was conceived with the same object and was widely appreciated. In Carol Reed's film *The Way Ahead* a platoon of soldiers is depicted solemnly listening to the programme and a description of an English rural Spring minutes before going into action in Tunisia. *Weekly Newsletter*, also started in 1940, relayed and commented on home news for Forces overseas.

Obviously an important aspect of this keeping in touch was the news bulletins themselves and in a wartime atmosphere the twenty minutes devoted to 'the nine o'clock' became sacrosanct in many homes. There was little criticism of the newsreaders, though some listeners objected to the news itself, particularly in the bleak weeks after the fall of Dunkirk, and again after Singapore's surrender in early 1942. One confessed he found bulletins so unbearable that he preferred to walk in the streets outside till they were over. Presumably he did not switch the set off in deference to the rest of his family. This 'defeatist' attitude was roundly condemned by most listeners, who were more concerned about the call sign.

Since the ringing of church bells was to be the signal that German invasion had begun the sound of Bow Bells could no longer be used between programmes. For a while the ticking of a clock was substituted. This was abominated by many. It seemed heavy with menace, almost an *Appointment With Fear*. 'Is this ghastly and depressing tick tock meant to represent Hitler driving nails into our coffin?' protested F. Butterfield of Bexhill-on-Sea. Alternative suggestions were not lacking. One listener suggested the Second Movement of Haydn's 'Clock' Symphony and another 'the roar of the British lion or perhaps the barking of a bulldog'.

There is a temptation to dismiss all this as trivial, but what it shows is that even before Dunkirk the British listener regarded the BBC as belonging to him in a very particular way, as a show that he expected a part of. The 'wireless' became almost one of the family, and what a listener heard on it took place in his home, among his family. In a pre-television age such a thing had never happened before and it is almost impossible to calculate the effect of it. Apart from keeping people in touch, the most obvious morale builder that radio could deploy was unalloyed entertainment. All manner of variety programmes proliferated, some using such well known names as Arthur Askey while others like Jack Warner made new reputations and yet others from the services, like Maurice Denham and Corporal Max Wall, got their first big chances.

Of all the shows none was more celebrated and popular than Tommy Handley's *It's That Man Again* (*ITMA*), a phrase first used by the *Daily Express* of Hitler. Though this show was not broadcast between February 1940 and June 1941 it was touring the country in a stage version for much of this time and forty-five minutes of the show were broadcast live from Manchester in May 1940, all of which was more than enough to keep it alive in the minds and affections of its devotees. When it returned it scaled peak after peak of new popularity. Handley was much given to intensive study of the newspapers even half an hour before a broadcast so that he might include breathtakingly topical gags. The show's writer, Ted Kavanagh, created over the years a wealth of comic characters whom, despite their craziness, the audience found instantly recognizable.

One of the very first of these was the Civil Servant 'Fusspot', whose repeated catchphrase was 'It's most irregular'. In a world of wartime restrictions listeners felt they knew him and were eager to share in the lampooning. Catchphrases were the other great feature of *ITMA*. To be able to use these in all manner of differing and even tragic situations revealed you as ready to be part of the nation-family. It is doubtful that such a show would have been successful before the war (indeed, in its pre-war guise it was not successful) but by using the English language, as Priestley too was to use it in a different radio context, it smashed down barriers. *ITMA*, with its *commedia dell'arte* style commentary on the war's progress and eccentricities, made variety acceptable to a much wider audience than the working class that had hitherto been its mainstay.

No figure of authority ever ventured criticisms of Tommy Handley. A girl singer of homely appearance, whose songs had to be transposed several keys down to accommodate her low voice and who was really happy singing only slow numbers, was easier meat. Vera Lynn, an East End girl, had been discovered by Howard Thomas and in late 1941 she was given a programme of her own called *Sincerely Yours*, her unmistakable style coming from her own vibrant sincerity. She was very soon a success with the troops and seen by *Women's Illustrated* as 'a symbol of all the things we are fighting for'. Others did not see it that way.

Just as 'Bomber' Harris protested about Rattigan's realistic portrayal of the fears of aircrew in *Flare Path*, so the notion grew that her sentimental songs might make the troops homesick, weaken their martial spirit and make them desert *en masse*. The BBC Board of Governors minute that observed '*Sincerely Yours* deplored, but popularity noted' was at least more circumspect than Earl Winterton who, throwing Tory chivalry to the winds, grumbled about 'the caterwauling of an inebriated cockatoo'. Even Vernon Bartlett, the Independent MP who as a journalist should have known better, wrote about 'the sentimental sloppy muck in the Forces Programme'. Though at one time she received a thousand letters a week seeking advice on service matters as well as personal problems, such critics did not consider that she aided the war effort. During the general election the aftermath of such disapproval had not been dispelled. In his campaign at Walthamstow West Charles Curran, the Conservative candidate, dismissed the Left as being 'led by Vera Lynn politicians who believed wishing would make their dreams come true', the last phrase being a reference to one of her songs.

Less contentious were such radio entertainments as *Workers' Playtime*, an unsophisticated variety half hour, and *Music While You Work*, which was no more than its name suggests. *Works Wonders* was a variety programme put on by the workers themselves in their factory surroundings. Minister of Labour Ernest Bevin approved of all of these, as did Minister of Aircraft Production Lord Beaverbrook, not because they thought that music or laughter was good for factory workers but because the shows were seen solely as an aid to increased production. Though *Workers' Playtime* could attract such topline names as Tommy Handley, Jack Warner and Arthur Askey, they were never popular with professionals. The nature of their business usually decreed late nights but a show from a factory involved arriving there at eight am to be ready for lunchtime. If the factory were at all remote artists and technicians were flown there, which involved an even earlier start. Yet the show was so popular it was soon being transmitted three times a week. Basil Dean told J. B. Priestley that there were 120 concert parties entertaining war workers in every part of the country.

Wartime broadcasting was more than just music and laughter, however. There were, for instance, documentary and drama. Drama tended to be weak and consisted to a great extent of adaptations from stage successes and current film releases, which appeared to have no adverse effect on cinema box office. A radio version of *Next Of Kin* was one of the first to be adapted and in January 1945, with a timing many must have considered apt, *Love On The Dole* was broadcast.

Radio documentary was more distinguished and covered a very wide field. It included *Shadow of the Swastika*, a dramatized history of the Gestapo as anti-enemy propaganda, or the patriotic *The*

Story Of The Hurricane. The Features Department, which put these programmes out, also favoured 'Celebrations'. One wonders that so much could be found to celebrate in wartime. After Russia's entry into the war Red Army Day on 7 November was regularly 'celebrated' on BBC radio, with articles backing up the programme in the *Radio Times.* 'Assistance rather than our admiration is what they want,' declared that journal in 1942. They got both.

Nearer home, the National Fire Service was also 'celebrated', the programme mounted in its honour being written and in large part performed by NFS personnel themselves. This was all part of the campaign to bring the 'ordinary man' into the studio. It was no longer enough to be a listener. He must emulate the title of the *Radio Times* gossip page and be 'both sides of the microphone'. This had really begun as early as June 1940 when a series called *Go To It*, introduced by Herbert Morrison, had first brought all sorts of workers to the microphone to talk in a manner that would help increase production. Other programmes such as *In Britain Now* copied the idea and in no time the notion got about that demotic English was the simple key to evincing the common touch.

Brendan Bracken, the Minister of Information in 1942, conceived the idea that a news announcer who did not use received pronunciation would be just the thing and accordingly the choice fell on Wilfred Pickles of the BBC Northern Region. His salary was increased to £800 per annum. It was also considered that no German would be able to imitate Pickles's Yorkshire accent. Many people in and about the BBC seemed obsessed with the fear that Germans would impersonate their announcers and fool them with false news. In the event Pickles's first news bulletin contained no greater cultural shock than the 'Good neet' he signed off with, and before long he returned to the Northern Region and a comedy programme.

The fear of German announcers had no doubt originated with the considerable success of William Joyce, whose sneering tones soon had him dubbed 'Lord Haw-Haw'. Early in the war, when many people had found themselves separated from their carefully acquired gramophone records, there had been many complaints about the poor quality of the music to be heard on the BBC. This separation, incidentally, gave rise to record requests and, when coupled with messages to parted friends and family, gave birth inadvertently to the strange new trade of what came to be called disc-jockey. Many of the then musically deprived declared that they

listened to German stations for good music. Soon they were
listening to more than music.

William Joyce had flirted before the war with Mosley's Blackshirts and now was happy to broadcast anti-British news bulletins
from Hamburg. He had millions of British listeners, some of whom
claimed in traditional British style that they wanted to hear the
other fellow's point of view while others reckoned he was as
good as a comedian. The BBC did not find him funny and sought
a way to counter his siren song. On the Forces Programme they
responded with Gracie Fields and Vera Lynn or comedy programmes such as *Hi Gang* featuring the Americans Bebe Daniels
and Ben Lyon, who were careful to announce in advance that their
BBC fees would go to war charities. At the same time the Home
Service sought to deflect Haw-Haw's appeal by putting on after
the popular nine o'clock news a pep-talk from some well known
name, which consequently was known as the *Postscript*. One of the
first to try was Norman Birkett, the famous advocate, who soon
abandoned his first pseudonym of 'Onlooker' and then the task
itself, claiming that many of Haw-Haw's criticisms of English life
as revealed, for instance, by the evacuation scheme and unemployment were perfectly valid and unanswerable. His successor, J. B.
Priestley, was to find a way to answer them and carve a new reputation into the bargain.

Already influential in literature and the theatre, Priestley was by
no means a stranger to broadcasting. He had written the first novel
specially intended for the air *Let The People Sing* and readings
from it had begun as war broke out. On St George's Day 1940 he
had broadcast a special programme called *A New English Journey*,
which even then had evoked an enthusiastic response from listeners.
'You cannot give us too much of J. B. Priestley,' declared one. The
Postcripts had begun just before, in March, and that verdict was
soon everywhere endorsed. He spoke without affectation in down
to earth tones a world away from the oratory and rhetoric of
Churchill, which were winning plaudits at the same time. Churchill
spoke defiance but Priestley dealt in doggedness that did not, however, exclude looking forward to a better world. While Churchill
spoke in defence of the old ways Priestley was one of the first to
ruminate about what the new ways should be and which of the
traditions should be discarded.

His audience grew to over twenty million, few of whom would

hear anything against him. When it looked as though he might be in trouble, they sprang to his defence. The first hint of trouble came with the broadcast of 28 July, 1940, when Priestley remarked: 'Among bundles of very friendly letters just lately I've been getting some very fierce and angry ones telling me to get off the air before the Government "Puts you where you belong" – the real Fascist touch. Well, obviously it wouldn't matter much if I were taken off the air.' Immediately letters flooded into Broadcasting House. 'J. B. Priestley tells us that some miserable persons want you to put him off the air. I beg of you to do nothing so devastating,' implored Katherine Lewis of Hereford, while a listener in Wilmslow was more belligerent: 'If J. B. Priestley is allowed to go off the air the whole BBC should be clapped in jail on the grounds of doing an action certain to cause despondency.'

This suspicion of what the BBC might be planning, though Priestley had not accused them, was well grounded. When he began a new series of *Postcripts* in January 1941 Sir Richard Maconachie, who was Director of Talks, seemed able only to note that Priestley was unpopular with Right-wing MPs, who had nobody to match him. After the sixth talk in the new series he was stopped. Neither the BBC nor the Ministry of Information was ready to take responsibility for this action and each blamed the other, but the relevant BBC minutes record unequivocally: 'Priestley series stopping . . . on instructions of Minister.'

An American ex-boxer and journalist, Quentin Reynolds, also achieved fame in the *Postscript* spot by apostrophising Hitler as Mr Schicklgrüber. He had been discovered by Harry Watt, for whom he recorded the commentary to *London Can Take It*. His instantly recognizable and husky voice that delighted listeners was also created by Watt who, fearing his audience would be deafened, persuaded Reynolds to whisper into a microphone held close to his enormous chest.

Almost as popular as Priestley because of his earthy no nonsense delivery in a plummy baritone was the 'Radio Doctor', Charles Hill. No doubt familiar with the British obsession for regular movements, he would boom about bowels and make jokes about prunes being black-coated workers. He seemed such a jovial sort, just the kind of friendly doctor you would hope to find in a National Health Service that people were increasingly talking about. Nobody then guessed of his implacable hostility to such a scheme and the trouble he was to cause Aneurin Bevan who, as Minister of Health, was to make it a reality. His seemed to be plain speaking of another sort and cheap at the price of £5 for a five minute talk after the *Kitchen Front*.

Unquestionably there was a widespread desire for education, but the pre-war Reithian concept of education in broadcasting, a conventional classroom approach, was no longer enough. The well educated few could no longer go on simply addressing the many in a formal way. In the early part of the war this didactic approach had revealed itself in the broadcasting of inter-unit spelling bees and even tongue-twisting bees. Something more was needed. Dr C. E. M. Joad, a pre-war pacifist and Left-wing philosopher at Birkbeck College and destined to find radio celebrity himself, declared in an interview in July 1942: 'A robust and honest student curiosity has awakened in the most lively sense throughout the community.' Scattered about the world, fighting for something better than had gone before, the BBC's listeners did not only want to know what their countrymen were doing. They wanted to know what they were thinking as well. This implied discussion, and in September 1942 A. D. Lindsay, the Master of Balliol, in a broadcast talk denied that democracy was government by voting and asserted that it was government by discussion.

There were still those who wanted pure learning, like 'A Soldier in Cornwall', who in January 1942 suggested 'that you broadcast lessons in the Russian language. Whichever way the war in the East goes, a working knowledge of Russian is essential.' But the typical educational programme for servicemen relayed by the BBC was represented by *Radio Reconnaissance*. This began on 4 February, 1941, after consultation between the BBC and educational experts of the three services. Listening to the programme, which went out every Tuesday and Thursday, was officially recognized in Army Orders as a desirable part of the training of any fighting man. Thus it coincided with the creation of that other reconnaissance of citizenship, the Army Bureau of Current Affairs. The programmes included a short commentary on the news that was usually given by Commander Stephen King-Hall, a veteran of the Battle of Jutland, which was followed by a talk often as part of a series. A typical one was *Science And The Fighting Man* by Ritchie (later Lord) Calder, the popular science writer. Information was often presented to stimulate discussion after each broadcast in true ABCA style. The programme on the controversial sinking of the *Bismarck* provided a topic till long after 'lights out' in one unit, whose 600 men were always paraded for the broadcasts.

Another discussion programme was specifically aimed at 'the fifteen to eighteen age group' before the teenager had been invented. This was *To Start You Talking*, first broadcast in October 1942, which was as much the Year of Discussion as it was the Year of Beveridge. *To Start You Talking* used dramatised situations to illustrate the problems being debated. These included sex equality, full employment, class distinction and town planning. The series was still going strong three years later and a selection of the programmes was published in book form just before the general election. Though young people were certainly interested and active in that election as never before, neither the programme nor the book was likely to have appealed to young people alone.

The greatest discussion programme of all was the *Brains Trust*. This was conceived as a panel of three regular and two guest experts, airing their learning and knowledge informally by answering questions from the public on all manner of subjects. It was the great thirst for knowledge and information among servicemen that had first prompted BBC researchers to suggest such a programme. The three regular Brains Trusters were Dr C. E. M. Joad, Professor Julian Huxley and Commander Campbell. Joad introduced a new broadcasting catchphrase 'It depends what you mean by – ' and much of his popularity was due to this philosophical gambit. The mere fact that it was so popular indicates the serious approach of those who sought for answers, an attitude that was to be so noticeable among the electorate in 1945. The 'question master', a title the *Brains Trust* invented, was Donald McCullough, who till then was mainly known for providing the text for a book of pre-war cartoons by *Punch* artist Fougasse. He was to stand unsuccessfully as the Conservative candidate for King's Lynn in 1945.

The first *Brains Trust* was broadcast on New Year's Day 1941 and scheduled for a six-week run. It so exactly hit the need of the moment and met such instant popularity that it ran for eighteen months without a break, during which time its length was increased by fifteen minutes and a repeat transmission during the week was introduced. Joad and Campbell did not miss a session, though ill health caused Huxley to miss a few. Though the programme had world wide appeal and was sent out on Eastern and Pacific short waves and was then re-transmitted by Australia, its greatest popularity and influence was within the British Isles, where its audience rose from one to eleven and a half million. Imitation Brains Trusts sprang up all over the place, in village halls, in schools, in Army camps. There was even a mid-Atlantic Brains Trust aboard a troopship. Brains Trusts were a form of discussion that particularly recommended itself to the forces. In January 1942 Joad took part in such a Forces' Brains Trust run by a battalion of the Royal Ulster Rifles, which was subsequently broadcast.

A year later the idea was taken a step further by the BBC with a *Listeners' Brains Trust*, in which the Brains Trust team asked the questions and listeners as personified by 'an entertainer, a soldier, a housewife, a business man and a factory worker' supplied the answers in 'exactly the same conditions as those observed by the original *Brains Trust* itself'. The representative 'soldier' on this occasion was Sergeant Eric Ford, who was chosen because he had done well in his unit's own Brains Trust and because he was conveniently near the BBC at the Hyde Park Anti-Aircraft Site. He was amused that the producer Howard Thomas, no doubt following the current fashion for representative types and demotic English, considered that he did not sound enough like most people's idea of a sergeant. Thomas asked him if he could not get a lower class burr, or at least some kind of regional accent, into his precise teacher's English.

The *Brains Trust* very nearly destroyed the old style of debating society and most public meetings soon adopted a Brains Trust style. In September 1942 the *Radio Times* was boasting that on a recent count no fewer than five Brains Trust-style meetings were advertised in the same week's issue of the *New Statesman*. The number certainly did not abate in the weeks before the election. The success of the BBC's own *Brains Trust*, however, proved its own undoing and soon those who had silenced Priestley moved in to emasculate this latest threat to the old ways. First, the type of question was more strictly regulated, discussion of politics being forbidden. Then, since it was considered that the regular trio of Joad, Huxley and Campbell were having too much influence among the forces, they were used only one at a time, authority not quite daring to sack the lot. It was the beginning of the end of the programme's popularity, but it was too late to take away the people's own Brains Trusts.

This kind of tampering with popular programmes may have been the reason why George Orwell, who briefly worked for the BBC, based the *1984* Ministry of Truth on the Corporation, as he later confessed to Malcolm Muggeridge. It did not go unnoticed, least of all in Parliament, where in 1944 many felt that a great era of broadcasting had reached its zenith in 1942 and that the attempt to restore authoritarian control as victory drew near was to be deplored and resisted. In July 1944, during a debate on the Ministry of Information's role, almost all adverse criticism was centred on the BBC. A Conservative Member, the aptly named Captain Plugge, made one of the earliest pleas for commercial broadcasting in this country and the Liberal Tom Horabin roundly accused the BBC of emasculating politics. 'The BBC has what it calls political programmes,' he said, 'but whenever I have listened to them I have found that they were politics in the abstract. People talk learnedly about Socialism, Liberalism or Toryism in a way that does not mean anything to the people at all and does not touch their lives in any shape or form.'

Less than a year later, during the campaign, politicians and BBC alike were able to put this declaration to the test in what *Time And Tide* was to call 'The Microphone Election'. Broadcasting had become so important to the nation by 1945 that it was quite impossible for politicians seeking election to ignore it. Although there were no election broadcasts during the week the country went to the polls, there were party political broadcasts every night, Sundays excepted, for most of June. They lasted for between twenty and thirty minutes in the peak listening spot immediately after the nine o'clock news. The two main parties had ten broadcasts each and the Liberals had four. Both the Communist and Common Wealth Parties were allocated one each. Labour's final broadcast was made not by Attlee but Morrison, who had written the manifesto and organized Labour's campaign.

The only one of all these speeches that is remembered today is the first one of Churchill's, which many at the time considered did more than anything to rob the Conservatives of victory. This was the occasion when he spoke of Socialism necessarily being maintained 'by some form of Gestapo'. A Conservative-inclined colonel on General Eisenhower's staff protested at 'Churchill's trying to tell me officers I've been working with for years, decent capable men whose potentialities I know, are about to erect a Gestapo

machinery because they're Socialists. I know it to be nonsense.'
There were many more like him.

There was another aspect too. Churchill's style was declamatory
and oratorical, of the old school, fine for defying ruthless dictators,
though even in his heyday many found the delivery melodramatic
or even comical. Harold Nicolson thought Churchill a poor performer on the air and was shocked that his famous 'We shall never
surrender' peroration was almost word for word the same speech
that he had made earlier that day in the House of Commons, and
more poorly spoken. Many Churchill supporters thought that the
fire and gusto departed to a considerable extent from the wireless
speeches after the turning point of the war, once people had begun
to look ahead to the fruits of victory. Undoubtedly tired, the old
man revealed marked lack of enthusiasm for broadcasting and by
1945 he could not hope to produce the new and natural fireside
chat style as pioneered by Priestley and to which Attlee, while
somewhat less than inspiring, came much closer. Where Churchill
exhorted people, Attlee made them feel they had something to
contribute.

7

Calling In The Experts

'The day war broke out,' remembers a resident at the Hans Crescent Hotel in Knightsbridge, 'we all went down into the cellar, where they'd set up a bar. Wet blankets were hung up all round the windows, expecting a gas attack or something. We heard the siren go and I think we heard a plane. We were all slightly a-tremble and we were all knocking back large gins and tonics.' Luckily it was a false alarm. It was the beginning of the phoney war, of inadequate air raid precautions, of propaganda leaflet raids on Germany, of the blind faith in blockading Hitler's economy and sending a British Expeditionary Force to France. Our political and military leaders were slow to get the measure of events.

This was the Blimps' war. In the grip of tradition, they had no grasp of the situation. Their ideas were washed up on the beaches of Dunkirk, leaving Britain at its most vulnerable. It was saved a few months later by the youngest of the three fighting services, the RAF. Yet victory in the Battle of Britain did not belong only to the few, the young men who flew the Spitfires and Hurricanes. It was a victory for technology, for the designers, the engineers, the mechanics who made and kept these single-seater fighters flying. The triumph was shared, too, by the back-room boys who worked on one of the most closely guarded secrets of the war: radar. This 'radio detection and ranging' system tracked the approach of Goering's Luftwaffe and enabled the precious aircraft that we had to be profitably deployed. Details of it were not officially released until 15 August, 1945, the last day of the war. In September 1940 it was one of the new ideas victorious in the skies over Britain. Youth and science gave the nation that vital breathing space without which our land turning point of El Alamein and the rest of the war would have been impossible.

The RAF was the modern service. A sergeant who volunteered

for a pilot's job in 1939, failed on his eyesight and spent the war
setting up and operating radar stations found it

> very democratic, right from the first. There certainly wasn't
> as much tradition as in the Army. I think the officers tended to
> come from university rather than upper class military families.
> Technical know-how was what counted.

A Flight Lieutenant had a similar experience:

> The war saw the weakening of the public school influence. In the
> RAF technical and managerial ability was becoming more im-
> portant than one's background. We had one man who had been
> the 'Boots' in a public school and became a very respected
> Flying Officer.

The young Battle of Britain pilot Richard Hillary, shot down,
badly burned, and patched up by the great plastic surgeon Archibald
McIndoe, was entitled to ask during 1941 in *The Last Enemy*:

> Was there perhaps a new race of Englishmen arising out of this
> war, a race of men bred by the war, a harmonious synthesis of
> the governing class and the great rest of England: that synthesis
> of disparate backgrounds and upbringings to be seen at its most
> obvious best in the RAF squadrons? While they were now
> possessed of no other thought than to win the war, yet having
> won it, would they this time refuse to step aside and remain in-
> different to the peacetime fate of the country, once again leave
> government to the old governing class? I thought it possible.
> Indeed, the process might be said to have already begun. They
> now had as their representative Churchill, a man of initiative,
> determination, and no Party. But they would not always have
> him; and what then? Would they not see to it that there arose
> from their fusion representatives, not of the old gang, deciding
> at Lady Cufuffle's that Henry should have the Foreign Office
> and George the Ministry of Food, nor figureheads for an angry
> but ineffectual Labour Party, but true representatives of the new
> England that should emerge from this struggle?

The Germans were thought of as a scientific enemy. Against them
we were led by the classically educated who had muddled along,
drifted into war and made a hopeless mess of waging it. This was
the theme of *Science In War*, a Penguin Special brought out by
twenty-five anonymous scientists in mid-1940, that period of
national self-criticism. People like Solly Zuckerman, a zoologist
specializing in apes, and Professor J. D. Bernal, a Communist

physicist, offered specific criticisms on the conduct of the war and general comments on the traditional ways of doing things. They argued for a rational, matter-of-fact approach to many problems. There was plenty to be critical about.

From the autumn of 1940 the bombing of London and other cities showed up the weaknesses of air raid precautions, shelters and medical services. Among other things the Government advised everybody to set aside one spare room – how many had one? – to be kept gas-proof. The solid-looking brick boxes called 'surface shelters' were repeatedly condemned as unsafe and useless by a Communist biologist, Professor J. B. S. Haldane, whose *Air Raid Precautions* had been a Left Book Club choice in 1938 and who was also chairman of the *Daily Worker* editorial board. In its ignorance the Government itself had to seek help. David Stark Murray of the Socialist Medical Association:

> When it became clear that Hitler meant business the Government came to us for advice on how to deal with gas and bomb casualties. Because we were the ones who knew. We'd already been at the business end of Hitler's bombs. The SMA set up Spanish Medical Aid Committees during the Civil War. It was one of our members who took the first ambulance to Spain from here. We set up the first blood transfusion service there. We had people like Haldane with us, who was able to lecture on gas and explosives. All this was indirect propaganda for a more efficient national organization of medical services.

The SMA concerned itself not only with bombing questions but also with nutrition, the effects of evacuation on children and the dangers of tuberculosis. The incidence of TB, which had been falling annually up to 1939, rose during the first year of the war. In reporting on this the SMA delved into industrial conditions and related social and financial problems that had to be tackled. A long memorandum on the whole subject of nutrition was sent to the Minister of Food, outlining the dangers of malnutrition and calling for adequate diets for pregnant women, children, adolescents, the sick, and industrial workers. The arguments were supported by convincing figures from scientific sources in many countries. Nor were the arguments confined to memoranda. With paper scarce, public propaganda was intensified by meetings. In one year Stark Murray addressed no fewer than a hundred.

Most of the criticism came from young scientists, whose views had been formed in the thirties. Some of them were Jewish refugees from Hitler. Not unnaturally, they tended to be Left-wing and had perhaps come together in pre-war science groups formed under the aegis of the Left Book Club. A typical selection of them was to be found on Sunday mornings at Malvern College in Worcestershire, where the Telecommunications Research Establishment was evacuated to carry on undisturbed with its vital radar work. In the superintendent's office there was a free-for-all discussion in which anybody, irrespective of rank or status, could join in to help solve an operational problem. The meetings, dubbed 'Sunday Soviets', were a lively opportunity for young boffins to put their ideas across and get noticed.

Radar was the prime example of the new devices that were so complicated that scientists had to be called from their laboratories to help work out the best methods of operation. The new devices in fact made possible warfare of a different kind and scientists found themselves involved in matters that would have previously been thought the exclusive province of the brasshats. This helped advance the view put forward in *Science In War* that scientific methods should be applied in the general conduct of the war. 'University types in flannel bags' began to apply operational research techniques to non-technical subjects, defining objectives, collecting facts and figures, evaluating, deciding the most efficient use of available resources. One of their early jobs was Ack-Ack Command, where legend has it that their researches revealed a spare man in every team for a particular type of gun. Historical investigation showed that his duty was to hold the lieutenant's horse.

The science involved in operational research was in fact fairly simple, yet its application was far-reaching. As the war effort became increasingly technical so operational research units became an established part of it. Their new ways of looking at and doing things showed the practical weaknesses and inefficiencies of tradition. They achieved results and more than justified their existence. Their numbers and importance grew as the decisions became bigger and the consequences of failure more catastrophic. From applying the techniques to tackling the U-Boat menace it was but a short step to wondering why they could not be used in the daily fight against poverty, disease and ignorance. The idea of efficiency investigations was not new. What was new was that they were applied to the benefit not of the producer but of the consumer, in wartime the Services, whose needs were paramount. As one worker in the field put it: 'Operational research is different in intention from market research or mass observation, because of its responsibility for the consumer's interest.' This had its peacetime implications too.

Pre-war capitalism, with its 'huge vested interests in destruction, waste and disease', had been called by Shaw 'Breakages, Limited'. Even making allowance for Shavian exaggeration this kind of system was ill-equipped to combat Hitler's orderly state-backed economic order. At the beginning of the war we got by on a mixture of muddle and hard driving by men like Lord Beaverbrook, who made spectacular buccaneering raids on one industry after another to pep up production. A Government inspector once had occasion to query the price of screws being produced by the Goldsmiths' and Silversmiths' Company. The unit price was so much higher than run of the mill screws that they might have been made of gold or silver. Accordingly the inspector visited the company's Regent Street offices to make enquiries. He was ushered by a flunkey over a deep piled carpet, up several flights of stairs to an attic where an old boy with a lathe was carefully turning out individual screws. The inspector decided on the spot that, serious though the war effort was, we could do without this individual contribution. Beaverbrook's was essentially a short term approach, extracting the immediate maximum from the existing system to get the aircraft we badly needed at the time. People worked all the hours God sent and not necessarily the most efficiently. It soon became clear that some other system was needed.

Companies were registered for production and the Government stepped in to control the supply of machines, material, men and money. To get what they wanted companies had to go through procedures. If a man wanted to leave a key job his case had to go before a tribunal. There were permits for supplies of raw materials. The supply of plant was a problem. Companies could not go out and buy it. It was allocated by the Ministry of Supply. Managing directors had to go along and fight for what they wanted, argue about meeting the targets laid down for them. Planning, statistics and controls were the order of the day.

The Civil Service became involved in industry; businessmen and trade unionists were co-opted into the Civil Service. Full time trade union officials were useful on the staff of the Ministry of Labour

for their knowledge of particular industries or problems. In their
new jobs they often found themselves dealing with old colleagues.
Even Lord Beaverbrook had Jack Stephenson, general secretary
of the Plumbers', Glaziers' and Domestic Engineers' Union, on his
staff at the Ministry of Aircraft Production. Not that it was a
simple matter of the newcomers teaching the Civil Service its new
job. The Civil Service was slow to begin with but when it was
geared up it was a well oiled machine that worked efficiently.
Though the permanent officials often did not grasp the importance
of technical issues in some fundamental decisions, they were able
to help industry do its job in many ways. One industrialist's experience was common: 'Before the war the company made small
profits and the rate of investment was small. When you had to go
to the Ministry of Supply for plant you went for good stuff. We
got all sorts of machine tools – on hire or with a grant – that we'd
never have afforded before the war. One was able to get the
technical point of view put across. It was accepted. In this way the
Ministry stimulated technology. Money became a secondary consideration.'

Above all the job had to be done. People learned to work far
longer, in a sense enjoying it. They were doing something. Morale
was high. A managing director in the engineering industry:

> One of the main reasons was that managements were going round
> saying: 'Look, you haven't applied for this job as supervisor . . .
> Oh, come on. You can do it. It's more pay. Come on. We need
> you.' We were searching for talent, as were most factories. Try-
> ing to get people to take on a greater level of responsibility. We
> were pulling them up all the time. Everybody felt wanted. There
> were promotion prospects. Able people who wouldn't have had
> the chance before came forward. Anybody who had the talent
> was used. Ideas were welcomed. Suggestion schemes blossomed
> in factories. Both employers and employees were more interested.
> Awards were made. People felt proud. They had made a con-
> tribution. In normal circumstances they would have kept back.

Here were the beginnings of a new employer/employee relationship, seen perhaps at its best in the Glacier Metal Company, which
made bearings for vehicles and weapons but was better known for
its enlightened outlook. At the outbreak of war a thirty-one year
old Scot, Wilfred Brown, had just become chairman and managing
director:

We started the basis of our new management methods right in the war. That was the stimulus. You had to get people with you. You just had to make them understand what it was all about. There was plenty of patriotic fervour about but it got misdirected unless there was some sort of forum in which you could really get the point across. We had been a very bad company before the war, treated labour very badly. I had grown up in it. I had some backlog to catch up on. I had to create some goodwill.

When Bevin insisted that all companies set up Joint Consultative Committees I knew this was useless because negotiations were excluded from it. The real negotiations – pay and conditions – were done by the shop stewards committee. The JCCs were a by-pass. In 1941 we set up a body that dealt with everything on a unanimous voting basis. We couldn't make any change in the company unless people agreed. This proved extremely effective. Representatives of the people in the plant agreed and then things happened. We got on with it. It was a democratic company. There may have been others doing it but one was rather isolated, so damned busy. There were no conferences going on to exchange ideas.

Wilfred Brown, in spite of getting an MBE for his efforts in civilian war production, later admitted he felt sensitive about not being in uniform. He also had to stop some of his key men rushing into it. Like all the others doing a vital job in civvies they need not have worried.

Scientists too were becoming more interested in society. They could see around them the devastation, suffering and unhappiness that the perversion of science was causing and in response were becoming more socially responsible. Lancelot Hogben, author of two of the best-selling primers for the Age of Plenty, *Mathematics For The Million* and *Science For The Citizen*, was always trying to get Kingsley Martin, editor of the *New Statesman*, to make his readers more aware of new technological possibilities. In an angry private letter, written in 1937, Hogben argued: 'The central problem of social spring-cleaning at the moment is how to replace the literary-legal intelligentsia of old school tie socialism by a technical "expertensia" in tune with the social aspirations of the salaried middle class . . .' He went on: 'But you won't do it, because fundamentally, my dear Kingsley, you and your entourage expect your readers to pick up an elusive reference to the seventh mistress of a seventeenth century minor French poet, and refuse to reckon with the fact that hundreds of people who don't give a damn for your French poet or his mistress know much more about a kilowatt, a calorie or a bacteriophage than you do.'

Come the war, this was even more so as Hyman Levy, a Marxist professor of mathematics with a humanitarian interest in science and society, stated:

> Hundreds of thousands of young men and women have been drawn from the shelter of their homes, where their contact with science was the mere switching on of an electric light or the turning of a knob of the wireless. Today these same young men and women are attending lectures in mathematics and science, predicting weather conditions, understanding and handling the most complicated apparatus in connexion with gunnery and aircraft. Delicate processes are being carried through by them in factory and workshop. They have become technically minded and operationally skilled. We are building up a population for the new scientific and technical age with terrific rapidity. Young men and women are pouring out of the universities into research and testing institutions, eager to play a part in the new fields that have been opened up to them. The significant point is that we have added to our population of highly skilled mechanics a vast population of technicians, while at the same time we have multiplied the size of our scientific profession.

Like Richard Hillary's young RAF types, these people were a new social and political force, as some of their betters were ready to acknowledge. C. H. Waddington, zoologist and operational researcher, said in his Pelican *The Scientific Attitude*, written just before and after Dunkirk and published in 1941: 'If power were to be in the hands of those best able to use it sensibly, nine-tenths of it would go to the offspring of the middle and lower classes. In a scientific society, "power would be in the hands of the people." ' But under our existing educational system, weighted in favour of the upper classes and the classics, these people were the least able to develop their abilities. Their intellectual potential was wasted. To Sir Lawrence Bragg, who in comparative ease at the age of twenty-four had shared a Nobel Prize with his father, the hardest post-war problem was going to be to convince our political leaders and civil servants of the place of science in the new world. They had to be re-educated.

From early on in the war scientists were discussing the kind of

peacetime world they wanted. In 1941 many of them assembled at
the Royal Institution in London for an international three-day
conference on *Science And World Order* 'to demonstrate the common purpose of men of science in ensuring a post-war order in
which the maximum benefits of science will be secured for all
people'. The audience was notably young and Left-wing. For their
model of a scientific society they often looked to the Soviet Union,
where it seemed that co-operation had replaced competitive chaos
and a Plan had succeeded. There poverty did not exist amidst
plenty, shortages were not artifically induced and wealth was not
wasted. The scientist had a status in society. His discoveries were
welcomed and put to work for the good of mankind as a whole.
Was not this the international brotherhood of man, a world in
which science knew no frontiers? Or as Professor Hyman Levy
asked at an Association of Scientific Workers conference in 1943:
'Where indeed would we be today were it not for the planned economy and the planned science of the Soviet Union and its Red Army
thrown with all its tremendous power into the scales on the side of
world emancipation?'

At the same conference a professor to whom politics were an
unwelcome responsibility felt that 'scientists should not only influence legislators from the outside but that they should also be
of and among the legislators, influencing legislation in Parliament
itself. Science affects the community not only in material ways but
also in the mental and spiritual spheres, and it has both a right and
a duty to claim a place alongside the Established Church in the
Upper House of Parliament. If bishops can be life peers why not
scientists?' This was one side of the interminable argument whether
the expert should be on top or on tap.

Health was a major subject in which they were prepared to weigh
in with scientific evidence. They had seen the Germans promote
Strength Through Joy and create at least the physical impression
of a better people. When it came to checking Britain against known
health standards we compared badly with other democracies, let
alone our enemy. In terms of the general death and infant mortality
rates we were worse off than Australia, New Zealand (both new
Dominions with Socialist governments) and the Scandinavian
countries. A pre-war survey by Sir John Boyd Orr had shown
that nearly half the population of the British Isles was to some
degree inadequately nourished. Writing in the first issue of *Picture*

Post for 1941, an issue devoted to A Plan For Britain, one of our best known scientists, Julian Huxley, boldy emphasised two unfortunate facts: 'Children are the greatest single cause of poverty in this country. And children suffer most in their health from poverty.'

From this Huxley went on to develop arguments for family allowances and for a positive health, as opposed to a disease, service based upon the family. Under a real family and population policy health centres would be created in which the full benefits of medical science would be available to everybody. So strongly did this idea develop that within two years Beveridge was to make the assumption in his Report that after the war 'a comprehensive national health service will ensure that for every citizen there is available whatever medical treatment he requires, in whatever form he requires it, domiciliary or institutional, general, specialist or consultant'.

Yet when experts were dealing with people who were not in strictly scientific situations they were less expert. Housing and the environment were a case in point. Writing in the same issue of *Picture Post*, the young architect and planner Maxwell Fry envisaged an attack on the slums and a bold building plan to civilize our industrial towns in twenty years or less. 'The main roads of the country can be tree-lined parkways, even into Wigan – yes, and right through it . . . Planning can eliminate waste in other ways by cutting out needless streets and regrouping buildings in communities, as has been done at Leeds and Liverpool, though not as yet on a large enough scale.' Instead of jerry-built streets with no gardens and not enough light and air new flats would stand in a park. Courts and alleys would be swept away. This clean-sweep planning appealed to the tidy, efficient mind at the drawing board, but it was not what the people wanted.

Arnold Whittick, a specialist in modern architectural history and planning who during the course of the war spoke to something like a quarter of a million people in all three services, always welcomed questions and discussion after his lectures:

Where they expressed their views mostly was on the type of house they wanted. They had a feeling that they deserved good accommodation. It was a very practical concern they had: better housing. They were very insistent on a fair degree of privacy: a house with a garden. They didn't like the idea of flats. That was a universal feeling. During a discussion on the relative merits of the flat and one-family house one man said to me: 'What are we fighting for?' After I had given my reply, he said: 'We're fighting for freedom, aren't we?' I then said: 'You mean the one-family house means more freedom than the flat?', and many men called out 'Yes'.

Apart from a few meetings addressed by professors – Harold Laski on *The Place Of The Scientist In Post War Administration* and J. B. S. Haldane on *Engels' Contribution to Science* – science and technology were not specific issues in the election campaign. The Labour manifesto gave them a short paragraph and the Conservative declaration only a glancing reference. Since 1943 Group Captain Frank Whittle had pleaded that the jet engine he had invented should become public property but that never became a public issue. The general notion of planning was an important one though. It was summed up in the platform arguments about Mulberry Harbours, the pre-fabricated harbours towed across the Channel to help the Normandy landings of 1944. To the Conservatives they were a triumph for private enterprise; to Labour it was a fine example of what could be achieved with proper planning in the national interest.

More important than the specific argument were the new technological groups seen by Richard Hillary and described by Hyman Levy. In the 1935 election the Labour Party had spent a lot of time discussing the production of specially watered down propaganda for the deserts of suburbia. The 1945 election showed this was unnecessary. In her post-election Fabian pamphlet Margaret Cole declared: 'The "intermediate" people, the scientists and technicians, the middle and lower ranks of administrators, those who live in the £600 to £1,000 houses in the suburbs, have largely been converted, not by any propaganda specially designed for them, but by the march of events, to belief in the necessity of social planning, if the purposes of their own skills, no less than the welfare of humanity, are to be achieved.'

H. G. Wells, an early Fabian who had seen in science man's route to salvation, had reason to rejoice. Here at last appeared the kind of victory he had worked for. But he was a dying man, able only to rail at his foes. One of them was Churchill, who might not have admired the man but loved his science fiction and reckoned he could pass an examination in it. Just before Christmas 1944 H. G. Wells published in *Tribune* an article *Churchill Must Go*, with

The war forced people to live much of their lives in public. Those who needed help with urgent social problems (above) could go to a Citizens' Advice Bureau, which in Bath used a converted horse box as a mobile office. (Below) For people sheltering from the blitz in the London Underground, the long nights were whiled away by entertainers.

The outlook of women was enlarged. In the Services (above), many had their first taste of social and political education at ABCA sessions. In factories (below) they could share in the enthusiasm of making weapons for 'Uncle Joe' Stalin.

GREETINGS TO OUR ALLIES IN U.S.S.R.
Нашим Союзника

views so virulent that the editor pointed out in bold type that they were personal and not necessarily the paper's. One of the minor criticisms was that 'Winston Churchill, the present would-be British Fuehrer, is a person with a range of ideas limited to the adventures and opportunities of British political life. He has never given evidence of thinking extensively, or of any scientific or literary capacity. His ignorance of contemporary social and physical science is conspicuous, and so he is naturally a Fellow of that profoundly snobbish organization, the Royal Society'.

Labour's electoral victory brought Wells no lasting satisfaction. In the shadow of the atomic bomb the outlook for *Homo sapiens* was grave and tragic. At the end of his life, when he could see science more powerful than ever, the prophet was disillusioned. His mind was at the end of its tether, his faith gone. But others had found theirs.

8

A New Heaven And A New Earth

At the Chelmsford by-election of April 1945 a villager strung up a
banner: 'This is a fight between Christ and Churchill'. The message
was an extreme statement of a view held by many. In what had
been a comfortably held Conservative seat the opposition was
conducted by the Common Wealth Party with the fervour of a
crusade. This was the first by-election to be held in England on the
new electoral register that enfranchised those who had moved or
come of age since 1939. The victor was Wing Commander Ernest
Millington, before the war a Christian pacifist idealist, admirer of
George Lansbury and campaigner in favour of the Popular Front
against the Nazis, for which he was expelled from the Labour Party.
Yet he saw no contradiction in joining the Territorial Army after
Munich. Since then he had transferred to the RAF and taken part
in the first thousand bomber raid on Essen. Once he had crash
landed back at base with two engines on fire. When asked to come
to an adoption meeting at Chelmsford he said: 'Look, I'm a Wing
Commander in charge of a bomber squadron fighting a war. The
adoption committee will have to come to me.' He did not think
they would stand for it but they did. He met them at the station
and took them to a local hotel, where he announced: 'Look we're
operational and I have to take off with my squadron at three
o'clock.' There was a question and answer session that he cut
short by getting up, looking at his watch and saying: 'Sorry, but
I have an appointment with Hitler.' He went back and flew off with
his squadron, thinking his attitude would put them off but, no, they
were swept off their feet.

In all the pressures and enthusiasm of fighting the war he had
not lost his Christian idealism:

Common Wealth was non-Marxist, non-trade union and had a
great sort of Christian Socialist evangelical pull. Parsons liked it.
The founder of the movement, Sir Richard Acland, had a

brother-in-law who was a priest, the Reverend Joe McCulloch. Acland used to come out with great evangelical statements like 'What is morally wrong cannot be politically right'. This went over very big. The working classes loved it. In the campaign I had parson support. Very important in an area like that. Previously the Church of England had been 'the Conservative Party at prayer'. Not any more. Parsons had been at war, too. I think many felt that people must not have put aside Christian teaching to go and kill unless it were to create something better.

Perhaps that was why as soon as the general election was announced a few weeks later the Bishop of Chelmsford, Dr Henry Wilson, appealed to his clergy not to engage in it publicly. 'I feel clergy make a grave mistake when they attach themselves publicly to any political party,' he said, adding that it was 'unbecoming' for a clergyman to sit on a party platform. He went on in his *Diocesan Chronicle*: 'I have only ever once attended a political meeting and that was thirty-nine years ago. I left wondering how any sensible person could think it profitable to attend such a silly business.' These remarks earned him a place in the *New Statesman* This England column and this comment from one of his local papers: 'Isn't thirty-nine years ago rather behind the times?'

As a churchman he certainly was. His own church leaders had joined with others as recently as 1940 to express their thoughts on the 'Foundations of Peace'. Under this heading a Christmas letter had appeared in *The Times* signed by Archbishop Lang of Canterbury, Archbishop Temple of York, the Roman Catholic Archbishop of Westminster Cardinal Hinsley, and the Moderator of the Free Church Federal Council. These four churchmen listed five standards they believed should be adopted in the organization of society: extreme inequalities of wealth to be abolished; equal opportunities of education; social care to safeguard the family as a unit; restoring the sense of divine vocation to man's daily work; use and conservation of natural resources for all.

Their thoughts were intended to outlive the twelve days of Christmas 1940, at least as far as Archbishop Temple was concerned. Early in the New Year he was to chair a conference at Malvern College of clergy and laity to 'consider from the Anglican point of view what are the fundamental facts which are directly relevant to the ordering of the new society that is quite evidently emerging, and how Christian thought can be shaped to play a leading part in the reconstruction after the war is over'. On the third day of the conference Sir Richard Acland presented a paper denouncing the profit motive and claiming that 'Common Ownership' was a matter of fundamental Christian principle.

At that stage Temple was not prepared to be so definite. He summed up the deliberations of the Malvern Conference in his 'Findings', which attacked materialism, urged congregations to take part in social work and made a vague reference to the private ownership of industrial resources being a possible 'stumbling block' to the leading of a Christian life. Nevertheless his appointment a year later as Archbishop of Canterbury was to George Bernard Shaw 'a realized impossibility'. To the *Daily Herald* he was 'the Red Archbishop'. He was the only holder of that office known to have carried a Labour Party card. As the Bishop of Manchester in the twenties he had seen social distress at first hand and had tried to do something to alleviate it, playing a leading part in the Conference on Politics, Economics and Christianity (COPEC). In the 1930s as Archbishop of York he had carried on with this work, branching out into other causes. Tom Skeffington-Lodge, a radical Anglican born and bred in Wensleydale, where he shared the same governess with Richard Acland, was active in one of them: 'When the Spanish Civil War came on I felt very involved indeed and I feel I was privileged to be a member of the Yorkshire Committee for Spanish Relief, of which William Temple was the chairman. That committee was completely anti-Franco, although not ostensibly so. Its name implied that we were willing and anxious to help all sufferers in Spain as a result of the Civil War but there was a very heavy anti-Franco bias among all its members. Temple was quite open about it really.'

His background was well known to Churchill, who although not a practising churchman himself realized his responsibilities and took pains in selecting suitable men. As well as listening to Brendan Bracken, among other things an ecclesiastical tipster, he employed a full-time patronage secretary to wander about the country with his eyes and ears open for likely candidates. When Archbishop Lang resigned, Temple's appointment was not an ill-considered decision. Asked why he had made a Socialist Archbishop of Canterbury, Churchill replied: 'Because he was the only half-crown article in a sixpenny halfpenny bazaar.' Temple was the only candidate whose father had held the office.

Churchill soon had reason to regret his decision. A few months later the ninepenny Penguin Special *Christianity And Social Order* was on the bookstalls. Secure in office and having checked his text with Keynes, the economic philosopher of the New Deal, Temple was now more forthright. He openly advocated family allowances, better housing, holidays with pay and raising the school leaving age. Although he emphasised that he wrote as a private citizen, the Primate's prestige could not help rubbing off. The paperback sold some 140,000 copies.

He followed this with a series of public meetings in London and the provinces, attracting large crowds. His address championed the poor, the oppressed and the exploited, and demanded a fairer ordering of society in which all would have the opportunity to play a full and satisfying part in the life of the community. 'The old Archbishop, heaven knows, was foolish and wicked enough, but the new obese one is positively dangerous,' wrote 'Chips' Channon in his diary. 'He now openly preaches Socialism from a platform which he shares with Cripps – Is England mad, and doomed? But perhaps it is as well that the Revolution should come from the top, rather than the bottom.'

Though he suffered from gout and other ailments, he carried on spreading his gospel. Donald Soper was a co-speaker in the heart of Mammon: 'It was at a big open air rally in the City of London, almost at the corner of King William Street, in a bombed area, in ruins. The windows of the surrounding buildings were absolutely crammed with people listening. He was known then to be a supporter of Labour. His prestige was very high. That was probably the last public meeting he ever addressed.' He died suddenly in the autumn of 1944. There was a considerable sense of public loss. He was the outstanding ecclesiastical figure of the war, whose name was to be remembered like the popular chaplains of the First War. To many ordinary people he had a wonderful way of putting things. He expressed their aspirations for a better society.

Behind him at Canterbury Temple left the 'Red Dean', well known because of his support for Russia, the success of his Soviet Aid Fund and the popularity of his paean, *The Socialist Sixth Of The World*. Temple, who had known the Dean since they were contemporaries at Manchester in the twenties, never approved of his 'Redness'. To the Dean the Soviet Union was a great experiment in a new order of society, where a new attitude towards human life was the natural counterpart of the new economic morality. Capitalism outraged Christianity, making impossible the Christian demand for justice, freedom, a creative abundant life, and an ever-widening fellowship for each human soul. Looking back on him, one sympathetic churchman's verdict was: 'A very much more simple man than most thought. His flirtation with Communism was emotionally praiseworthy but intellectually it was pretty thin.' During the war, though, thousands fell under the spell of this tall, sincere Establishment figure. It was a simple faith. The heroic Soviet Union was the nearest thing to paradise on earth and they felt that what he said must so obviously be right.

There had always been Left-wing clergy in small scattered groups, a fringe. One of the things Temple did was to make radicalism more open and respectable, with a broader degree of acceptance within the Church. A group that emerged soon after his appointment as Archbishop of Canterbury was the Council of Clergy and Ministers for Common Ownership. It was formed in May 1942 at a conference held in Leicester, where the following declaration was adopted: 'We believe that the private ownership of the great productive resources of the community is contrary to Divine justice, and inevitably involves man in a self-centred way of life. We believe that the common ownership of these resources, with due regard for the freedom of the individual, more nearly expresses the will of God for man's life on earth as revealed by Jesus Christ. We pledge ourselves, as an essential part of our Christian duty, to work for this end.' The president of the council was the Bishop of Bradford, Bishop Blunt, who had lived up to his name in 1936 by breaking the uncomfortable official silence on the association between Edward VIII and Mrs Simpson.

The Bishop was also active with other clergy and laymen in another body with similar aims, the Socialist Christian League. Skeffington-Lodge, until he volunteered for the navy after the fall of Chamberlain in May 1940, was its chairman:

> It wasn't a very big organization but the significant aspect of it was that it was part of the Labour Party. It was an affiliated organization. When you look back at the history of the Labour Party what differentiated it and still does from the other social democratic parties of the West is that its outlook is not exclusively and never has been Marxist-inspired. It has rather been Christianly-inspired and came to birth originally as a result of the

Christian convictions of its pioneers and founders, who saw the Tory Party and to a slightly lesser extent the Liberal Party passing by on the other side in the face of appalling squalor.

Like Common Wealth, these movements were inspired by high ideals. They wanted not merely a re-ordering of the economic system but nothing less than a change of heart, a revolution in the human spirit. Their philosopher was R. H. Tawney, Socialist, moralist, close friend of Temple, worker in the WEA and professor of economic history at the London School of Economics. Christian Socialism had its roots deep in the traditions of English Nonconformity, traditions of democracy and the people and good works. The Independent Labour Party even had its own church. 'My father was a member of the ILP and used to take me to the ILP Labour Church every Sunday,' remembers Jim Cattermole, a trade unionist who became a full-time Labour Party agent for the 1945 election. 'You'd sing hymns and hear the address, which usually contained a Socialist message, and put your money in the plate.' Down in true blue Sussex a part-time Labour agent, A. G. Johnson, told his agricultural audiences at Partridge Green and Dial Post that Socialism was nothing new. It had been started 2,000 years ago by the sea of Galilee, and the Man who preached it had been put to death by the wealthy. These same people would again say 'Crucify Him' if He appeared today.

To many true blue supporters the statements were blasphemy and to be asked 'Was Jesus Christ a Socialist?' was an invitation to throw a spluttering fit. It was a question often asked by ordinary people at the Tower Hill meetings of Donald Soper:

When people have been doing the wrong thing morally because they felt they had to – violence, hatred, killing and so forth – it is not only true that they become almost acclimatized to, habituated to it, but also there's the countervailing principle that because of human nature people want to get rid of it. They want to find some kind of respite from it or some kind of antidote to it. Therefore there was a disposition to think in every field in which people did their thinking – religious, social, economic – that there was a better way of living and this better way of living had better now be started because we'd had enough of the other. In this respect it's not surprising people looked to Jesus or asked the question 'Was Jesus Christ a Socialist?'

In this mood more clergymen were prepared to declare their allegiance. One of them was the Rev Mervyn Stockwood, the future Bishop of Southwark, who boldly announced that he was going to vote for Sir Stafford Cripps in Bristol East. It was not out of reverence for the teetotal, vegetarian, patrician Anglican: 'I shall vote Labour because I am concerned primarily with principles and not with personalities. As a Christian it is my duty to work for a Britain which will be characterized by justice, fair dealing, peace and prosperity. Theory and practice alike prove the inability of Toryism to rise to the occasion.' This was a conversion. On the night when the results of the 1935 general election were being declared he was wearing the tie of the Cambridge University Conservative Club. With L. John Collins, the nuclear-disarming Canon to be, he had drunk toasts to the Tory victory.

Wartime was a spiritual time. Closer to death, people learned to pray, not necessarily on their knees. In shelters to keep their spirits up people sang hymns as well as popular songs and for those wanting a deeper understanding there were essays in popular theology, like C. S. Lewis's *The Screwtape Letters*. Religious broadcasting flourished. Churches attracted bigger congregations than they had in peacetime. Roman Catholics in particular were pleased with the number of converts they made. In the early part of the war, churches too were places of sanctuary during raids, partly because they were substantial buildings and partly in a naïve belief that they would somehow be spared. Especially in towns and cities their halls became community centres, dispensing food and help and Christian fellowship. Most denominations came to the aid of their fellow men and women on the home front or in the Services, often expressing their practical Christianity in the provision of a canteen. In the words of Lt-Col, later General, Frederick Coutts of the Salvation Army: 'The cuppa char and the wad became almost symbols of Christian service. The very friendly approach which marked our people was welcomed by the Serviceman in a context where friendship had assumed a new value. In the Services people expected to be sworn at, pushed around. When someone addressed one as a human being this was welcome and restored one's self respect a bit.'

There was still opposition to the pacifist stance of churchmen like Bishop Bell of Chichester. The Rev Reg Sorensen, Unitarian, pacifist, one of the old school of Christian Socialists, a political animal because he was a religious being, became a well known figure in his Leyton constituency, where he campaigned in an old red Austin Seven that often wanted pushing. His women supporters wore red blouses. At one of his meetings someone asked: 'Is it true that your two sons were conscientious objectors?' Rev Sorensen replied yes it was true but he was no more responsible for his sons' opinions and deeds than Mr Amery (the Conservative Minister whose son, John, turned traitor) was responsible for his. Then he went on: 'But that's unfair to them because one son is at this moment in Buchenwald with the Friends Ambulance Unit and the other one is in China doing hospital work.' In fact he never came back from China. The ambulance 'plane he was in was shot down. Such points of view were better understood than in the First World War.

In the country at large religious influence tended towards change. Wartime experience had stirred the Nonconformist conscience. There were still those in the Labour Party who had learned their public speaking as lay preachers, especially in Durham and the Welsh valleys. One of them was the nineteen-year-old Clive Jenkins of Port Talbot: 'People belonged to four things in South Wales: the unions, the Co-ops, the Labour Party, and the chapels. There were Methodist, Baptist, Presbyterian and some smaller sects. Everybody was in a chapel except those people associated with the English management class, who were C of E and went to a rather grander church. I was on the Methodist circuit as a fill-in preacher from the Youth Temperance Council.' In Cornwall Nonconformity was often associated with Liberalism. The Quaker chocolate families, the Cadburys in Birmingham and the Rowntrees in York, were also Liberal but the Society of Friends had become a younger, more radical movement. In Reading the Labour candidate, Ian Mikardo, was aware of the Quaker influence going back to William Penn. In other urban centres, especially London, many of those on the Left were Jewish refugees from Hitler.

Skeffington-Lodge, an Anglican who never approved of holding political meetings that clashed directly with the hours of normal church services, was well aware of the Nonconformist influence: 'I did have quite a number of people belonging to the various churches in Bedford and the villages who were emphatically in favour of my winning the seat. The Methodists were particularly strong. I think this goes back to the time of Bunyan.' This was no

D*

flight of fancy. J. Wentworth Day, a High Tory who lived in Essex, did not find it remarkable that the East Anglian agricultural workers went Labour: 'Always had been Left. Nothing new. A historical thing. Goes right back to Cromwell. There are deep roots of Nonconformism and Liberalism. Specially in Norfolk. I always say it was due to the *nouveaux riches.* Families who treated them very badly and were extremely avaricious.'

In Lancashire the Nonconformists were a distinct element within the Labour Party, as Bob Walsh, editor of *Catholic Worker,* observed: 'At regional level you could see the influence of religious differences: Irish RCs from the larger towns and Nonconformists from the small towns. The differences weren't openly expressed but they did influence people's thinking. There were still suspicions about RCs.' This was particularly evident in Liverpool, where there was a strong Orange working class Tory group led by Alderman Longbottom. Between the wars the Orange Order had maintained a tight control over immigrant Irish workers.

The sectarian issue was at its sharpest in Northern Ireland as a contemporary Labour writer, Sean Herron, recorded:

> The Unionist programme for the future of Ulster is always simple. It consists of the 'maintenance of the constitutional position', which in brief means Partition. The Union flag drapes every Unionist platform, the candidate's photograph is superimposed on a Union Jack and stuck on every gable and wall, King William (or 'oul Billy', as he is called by those most familiar with his activities) on his white horse leads columns of seventeenth century soldiers, to every Unionist meeting, and the lambeg drums with the overburdened drummers bleeding at the wrists provide the impression of the seventeenth century artillery. Behind them march pipe bands, flute bands, accordion bands and whatever other bands the Orange Order can produce.
>
> Banners with large portraits of the King and Queen Victoria . . . are 'danced' in the processions (this gives the impression that the banner bearers are mildly and happily inebriated – a point of view we as children always held) and the Unionist candidate goes before, in a brougham or 'brake', drawn by black Belgians, normally used for drawing hearses, surrounded by happy and normally ragged children, in whom the candidate delights for the period of the election. And always the amplifier van patrols the street shouting 'Vote for . . . and keep Ulster in the Empire'.
>
> Out in the country constituencies, while Belfast Unionists are

complaining bitterly of questioners as 'hooligans trying to break up our meetings', Orangemen are chasing Labour candidates out of town, clergymen who are taking the Labour platform are being warned of violent revenge by anonymous letters (Protestant clergymen at that) and the pipe and drum bands are taking their place beside Labour meetings to drown the speakers. Two young men were removed from one Unionist meeting by the police, for having asked the candidate what he proposed to do about unemployed aircraft workers. Food is plentiful in belligerent Ulster, and the Labour candidate for North Antrim was chased out of Dervock by Orangemen with adequate supplies of eggs.

Antrim was to have the doubtful distinction of the largest majority in the United Kingdom, 38,856. In those figures, the gerrymandered constituencies, the high unemployment, the poor housing and all the other inadequacies lay the seeds of future troubles.

John Boyd, a member of the Amalgamated Engineering Union, of the Labour Party and of the Salvation Army, saw from Motherwell, Lanarkshire, the sectarianism spread into parts of Scotland:

During the Depression, the hungry thirties, when Scotland had an equal if not worse share of unemployment than Wales, when people were idle and moved around aimlessly – I was a year idle – there grew an ugliness that I hope never returns. In Glasgow, in South-West and South-East Scotland, gangs of unemployed people developed. They began to dislike each other out of religious bigotry and it led to fighting. When the election came the general buoyancy, the desire for change, was diluted in Scotland by the Orangemen who had to be loyal to King and Country, epitomized by the Conservative Party, which received the support of some workers. Some would not vote Labour because they felt it was the party of the Irish labourer and the RC. It was probably one of the reasons why the Conservative Party did less badly than might have been expected in the prevailing mood.

In Wales Labour won seventy-one per cent of the seats against fifty-two per cent in Scotland. For many years Scotland, Glasgow in particular, was to be typified for southerners by accounts of Gorbals gangs with weapons like sharpened bicycle chains over their shoulders.

On the whole the United Kingdom was fortunately spared the direct association of religious groups with political parties. The only real denominational issue in the campaign was the Roman Catholic concern with the financing of their schools in the implementation of the 1944 Education Act. This issue was brought to the notice of all major parties. None of them included religion in their manifestoes. This was perhaps an omission on the part of the Conservatives, who had always had the maintenance of the Christian religion as part of their platform along with their regard for Empire. Rather did the parties give a nod towards the subject. In St John's Hall, Penzance, there was a meeting to discover 'Christianity – What Candidates Think?' The vicar of St Mary's presided and the questions came from the Industrial Christian Fellowship. Not surprisingly the three rival candidates were all in favour of Christianity, the Labour man stating that Nazism was a pagan religion. The vote of thanks was moved by the Rev Vaughan Johnson and the Rev G. H. S. Buckley was at the piano. Many similar meetings were held throughout the country.

The *Daily Mirror*'s 'Vote for him' campaign claimed to have clergy support. This was more than journalistic generalization. Religion was not a specific issue in the campaign but it did have background influence. As Frederick Coutts saw it:

We have a residual legacy of the Christian faith that influences our daily lives, our behaviour as between man and man. It's like the Gulf Stream, of which we don't think from one year's end to the next. Yet it's there, exercising a moderating influence on our climate. In some places it's more evident than in others. They tend to be the small, more personal communities, where the clergy is stronger on the ground. It's not so strong in the cities, where the fellowship of common danger did not live for so very long after the war. The 'Christian' concern in 1945 was more a humane concern.

His view is echoed by Donald Soper:

In wartime religion had become a part of people's lives, a very naïve and simple kind of religion in many cases, one that wasn't sufficiently deep. The fellowship, the community was occasional. We knew it here at Kingsway Hall on the roof tops: the sense of belonging, the sense of fellowship in the blitz. Take away the roof top, take away the blitz, and then you find whether that community is based upon something deeper. 1945 was the last of the old-fashioned types of election at which religion as an ecclesiastical entity played a part.

9

Learning To Be Citizens

In Port Talbot towards the end of the war, when the worst of the bombing was over, there was something called the Forum. We had our own debates for say three weeks and then a celebrity for the fourth. We used to go and have supper with the celebrities afterwards in a local hotel. It was there that I first met Julian Huxley and Professor Joad. I was astonished to discover that we paid them a fee and expenses. I was very naïve. I didn't know that people got paid for lecturing. We were paying them £50, which was a lot of money in those days. The hunger for listening to people in wartime was so intense we used to make great profits after having paid the enormous fees. You could sell tickets for a shilling (5p), or two shillings (10p) perhaps. You could pack a chapel hall. There was a great culture hunger.

So Clive Jenkins evokes the almost romantic appeal for education that developed in the war years.

Before the war, even in Wales one suspects, feelings had not been quite so intense. True, instruments of adult education existed going back in unbroken line to the Mechanics' Institutes of the last century. Trade unions and the Co-operative Movement had always striven to provide every possible educational facility for their members. For those who did not care for such political affiliation there were other educational bodies, of which the most well known was the Workers' Educational Association, founded by Albert Mansbridge in 1903. As secretary to the WEA he was invited during the First World War to assist with educational services in the British and Australian Armies, an event to have far reaching echoes in the second world conflict. Despite the variety of courses available through the various agencies, which had co-operation from the universities in the shape of extension courses and such residential colleges as Ruskin and Coleg Harlech, there were in 1938 still only 56,000 adult students.

Though there were signs of this figure steadily increasing there was no indication of the overwhelming desire for knowledge and learning that came in the immediate wake of the social upheaval Hitler's war created. During the long hours of fire watching, working with the NFS or Home Guard, all manner of subjects were discussed and clerks and manual workers found themselves debating with doctors, lawyers and all kinds of professional and educated men. To those who had never thought about it, to those who had never before had time for it, education suddenly became very desirable. Perhaps more than anyone else the trade unions were the best equipped to deal with this increase in demand. The war had brought larger membership to the unions, which meant more money. Determination to beat the enemy meant fewer strikes, so financing these did not deplete union funds. Many unions decided that their wisest investment was education.

Much of this was done through the National Council of Labour Colleges, whose most famous pupil must surely be Aneurin Bevan. Based on the picturesque Scottish village of Tillicoultry, having been bombed out of Hampstead, the NCLC was run by its frugal and dedicated general secretary J. P. M. Millar, a good steward of union funds. Together with his wife, Christine, he had written postal courses in English the working man could comprehend. Free through union membership, the sets of lessons when put together made a book. Jimmy Millar's overriding idea was one of independent working class education free of all state interference. He wanted the TUC to finance the rationalization of working class education and bring together the trade union educational enthusiasts from the WEA, whose state subsidy he scorned. The Colleges grew throughout the war with the help of union finances, only Bevin's union, the Transport and General Workers' maintaining any significant links with the WEA.

In practice what this meant was that the NCLC provided a political education of Leftish bias, considered by some to be Marxist, while the WEA provided a more general education, which might incidentally lead one to a Leftish outlook. Yet with both movements, as with others, the prime motivation seems to have been to find out. 'Why are we fighting this war?' seems to have been a popular and perhaps natural subject with lecturers at the outset.

Desmond Neill had all sorts of people coming to the adult education classes held in the Quaker settlements at York and Leeds throughout the war: 'In York those attending were railway workers; Rowntree and Terry employees; a large proportion of women whose husbands were away in the war taking the opportunity to get out in the evenings and to exercise their minds; older men; but not many in their twenties. They were away at the war. In York and Leeds those who came were by no means just middle class. There was a good sprinkling of clerks and manual workers.' The swelling numbers were perhaps remarkable in their determination not to miss the classes.

Initially, under the stress of air raids, many of the subjects studied seem to have been escapist, local history, music and literature being obvious favourites, and the time honoured rule of the WEA that a student must turn in a piece of written work at each meeting was now more honoured in the breach than the observance. After the publication of the Beveridge Report in 1942 a new interest was born in economics and the problems associated with what soon came to be known as 'post-war reconstruction'. Ever since Russia had entered the war there was also a great public desire to know 'the truth' about that country and whether its political functioning was more efficient than our own. In March 1945, John Parker, MP for Romford, on his return from a visit to the USSR with a Parliamentary delegation, gave a talk to a packed meeting at the Dagenham Civic Centre. His audience heard how Russia was 'run by the young'. He had seen children of twelve rivetting in aircraft factories and had noticed that all the managerial class seemed to be between twenty and forty. This was heady stuff and just what people, especially the young, wanted to hear.

'What about Russia?', soon to be a favourite heckling gambit at political meetings, was rhetorical and not designed to elicit information on the less than warm reception that servicemen on the Murmansk run were apt to meet. As early as August 1941 the poet Stephen Spender, serving in the NFS, had observed how Russia's coming into the war had 'heartened even the most anti-Bolshevik. At last we're fighting with people who really believe in something. They may be wrong. But they believe.' Two years later Spender might have modified his views, but his NFS colleagues had not. According to Harold Nicolson adverse criticism of the USSR was rated 'Fascist talk'. In terms possibly not as exaggerated as they sound he wrote: 'They worship the very thought of Stalin. Russia is their only religion.' Red Army Flag Days were well supported and any civic dignitary like the Mayor of Walthamstow who slighted a Russian visitor had some shamed-faced explaining to do. While the British were getting their aid from the USA and giving their admiration to the USSR the WEA 'book boxes' could not contain volumes enough about the Socialist Sixth of the World.

Discussion had always formed a part of adult education and after the Beveridge proposals, possibly the subject of more discussion than anything else, civilian debating societies flourished. At Leyton in East London the Labour Party organized a series of speakers to talk and debate on every conceivable subject at the new library that the Party had been instrumental in getting opened. In Birmingham a debating society was created almost inadvertently from the correspondence column, 'Public Opinion', in the Birmingham *Evening Despatch*. Denis Howell, a future Minister of Sport, once had two letters published on the same evening:

> They used to print a whole page of letters. Tremendous arguments went on through the columns of this paper about the state of the country and particularly what was going to happen after the war. Reuben Osborn, a psychologist and author, wrote saying he found this correspondence absolutely fascinating but suggested speeding up things by getting some of the letter writers together so that we could argue the thing out. This became the Public Opinion Action Association. Its first meeting in 1944 was packed out, broadcast by the BBC, reported by the *Daily Mirror*. The first debate was on 'What is democracy?'

Wallace Lawler, later to become a Liberal MP but then a young man opposed to all political parties, became its chairman. Denis Howell felt:

> That group had a profound effect on politics in Birmingham. It met weekly, every Monday night. There were never fewer than 200 people there, because there was little else to do in those days. We'd been through the bad bombing period and people felt they could begin to come out at night. People from all walks of life and of all political complexions came. It was a marvellous experience in public speaking, learning the cut and thrust of debate. We had a number of debates on the Beveridge Report, post-war reconstruction and we also had a period of fifteen minutes like question time in the House when anybody could raise any current affairs subject.

If civilian life was so afire with this 'cut and thrust of debate' it would be unrealistic to have expected the Services to remain immune, though there were some who thought this should be so. From the beginning of the war it had been realized that soldiers not actually fighting would need weapons to keep boredom at bay, and perhaps to forestall the barrack room lawyer. In the winter of 1939 the universities, the WEA and other bodies had formed a Central Advisory Course for Adult Education in HM Forces. The fine sounding title concealed the fact that little was actually being done. Admittedly, lectures and courses for troops were arranged to combat what some were calling 'The Great Bore War', but it was done very much on an *ad hoc* basis and in a haphazard way. Remuneration and allowances were only about £8 a week for the lecturers but determination on the parts of lecturers and the lectured alike played its part, particularly after Dunkirk, once a feeling of public self-examination became entrenched.

The Education Centre at Dover became known as the 'Front Line University' and carried on through all the bombardments of Hellfire Corner. Like others of its kind it was largely a self-governing institution through its committee of soldiers. Built, furnished and maintained by them, it was probably more appreciated than would have been the case had it sprung from some chromium-plated act of philanthropy. A. T. D'Eye was one of the lecturers to members of the women's services in a hotel hard by Dover Harbour: 'On one occasion my subject was the British constitution. The siren went, we could hear the 'planes overhead, they dive-bombed the harbour, my knees were knocking but the women wanted me to carry on with what I thought for them must be a dull subject.'

There was a Site Visitor Scheme, which was reckoned particularly suitable for Ack-Ack and searchlight units. A local resident would undertake to drop in on a site on one or two afternoons a week and talk about some subject of general interest to the men and women over a cup of tea. The universities also helped. Among their lecturers were Commander Campbell of the Brains Trust and Sir Charles Petrie, the historian. Brains Trusts were popular and frequently spontaneous. They might discuss matters of great pith and moment or simply local grouses, and this went on throughout the war. You did not have to be an expert. Anybody could chip in any time, anywhere if the mood was right. Tommy Trinder sometimes made it part of his act: 'I remember at the end of a show I did at the San Carlo Opera House, Naples, I said to the audience of troops, "Well, now, we'll have Any Questions?" and I sat down on the edge of the stage and we rounded things off there and then with a ten-minute general conversation on all sorts of topics.' Amiable, relaxed and co-operative as all these activities were, it was clear that they were not going to be enough, particularly after the Dunkirk evacuation. After that most of the Army were going to be based in the UK for a considerable period. Their time had to be filled, preferably with something that would raise interest and morale.

In September 1940 a special committee reported that education was the obvious answer and that every unit should have its own education officer. As a first step the Education Corps was greatly expanded, civilian lecturers used increasingly and correspondence courses set up for those studying for professional and technical qualifications. But Sir Ronald Adam, the new Adjutant-General, wanted something more, and possibly mindful of the First World War and Albert Mansbridge, sent for a leading light of the WEA, W. E. Williams, who had been so closely involved with the birth and development of Penguin books and was secretary of the British Institute of Adult Education. He and Adam noted that nothing was so popular with the troops as discussion groups and Brains Trusts. What the men wanted was to find out 'the facts', a feeling that could be taken advantage of. Williams was to call the whole exercise 'a reconnaissance of citizenship'.

The Army and a great deal of the world outside the Army came to know it as the Army Bureau of Current Affairs or, more simply and affectionately, ABCA. Williams wanted it to be something more than just another military parade for the troops:

The Adjutant-General in the phoney war period asked me to tour the camps and decide what must be done in the way of education. Eventually I came up with ABCA. Sir Ronald Adam's last job had been defending the perimeter of Dunkirk. A professional soldier but a man of vision. He insisted on Army psychiatrists and Army education. I remember my wife and I both had eight days' leave at the same time not having seen each other for months. We spent the time down at Penrhyn in Caernarvonshire, walking over the mountains there trying to think of a name for this new set-up, talking and talking, racking our brains for a name. We knew it had to roll trippingly off the tongue and it had to be simple or it wouldn't catch on. And at last we thought of ABCA. We knew at once that had to be it. It *would* be an ABC of Current Affairs. And the initials were easy enough to remember. Eventually it even became a verb – to ABCA-ise – and I became ABCA Bill.

From the start the concept had strong official backing. Williams insists: 'Adam backed me. So did all senior officers. Except Montgomery! I had the hell of a row with him. You see at first many brasshats said, "But there won't be time for this." So I answered, "Then do it in the King's time." By making ABCA a compulsory parade, the same as any other, it ensured that everyone in the Army took it seriously. Montgomery wanted it to be part of Chaplain's Hour, which would have sunk it. No, I didn't get on with Montgomery. But generally from all senior officers I had total support. Their only concern was what was best for their men.'

After the resounding defeat in the 1945 election many Conservatives, casting round for explanations and faced with the assertion that it was the Service vote that had swung the verdict against them, blamed ABCA. It had fed them with Red propaganda, corrupted them into Bolshevism. This version died hard in Right-wing circles. A devoted constituency Party worker after thirty years vowed: 'Almost every education officer in the Army was Labour and was preaching Labour doctrines. Labour had the Army taped. The chaps used to go to these lectures because they'd nothing better to do. At the end of the war they were fed up. The wrong men got out first. Everything that went wrong was Churchill's fault. They blamed him and voted against him *en masse*.'

A full time worker at the Conservative Research Department was involved in RAF Education: 'Before ABCA I used to try and help fellows get over boredom by teaching a bit of local history and running discussion groups where we'd argue such topics as "Is it better to be rich or talented?" Once ABCA had started and my sessions were known about the CO sent for me and asked what went on. He asked if I'd like to do some ABCA style stuff and offered me some yellow covered books. I refused. Williams who headed ABCA was a tremendous Leftie.' A High Tory who was passionately involved in the 1945 election put the case in its most extreme form: 'Williams smothered the troops in seditious literature. One general burned 10,000 of those wretched ABCA pamphlets before his men, whom he'd called on parade, saying "This is rank treason". Williams was extremely cunning. He never wore uniform or accepted rank because he knew if he did he could be disciplined. Court-martialled.'

Such suspicions and prejudices pre-dated 1945 and were cherished by Ernest Bevin and Winston Churchill, who once issued an order of the day demanding to know details of the finances and personnel of ABCA with a clear threat to wind the organization up. Churchill's autobiography gives the text of the order without any indication of its fate. Williams reveals it: 'We survived because the Secretary of War, Sir James Grigg, tore it up. He was a very tough man with a fearful temper. He tore Churchill's order up because he thought he was intervening in things he knew nothing about. And he was right.' So Grigg, who was thoroughly detested by almost every soldier, for once played the hero in near total secrecy and saved ABCA.

Does ABCA really deserve the villain's role? To begin with at least, it was a modest project. Its staff consisted of its director, W. E. Williams, one lieutenant-colonel, two majors and two staff captains. By the end of the war the full staff of the Directorate never once exceeded a total personnel of twenty. Its first activity was the production in alternating weeks of two periodicals called *Current Affairs* and *War*, which were circulated to every regimental officer in the Army. *War* charted the progress of the fighting but in such a way as to suggest matters for discussion. *Current Affairs* invited a well known expert to write on a topical theme selected by the Directorate, whose sub-editors would shape it into a discussion brief. Typical titles were 'The Nation's Health', 'Spain', 'Social Security', 'The Scientist In War' and 'The Government Resettlement Plan'.

These formed the basis of the compulsory education period of at least one hour a week, and the briefs were used by platoon commanders, who were expected to lead the ABCA sessions and who eventually were trained to do so. Wall newspapers, exhibitions, reference libraries called 'information rooms', educational films – all played their part. Perhaps the most famous ABCA brief was the one on the Beveridge Report that appeared in December 1942. The War Office withdrew it after two days, thereby creating a storm. Six months later it was replaced by another on social security couched in more general tones, and with a warning inserted by officialdom that there was danger in easy promises. Of this pamphlet Williams maintained: 'It was really nothing more than a summary of the Beveridge proposals. But do you know it remained the most popular? It was always in demand. By 1945 we were an exhausted nation. Only the thought of Beveridge kept us going.' Williams, who incidentally never voted for any party at any election in his whole life, successfully inveigled many famous names to write his ABCA pamphlets but did not see his job as a desk-bound one so much as a roving commission.

He was in fact the only civilian in the Army and eschewed uniform as a deliberate policy: 'I knew that the Army does not like imitation soldiers. They offered me Brigadier but I said "No" and of course they thought I was holding out for something higher so they came back with Major-General. I still said "No". I knew I would be taken more seriously as a civilian. Another aspect was that the ordinary troops wouldn't speak frankly to a red tabbed chap coming down from the War Office. But a chap in a civilian suit was something different.' This seems to have worked both ways. Frederick Coutts of the Salvation Army tells the story of a large ABCA meeting held in a huge aircraft hangar: 'An officer of the old school had addressed the men in hortatory terms and then called on the ABCA man to speak. He rose and began simply, "Gentlemen". That one word changed the whole atmosphere. The vast audience was in the palm of his hand, eager to hear what he had to say.' It is by no means impossible that the 'ABCA man' was Williams himself.

Yet at the time the efficacy of the whole ABCA scheme was not apparent. Actor Stephen Murray sat in on many ABCA sessions and felt: 'Those I saw were really not very brilliant and the men seemed bored and didn't argue. Of course, I may have been unfortunate.' A soldier who fought in the Italian campaign is more sweeping:

> Towards the end in Italy, in the early spring of '45, one or two NCOs were given the task of holding little ABCA 'indoctrination' meetings but they were very much a failure. In some of these gloomy villages one or two sergeants would go round asking if anyone was willing to come to a meeting. About three or four chaps would go then come out, not interested. Largely because of the people giving the lectures. They were mostly Central European refugee NCOs in the Intelligence Corps. We weren't

really interested in their opinions. I would say nine out of ten
chaps never heard of ABCA. A few who were mildly political
were aware of Beveridge and the goodies coming after the war.
But we never really believed it.

This would seem to be an extreme view since yet another veteran
of the Italian campaign has a totally contrasting story: 'During one
lull in the campaign the education officer, who understood I was
quite enthusiastic about the Soviet Union, asked me if I'd like to
give a talk to the troops. The hall was quite full. The education
officer wanted me to do some more but I had my own job to do.
Earlier, in Scotland, I'd talked to quite a lot of chaps stuck in the
field all night. The troops wanted to know and argue.' A. D.
Lindsay, who was to head the post-war academic experiment at
Keele, compared the work ABCA was doing with the Putney Debates and Cromwell's Puritan Army. W. E. Williams himself was
more than once heard to quote Cromwell's predilection for 'the
plain russet-coated captain that knows what he fights for and loves
what he knows'. In *Tribune* of 12 January, 1945 there appeared an
article *ABCA Alone Won't Do*, which among many other strictures
registered the criticisms that ABCA's efficacy too often depended
on the attitude of the commanding officers concerned, that many
of the troops were suspicious of ABCA and that only about fifteen
per cent of the troops were politically conscious.

This diversity of contemporary attitudes, and particularly the
critical stance of those supposed to have been most thoroughly in-
doctrinated, rather invalidates the view that has flourished on the
Right ever since 1945 of ABCA as a political juggernaut launched
by opportunistic Leftists. Even Williams was not satisfied with
ABCA. In an unpublished monograph on Army Education between 1939 and 1945 he asserts that 'Army Education was never
more than fifty per cent effective.' Nevertheless those who also
wished to undertake that reconnaissance in citizenship saw it as a
model and one that worked. The RAF set up its own education
scheme using the *British Way And Purpose* pamphlets. A course
in citizenship introduced in the winter of 1942, when education time
was extended to three hours weekly, these made much of the discussion of war aims.

The ABCA style translated least happily to the Senior Service,
which was perhaps also the most hidebound by tradition. Douglas

Long, a Marxist, was involved with ABCA's naval counterpart:

It was called EVT: Educational Voluntary Training. It appeared
in Admiralty Orders but nobody took much notice. I went to the
Captain and said, 'I think we should do something about EVT,
sir' and he grumbled, 'Who's going to do it?' So I volunteered.
Of course their notion was that it should teach the ratings how
to deal with civvy life. Many were straight from school after all.
But I taught them how they should vote. The men were enormously interested if top brass wasn't. For them it had all begun
long before, of course. On a North Atlantic convoy you might
have six men at action stations round a gun all night. What else
was there for them to do but talk? Later I was based at Chatham,
still doing education. Top brass still thought it was a matter of
teaching who'd won the Battle of Trafalgar and that they had
splendid educational facilities there. Actually there was an information room housing a library of books of the *Eric: Or Little
By Little* type. I tried to make it more practical.

The NFS also set up an education section modelled on ABCA.
Reg Underhill, later to be Labour Party National Agent, thought
it was 'not as professional, not as formal' as ABCA. Whatever its
shortcomings, ABCA was clearly a workable model of adult education and one that others could copy. The Nazis thought they
could win war by virtue of people's unquestioning obedience. The
British wanted to win by free discussion and questioning. In this
respect ABCA may have helped win the war. It is less certain that
it won an election for Labour. Many of the returned Labour MPs
certainly did not seem to think so or, if they did, were remarkably
unappreciative of the fact. Ernest Bevin, whose huge frame concealed many petty prejudices, was an uneducated man himself and
seems to have resented anyone else having or even desiring education and had made mischief for ABCA with Churchill. Incredibly,
the new Labour Cabinet of 1945 set about dismantling ABCA.

W. E. Williams paid a visit to the Labour Minister of War:

After the election I went to see John Bellenger – a tried party hack.
He wasn't the least interested in ABCA. It became clear to me
the Labour Government wanted to end it. This has never been
told before but it's an interesting reflection, isn't it? If ABCA
had *really* won the election for the Labour Party why were they
in such haste to wind it up despite the fact a conscript army
which now did no fighting still remained and was to remain

for many years? Bellenger had no time for it, wasn't interested. Nor had his number two, young Michael Stewart. Only the third man there was all for it. That was John Freeman, who'd been a Desert Rat, but he alone didn't carry enough weight against the others. In fact neither political party was ever helpful to ABCA. Only the Army was. I think the Labour Party resented anyone outside their ranks promoting the discussion of ideas that did not originate with them.

Another educational concept that evolved from the current craze for discussion groups and forums was nurtured by the Army. Unconnected with ABCA, it had the same motivations but lacked official backing and was ruthlessly suppressed. The Cairo Parliament strangely grew out of a Music Club, where troops on leave in the Nile Delta could relax. Somebody suggested a discussion group and this flowered into the idea of a mock Parliament with political parties holding mock elections for seats. In these the Socialists won an overwhelming majority and business was conducted as near the style of the real House of Commons as possible. The Socialist 'Chancellor', the young Leading Aircraftsman Leo Abse, later for many years to sit in the real House as MP for Pontypool, brought in a measure favouring nationalization of the Bank of England. Before debate could properly begin several brigadiers accompanied by military police marched into the large hut that served as a Chamber and announced they had orders to suspend the proceedings. Some 600 service 'MPs' were outraged.

An order was read out by the intruders demanding the word 'Parliament' no longer be used, that nothing be said contravening King's Regulations, that there be no Press reports, that soldiers undertake no political activities. But the orders magnanimously concluded the Assembly might follow the procedure of the Oxford Union. Anger erupted into uncontrollable laughter. The 'Prime Minister' and the leaders of the other two main political parties each in turn rose and delivered a protest speech, the most outspoken coming from the Conservative leader. All insisted their activities here were an aid to the war effort and educational as well as the right of any citizen army. The protest of the leaders was put to the vote and carried unanimously. Only the intruding chief brigadier voted for his own order! The Speaker of the House then confounded the defeat further by declaring that in any case the Order could only apply to future meetings and not to this one.

The brigadiers and their military policemen had to stand and listen to the debate on nationalizing the Bank of England, which was carried enthusiastically.

Next day all the prominent members of the Parliament were posted to trouble spots and Leo Abse, the 'Chancellor', was arrested. His demand for a court martial was refused. A complete censorship on mail to England was imposed to try and stop news of what had happened being made public. But news was smuggled in with the aid of the pilots of Transport Command and questions in the real Westminster were soon being asked by Aneurin Bevan, Emanuel Shinwell and D. N. Pritt. A debate was forced in which Sir James Grigg had shamefacedly to defend the Cairo antics. Nobody seemed to notice that it was as though both sides had acted out a charade of what had happened between King and Commons in the Parliament of three hundred years before. Abse was returned to England because it was said his 'enthusiasms' disturbed the Middle East troops. The Cairo Parliament was not allowed to meet and debate but it was impossible to stop people talking about it and its clumsy suppression. Possibly this action accounted for some of the talk about violent overthrow of the rulers if victory did not come through the polls in 1945.

Margaret Cole was to write a few months after the election: 'The British voter of 1945 is a different creature from his father of 1918 – he is very much better educated; secondary education, technical education, evening class education, reinforced by the education, however scrappy and uneven, which has been given in the wartime Services, is bearing fruit at last. Far more people can *argue* now than could twenty-seven years ago.' No doubt this was why so many commentators were to remark on the reasonableness of the electorate, their willingness to listen and their desire to know.

10

When This Lot's Over

During the week Arnold Whittick was lecturing to men and women in the Forces on housing and reconstruction and recording some of his experiences in letters to *The Times*. At weekends he went home to Kent and served in the Home Guard.

The Colonel was an architect, interested in a better planned Beckenham after the war. He noticed my letters in *The Times* with a local address and asked his fellow officers if any of them knew me. One of them did ('He's a private in your battalion') and was told to point me out on parade the next Sunday morning. The Colonel made a bee-line for me:

'Are you Arnold Whittick?'

'Yes sir.'

'You've written these letters to *The Times*?'

'Yes sir.'

'I'd like to discuss it with you. Would you come to tea this afternoon?'

'Yes sir.'

After that we had several meetings. With the assistance of the Town and Country Planning Association we set about forming a group: the Beckenham Planning Group. The Colonel thought we ought to get a good membership so he asked me if I'd address the battalion. I obviously agreed. So he marched them all on an icy, slippery Sunday morning to the King's Hall cinema in Penge. It was full. There was I, Private Whittick, 5ft 4in [163cm], in a baggy, ill-fitting uniform addressing them. All the brass sat in front in their smart uniforms. My small daughter was bursting with pride and my wife was feeling uncomfortable. Shortly after that we had an inaugural meeting in the library. All the early members were recruited from the Home Guard.

Beckenham 'Dad's Army' was one small non-political group interested in a better Britain. After the blitz of 1940-41 people's hopes were buoyed up by the promise that their stricken towns would, in Churchill's words, 'after the war rise up beautiful, re-splendent, phoenix-like, from the ashes of the dead'. Members of the Town and Country Planning Association expressed their individual views in the 'Rebuilding Britain' series of booklets published by Faber and Faber. The authors of *Our Towns*, learning the lessons of evacuation, wanted a campaign for better education, academic, social and moral, to be waged side by side with the battle against poverty and bad material conditions.

As early as New Year 1941, in response to Forces' questions on what they were fighting for, *Picture Post* published a special issue on A Plan for Britain. Introducing it the editor, Tom Hopkinson, wrote: 'This is not a time for putting off thinking "till we see how things are." This is a time for doing the thinking, so that we can make things how we want them to be. More than that. Our plan for a new Britain is not something outside the war, or something *after* the war. It is an essential part of our war aims. It is, indeed, our most positive war aim. The new Britain is the country we are fighting for.' The aims outlined covered full employment, all-in social security, a national health service, planned use of the land, better homes and towns, a complete overhaul of the educational system, and proper provision for leisure. All this provoked more correspondence by the sackful.

Post-war reconstruction, especially after the publication of Beveridge, interested all sorts of people. In a small way they could see it with their own eyes. It was possible and it could be done well. When newly-weds and those bombed out used their priority dockets for furniture they got good value. As Harry Pollitt wrote: 'With all the difficulties and limitations of wartime production, the mass-produced Utility furniture of today is a tremendous advance on the thinly veneered, shoddy muck which was all that most young working class couples could acquire in pre-Utility days.' Hugh Dalton at the Board of Trade had, with designers, established government standards and kept the private manufacturers up to the mark. The furniture may have been a bit austere but it was well designed and soundly made of decent quality materials, made to last. It showed a confidence in the future. And why shouldn't the Government organise a better deal all round for young couples?

There were plenty of ideas around. Papers on post-war reconstruction were produced by a study group at the Royal Institute of International Affairs. It was enthusiastically discussed at WEA evening classes around hissing gas fires in country libraries and schoolrooms. A. T. D'Eye was an Oxford extramural tutor with the WEA in East Kent:

> I don't think we missed a class there, even though we were in the front line of the bombing. One night Deal public library was bombed so the next night's class met at the Miners' Welfare . . . A miner was walking down from Elvington to Eythorne one night when a piece of shrapnel from a German shell fired across the Channel hit him in the thigh. I think that was the farthest inland, about five miles from Dover, a shell ever reached. It was fortunately only a superficial wound. We bound it up for him and carried on with the class.

In London bombing did not stop the talks and discussions. Barbara Wootton was then in adult education: 'We switched a number of our classes to Sunday mornings because this was less dangerous. Post-war reconstruction played a considerable part in those that I took because it was all that seemed important at the time.' The Rotarians had it as a frequent topic on their agenda. A Social Security League was formed to press for 'Beveridge In Full'.

The shape of things to come was also exercising the minds of those with conscientious objections to the war. Concerned with ethical and social responsibilities, the Society of Friends was trying to update its 'Eight Foundations of the New Social Order', originally drafted in 1918. The deliberations were done through its Industrial and Social Order Council of which Desmond Neill, a warden of Quaker settlements in Yorkshire, was a member:

> It was a controversial question because one can broadly say that until World War One the Society of Friends was on the whole Liberal but in the twenties and thirties a considerable number of Friends, especially the younger ones, were moving into the Labour Party. The old group of paternalist Liberals like Arnold Rowntree, the Harveys, were reluctant to see the Society committing itself sharply to policies that could be labelled Socialist. Those of us on the Industrial and Social Order Council were picked by our quarterly meetings from all over the country because we were concerned with social questions. We were supposed to be drawing up discussion pamphlets and within our body there was a fairly strong radical approach to society. We were trying to get the Friends to come to the point where they would make a new declaration on the social order . . . It was when we pre-

sented our redrafted eight points to the yearly meeting of the Society of Friends that the real conflict of opinion occurred. There was a considerable amount of reluctance to accept it.

The Quaker debates showed the essence of the conflict over post-war reconstruction. On what basis was Britain to be rebuilt? The old or a new? Where was the line between reconstruction proposals and party political propaganda? The Labour Party in Faversham, Kent, came up against the question when it tried to book a church hall for a meeting to be addressed by Professor Harold Laski. The church refused to let its hall for a political meeting so the Labour Party changed the title of his address to 'Post-War Reconstruction' and the booking was allowed. Laski's speech remained the same.

The electoral truce between the major parties did not stop post-war thinking. During the dark midsummer of 1940 Laski had asked in a Penguin Special *Where Do We Go From Here?* Some 80,000 people, intrigued by the catchphrase title, bought it to find out. G. D. H. Cole, the Socialist educator, was chairman of the Nuffield College Social Reconstruction Survey, which for three years brought together administrators, representatives of universities and local government to lay the foundations of a more satisfactory society. In that society the Co-operative Movement was interested in its own future prospects, which were discussed in the weekly *Co-operative News*, the monthly *Co-operative Review*, at the Movement's annual congress and by its own political party. Education was a topic of major concern.

The Fabian Society, one of the few outlets for intellectual political activity, grew not just in London but also in the provinces. Leeds Fabians, for example, were particularly interested in the break-up of Empire. The Society's national series of autumn lectures in 1943 and 1944 were devoted to the problems of post-war reconstruction. Lecturers included Aneurin Bevan, Sir William Beveridge, G. D. H. Cole, Jim Griffiths, Harold Laski and R. H. Tawney. Another specialist group that grew in numbers and influence was the Socialist Medical Association, with its eyes firmly on its principal goal of 'a new system of medical care'. Its work, especially among young doctors, helped to change the political atmosphere inside and outside the profession.

Within the Labour Party the man who lifted people's eyes to the future was Herbert Morrison. As Minister of Home Security he was well aware of the devastating effects of poor planning. In the

big raid on Coventry the unco-ordinated actions of the local fire
brigades had revealed a chaos that made a bad situation very much
worse. The extent of the shambles was so great that it had to be
kept from the public. Out of these ashes Morrison had created the
National Fire Service. For him reconstruction was a larger opportunity to shed his London County Council image and emerge as a
national figure worthy of consideration for the Party leadership.
On his initiative Labour's National Executive Committee set up a
new Central Committee on Reconstruction Problems with a veteran
of the two minority Labour Governments, Emanuel Shinwell, as
its chairman and Harold Laski as secretary. It first met in mid 1941
and soon spawned sub-committees to cover particular aspects of
policy.

In 1942 the Labour Party conference adopted *The Old World
And The New Society*, a general statement of reconstruction policy.
Later that year and into 1943, during the initial impact of the
Beveridge Report, Morrison carried his campaign to the country,
speaking not only on social security but also on the broader issues
of the kind of mixed economy Britain should have, the country's
economic prospects, the need for international co-operation and
the kind of international organization essential for world peace.
This culminated in a winding-up speech at the Labour Party conference of Whitsun 1943 in which he outlined the public ownership
policy of a future Labour government. It was a triumphant moment. The delegates gave him thunderous applause. He was giving
people the kind of lead they were looking for. So much so that
later that year Churchill took him aside and asked him to desist.
He refused.

About the same time that Morrison was beginning to face the
future R. A. Butler, a Conservative reformer, was getting members
of his party to sit down and do some thinking. Under his chairmanship a Conservative Post-War Problems Committee was formed.
From the autumn of 1942 sub-committees published reports on
education, youth, agriculture, demobilization and resettlement,
housing and the administration of justice. Putting education and
youth first showed the influence of Butler, who was still aware of
the severe shock that the revelations of evacuation had administered
to the national conscience.

Looking back, he was to write:

It was realized with deepening awareness that the 'two nations' still existed in England a century after Disraeli had used the phrase. The challenge of the times provided a stimulus for re-thinking the purposes of society and planning the reconstruction of the social system of which education formed an integral part. Realization of a full democracy – an order of society free from the injustices and anomalies of the pre-war period – was the ideal. Education problems were thus seen as an essential part of the social problem and the urgent need for educational reform was increasingly realized.

For wider appeal the Conservatives issued from late 1943 a series of sixpenny ($2\frac{1}{2}$p) *Signpost* pamphlets 'designed to point the road along which we must travel on our quest for a new and even better Britain'. Unfortunately the series had a muddled sense of direction, pointing backwards rather than forwards.

Dissatisfaction with the Party's general attitude was publicly ex-pressed by a young Conservative MP, Captain Quintin Hogg, a few months after he returned from the Middle East and spoke strongly in favour of the Beveridge Plan. Early in 1943 he wrote *An Open Letter To The Tory Party*. Quoting Disraeli from 1835 ('The Con-servative Party is the National Party, the really democratic party in England') he declared that:

The Conservative Party is either a national party or it is nothing. It is to this fact and to no other that it owes its continued survival after the disappearance of so many of its historical rivals. Once the suspicion is allowed to grow that it is a class party, that it is abandoning the high ideal for which it has stood literally for hundreds of years and is serving the interests of individuals, or of a section of the nation instead of the community at large, the Conservative Party is not only dead but damned. No electoral truce, no Parliamentary majority, and no skilful tactics will save it. Nor, you will agree with me, would we deserve in such circum-stances to be saved.

Castigating some Tory MPs for their attitude on Bevin's Catering Bill, designed to give a fairer deal to workers in that sweated in-dustry, he concluded his protest: 'Fellow members of the Con-servative Party, I appeal to you to put a stop to the tactics of a short-sighted and reactionary rump. Tell them that they are ruining the party. Tell them to take a long view. Tell them to stick to the principles of Disraeli.'

During 1943 some forty young Conservative MPs of like mind, among them David Gammans, Lord Hinchingbrooke, Quintin Hogg, Hugh Molson and Peter Thorneycroft, came together in the Tory Reform Committee. Its manifesto *Forward By The Right*, originally printed for private circulation, subsequently went into two larger editions. In addition pamphlets and bulletins were issued, for which the Committee later set up its own research organization. In *Full Speed Ahead – Essays In Tory Reform* Hinchingbrooke argued that between the wars the Conservative Party had been wrongly deflected from Disraeli's goal of one nation: 'I hope you are aware of the desire that exists in the Progressive Right to be rid of the incubus of finance and the control of big business, to make money the servant of enterprise, not its master, to rebuild our country after the war not with the thought of money gain but with the thought of social purpose.' This involved a measure of state control over certain industries to maintain the unity between capital and labour that had been found during the war.

To Hinchingbrooke, Britain's survival as a great power depended upon the inseparable factors of full employment, national unity and social reform. Hogg declared in the House that 'if you do not give the people social reform, they are going to give you social revolution' and went on to quote Disraeli again. The Conservative Women's Reform Group produced its own version of what to do *When Peace Comes*.

These were very much minority views among Conservative MPs. Diehards like Sir Herbert Williams distrusted the drift to 'pink Socialism', a phrase that did not disturb R. A. Butler intellectually but which he had to watch politically in his quiet manoeuvrings for the acceptance of more enlightened policies. In reviewing Hinchingbrooke's essays, A. G. Erskine-Hill, the *Signpost* author of *The Future Of The Small Trader*, agreed with Disraeli that the condition of the people should be improved but not 'at the expense of the personality and dignity and character of the individual, however humble'. There was also the question of financial expenses with the consequent burden of taxation to pay for an increase in state power. The characteristic sense of the British people would prevail, however. 'I am confident that no matter what may happen in the short run after this war, the people of this country will be only too glad to find that there is still a party which has not lost its moorings by going full speed ahead on an uncharted course, and

FAREWELL

"Since there's no help, come let us kiss and part."

On 30 May 1945 E. H. Shepard, best known as the illustrator of *Winnie the Pooh*, made this sharp comment on the forthcoming election in *Punch*.

Churchill, the conquering hero (above), was cheered by the crowds on his election
campaign tour, as shown here in Leeds. But it was the mild Clem Attlee (below) who
got the loudest cheers from party workers at Transport House on 26 July 1945.

which continues to believe in the continuity and stability of customary life, so far as that will be possible in a world buffeted by post-war difficulties,' wrote Erskine-Hill. With others he set up the Progress Trust to combat the Right Progressives.

The problems of Conservative policy came from the top, from Churchill himself. Soon after joining the Coalition the Labour Party leader Attlee realized: 'The Germans are fighting a revolutionary war for very definite objectives. We are fighting a conservative war and our objectives are purely negative. We must put forward a positive and revolutionary aim admitting that the old order has collapsed and asking people to fight for the new order.' Churchill always refused to make a statement on war aims, apart from those on the battlefield, on the grounds that precise aims would be compromising whereas vague principles would disappoint. In a Cabinet memorandum circulated at the time of the Beveridge debate he warned that 'a dangerous optimism is growing up about the conditions it will be possible to establish here after the war . . . It is for this reason of not wishing to deceive the people by false hopes and airy visions of Utopia and Eldorado that I have refrained so far from making promises about the future. We must all do our best and we shall do it much better if we are not hampered by a cloud of pledges and promises which arise out of the hopeful and genial side of man's nature and are not brought into relation with the hard facts of life.'

In the spring of 1943, however, Churchill did broadcast on his own Four Year Plan, which he envisaged being implemented by a continued Coalition or a National Government of 'the best men in all parties' who were 'willing to serve'. His Plan, which included an end to unemployment, a national health service, equal opportunities in education, was general in outline with a caveat on cost. Notably there was no mention of the Beveridge Report. Exactly a year later Churchill reviewed on the radio the achievements made or planned and announced that work was starting on the manufacture of pre-fabricated houses. These would supplement the post-war permanent construction programme and make a major contribution to tackling the enormous problem of rehousing.

The Coalition Government did achieve something. Following the 1942 publication of the Scott Report on *Land Utilization In Rural Areas* and the Uthwatt Report on *Compensation And Betterment*, a Ministry of Town and Country Planning was created in 1943. The

E

following year the Town and Country Planning Act incorporated some of the Reports' recommendations and helped local authorities by giving them increased powers in physical reconstruction, especially in blitzed areas. From what was done in 1944 it appeared that the social message was getting across: a White Paper was produced on social insurance; a Ministry of National Insurance was set up; there was a White Paper on a National Health Service; one on *Employment Policy*, which proposed sufficient state intervention to ensure 'a high and stable level of employment'; and R. A. Butler manoeuvred his Education Act through, giving the country a national system of free secondary education for every child.

The Coalition was also apparently looking farther ahead. In late 1943 Lord Woolton, the popular non-party Minister of Food, was appointed Minister of Reconstruction with a seat in the War Cabinet. Under his chairmanship a Reconstruction Committee was established. Its members included influential politicians like Sir John Anderson, R. A. Butler, Oliver Lyttelton and from the Labour side Attlee, Bevin and Morrison. The Committee discussed and approved White Papers and R. A. Butler recorded in 1945: 'The fact is that the Committee has done a good deal of useful work in framing the future social and political structure of the country.'

Lord Woolton went about making speeches on the subject. A selection of them was published under the title *The Adventure Of Reconstruction* on 26 July, 1945, the day the Labour victory was announced. His general objective was clear: 'Full employment and full opportunities for education, a rising standard of living, good housing and enough of it, improved standards of public health – all these go to provide the sense of social security which we want to build up in our time and to bequeath to the next generation as our contribution to the well-being of a great Britain.' Yet in fact he was not adventurous. He was at pains to point out that he did not want 'a brand new world'.

He did not appeal to the trade unions, which during the war had so far enjoyed a much closer relationship with the Government. Having to intervene in all sorts of activities on the domestic front, the Government sought the co-operation of the Trades Union Congress. George Woodcock, a former weaver, was then Head of the Research and Economic Department at the TUC:

The Government had two motives – morale and help. They wanted to keep us sweet, not on the outside criticizing and we put to them things they would have missed. For example, a pre-war government committee had drawn up a rationing scheme including special provision for heavy workers. We said, 'No. You can't do it. It would be fatal.' On the face of it the TUC would have been in favour but we could see all the problems. How do you define a heavy worker? The difficulties of house-wives meeting in a shop to get different rations for a domestic plumber and a ship's plumber. We had regular committees at the Ministry of Labour. We also had a Rationing and Prices Committee, which had regular meetings with the Ministry of Food and with the Board of Trade on clothes rationing. These committees were totally different from the *ad hoc* deputations between the wars. They were regular – monthly, fortnightly or even more often. You had an agenda so a matter could be carried over from one meeting to another. The idea of having a discussion was to do something about it.

The Government was able to achieve its objectives. At the same time the TUC bargained, meeting demands but also getting concessions. However, these tactics could only be used in a war situation. Woodcock again : 'In 1944 we produced the *Interim Report On Post War Reconstruction.* The Government was not at all interested in what we'd got to say. This is where the wartime arrangements didn't work. Kindly Uncle Fred Woolton was put into the Ministry of Reconstruction to smother it. We were plumping for the nationalization of coal, railways, electricity and not unnaturally they wouldn't wear it. They were aware I believe that at least the nationalization of coal and railways would have to come but they couldn't support it. It was a waste of our time.'

The idea of a planned peace was broadly agreed by all parties. In a sense everybody accepted in some degree Keynes's arguments for a managed economy and an interventionist government. The question was 'How much?' Was it to be Rationalization or Nationalization? Down among the grass roots of the Left there were firm views. One day in 1944 Will Cannon, a retired shunter and honorary member of the Reading Number One Branch of the National Union of Railwaymen, went along to his branch meeting. Under the item 'Correspondence' a letter was read from the secretary of the local Labour Party pointing out that as an affiliated organization they were entitled to put forward a resolution to go through the constituency Party to the annual conference. The chairman asked whether anybody had a resolution.

Will Cannon said: 'I don't like this economic programme they got. Why aren't they going to nationalize the railways, the coal mines, the steel and the rest?'

'All right,' replied the chairman. 'You write a resolution out.'

He did. It was not all that well worded but it went forward to the constituency Labour Party, one of eleven put forward by various union branches. After a warm discussion and marginal re-drafting to make it sound a bit better it was submitted to conference as the Reading resolution.

Grass roots opinion was going to be decisive in forming Labour Party policy and strategy. The Coalition consensus could not long outlive the end of the war.

11

Comrades In Arms

'We have the first dictator since Cromwell, and much as I distrust Winston I have even less faith in the Commons – a more moribund collection of old fogies and nit-wits I have never met.' This was the diary entry of a Conservative MP, 'Chips' Channon. Looking at his fellow Members in 1942 he might well have thought of the Lost Generation, the promising young men who were killed in the First World War. As the Parliament grew older it became more lifeless. Elected in 1935, it was the longest of the century. Of its three Prime Ministers only one, Stanley Baldwin, had been returned by the electorate as the leader of a victorious party. It was the same party that had welcomed back his successor, Chamberlain, from Munich and then two years later overthrown him. Churchill became the war leader of a party whose appeasement policy he had opposed. More and more, Parliament was unrepresentative of the country and by-elections were not changing the situation.

Within a week of war being declared the three major parties agreed to an electoral truce. When a Parliamentary seat fell vacant they would not put up rival candidates. Instead the party that had previously held the seat would chose its candidate, and he would be allowed a walkover. If there were to be any opposition it had to come from an Independent or a representative of a minority party. Thus there was often not much real choice at a by-election. The electoral register was also closed. No new voters were added when they reached twenty-one and those who moved from one constituency to another, which frequently happened in wartime, were not transferred to the register in their new area. People felt they had been disfranchised. The electoral truce produced some strange alliances. At the Wallasey by-election of April 1942, for example, Sir Richard Acland's Forward March movement supported the Independent, George Reakes, while Labour and the

Communists were supporting the Conservative candidate. In April 1945 Chelmsford Labour Party displayed copies of a telegram from Attlee still supporting the Conservative.

The truce fell hardest on the Labour Party. In 1942 the annual conference only narrowly rejected a motion to denounce it. Yet the Labour Party did not accept the electoral truce as a political truce. It was determined to retain its identity even though its leaders were serving in the Coalition. In Parliament MPs who were not members of the Government continued to sit on the Opposition benches and elected their own administrative committee to sit on the Opposition front bench. Outside Parliament the Labour Party held its annual conferences without interruption whereas the Conservatives only held theirs from 1943.

Preserving Labour's independence was not just tradition. It was an electoral necessity. Jim Griffiths, a Party stalwart since 1908, sat on the Opposition front bench, from which he had a good view of the ambivalent Churchill: 'He was of course Conservative leader as well as Prime Minister. Though not when he first took over the Government from Neville Chamberlain. Chamberlain remained leader of the Party till his death six months later. Then Churchill took on the Tory leadership. He didn't have to but he did, and I often think that the moment he did that there was no doubt we'd won the next election.'

Griffiths's fellow Welshman Nye Bevan never forgot that collections of Welsh miners' pennies helped to put him opposite Churchill, and was his most persistent wartime critic. He saw not only the two leaders in one but also a man who wrongly believed he had inherited the military genius of his ancestor Marlborough. Up to the end of 1942 this was a difficult image to sustain with the losses of Greece, Crete and Libya in the Mediterranean; the fall of Hong Kong, impregnable Singapore, and Burma in the Far East; the sinking of the *Hood*, the *Ark Royal*, the *Prince Of Wales* and the *Repulse*; the German battleships *Scharnhorst* and *Gneisenau* slipping through the English Channel and breaking the blockade. Officers and civil servants confided in Bevan, passing on much information that he dared not use. His criticisms of the conduct of the war, often apparently the lashings of a class warrior, were well informed. When he attacked things like the value of the strategic bombing of Germany he knew what he was talking about. He had the ability to absorb facts and, like Churchill, the gift of

language to present them. But it was a different language, by turns
beautiful, poetic, penetrating, fiery. Where Churchill was an orator
Bevan was a debater. His opponents had to listen to him. In his
demand for a 'Second Front Now' to help the Russians he had
support from the other end of the political spectrum in Lord
Beaverbrook. *Tribune* and the *Express* had a campaign in common.

During 1942 public dissatisfaction with the conduct of the war
was reflected in by-election swings against the Government. In
March the populist Denis Kendall, an aggressive industrialist who
wanted better management, was narrowly elected MP for Grant-
ham, Lincolnshire. He later proudly claimed he was the only MP
to have shot down an enemy aircraft from the roof of his own
factory with a gun manufactured by himself. In April two former
Labour men turned Independent won seats: the quirky W. J.
Brown at Rugby and George Reakes by a handsome majority in
Wallasey. A similar majority was secured in June at Maldon, Essex
by Tom Driberg, an independent Socialist who wrote for Beaverbrook and who capitalized on the disastrous fall of Tobruk four
days before the poll. At his eve of the poll meeting he was supported by Hannen Swaffer, a member of the Labour Party who
risked expulsion for his action, and by three men who were emerging as key figures in a new radical movement: Sir Richard Acland
MP, J. B. Priestley and Tom Wintringham.

Something had to fill the political vacuum created by the political truce. The Communists had already tried and failed with a front
organization, the People's Convention, which aimed at a People's
Government and friendship with the Soviet Union. When the Convention was officially wound up at the beginning of 1942 the Second
Front Movement was not broad enough to take its place. The
vacuum was filled by the merger of two organizations, the 1941
Committee led by J. B. Priestley and Sir Richard Acland's Forward
March movement. In the mood of despair after the loss of Tobruk
they came together in July 1942 to form the Common Wealth Party.
The new party intended to contest by-elections where a 'reactionary'
candidate was standing and was not opposed by a Labour or other
'progressive' candidate.

Priestley, too much of an individualist to work with committees,
resigned as president within a few months and CW, as its members
came to call it, took its character from Acland. Lanky, bespec-
tacled, earnest, he believed that we had to find nothing less than

a new way of living. Individuals could not go on living their lives in
the old way, in the old atmosphere, for the old motives. As earnest
of his own intent he left the Liberals and gave to the National Trust
the Devon estates that had been in his family since the baronetcy
was created in the Civil War. His typical follower was middle class,
professional or managerial, a person who had something to give.
Under the Self Assessment scheme he contributed what he felt he
could afford to CW. It was a movement composed of individuals,
never more than 15,000 in number, and not financed by any power
bloc.

They believed in fellowship. One of their slogans was 'Life Before
Property'. Common ownership of land and of all major resources
would remove the inequity of six per cent of the population owning
eighty-six per cent of the nation's wealth. In the new vital democracy there would be proportional representation, regional parliaments and joint consultation in industry. Power politics would be a
thing of the past. There would be no more secret diplomacy and an
end to public lying. One of CW's posters asked 'Is it expedient?'
and answered its own question by having 'expedient' crossed out
and the word 'right' written over. It was an ethical movement, its
character Puritan and Utopian. Its effect was to be inspirational
rather than practical, showing its strength in a number of by-elections.

At North Midlothian Tom Wintringham, now serving in the
Home Guard, just failed to beat the Conservative. A young service-
man, Lieutenant Raymond Blackburn, made a significant showing
at Watford using the Beveridge Report and a Youth Parliament.
The first victory was in the rural constituency of Eddisbury,
Cheshire, won in April 1943 by a young Battle of Britain pilot, John
Loverseed, on a platform of a Second Front, 'Beveridge In Full
Now' and the nationalization of agriculture. Though Labour had
never contested this apparently hopeless seat, CW now became a
'proscribed' organization, barred to members of the Labour Party.
Nevertheless local Labour Party members turned out to help a
young army officer, Lieutenant Hugh Lawson, win Skipton up in
the Yorkshire Dales for CW at the beginning of 1944. Harold
Nicolson recorded in his diary: 'I fear that Winston has become
an electoral liability now rather than an asset.' All Churchill could
do in the House was glare when Charlie White, the new Member
for West Derbyshire, was introduced. An Independent supported

by CW, he had defeated the son of the Duke of Devonshire in his pocket borough.

The electoral truce was now clearly breaking down. In March 1944 Transport House advised local Labour Parties to build up their organizations in readiness for a general election. The tone of debates in the House was sharpening and in the lobbies Members were beginning to speculate on polling results and other possibilities. On one occasion the suave Anthony Eden and the 'h'-dropping Ernest Bevin agreed that if Churchill retired then they could continue to work together in a Coalition. Neither was concerned which office he held. Bevin, though had to have one thing for the trade unions : nationalization of the coal mines. An observer of the conversation was General Smuts, the South African Premier, who later commented to Eden that it was 'cheap at the price'.

In October, however, both the Labour and Liberal parties announced they would fight the next election independently of all other parties. This was the time when it once more became necessary to prolong the life of the existing Parliament by legislation. In moving the bill, Churchill declared that as Parliament was entering its tenth year it would be wrong to prolong it much beyond the end of the war with Germany. This he envisaged happening by spring or early summer 1945, when the Labour and Liberal Ministers would leave the Cabinet. After the break up of the Coalition Conservatives would carry on as a Caretaker Government until the election. This would probably take place in October 1945, when public opinion had had time to quieten down after the victory in Europe and the war against Japan was likely to last for another eighteen months. Within a matter of months Churchill would regret these statements.

In the Labour Party there was a strong rank and file desire to get on with the job of reconstruction. This feeling had been pent up by the postponement of the Party's annual conference from its traditional Whitsun date, when rail traffic was building up for D-Day (6 June 1944). German rocket attacks then intensified the travelling problem and the conference did not assemble at Central Hall, Westminster until December. Delegates were unhappy with the cautious, vague approach of the National Executive's policy document *Economic Controls, Public Ownership And Full Employment*, which reaffirmed the principle of public ownership but only proposed acquiring the Bank of England. Twenty-one constituency

E*

parties and the National Association of Labour Teachers put down resolutions specifying a list of industries for nationalization. A composite version was moved by Ian Mikardo, the unknown candidate for Reading, where Will Cannon had first stirred the grass roots. The resolution, seconded by a teacher, Evelyn Denington, called on the National Executive to include 'the transfer to public ownership of the land, large scale building, heavy industry, and all forms of banking, transport and fuel and power' in the electoral manifesto. After a lively morning's debate Shinwell replied for the Executive and Laski asked Mikardo to remit the resolution. He refused. On a show of hands, it was carried by an overwhelming majority. As Mikardo was leaving the hall at lunchtime, like a man in a dream dazed by the revolution he had unconsciously wrought, Morrison came up to him, put a friendly hand on his shoulder and said: 'That was a good speech you made, young man. You did very well. But you realize you have lost us the general election, don't you?' Shortly afterwards Morrison was appointed chairman of the Policy and Special Campaign Committees, with responsibility for drafting the Party's election manifesto, which became *Let Us Face The Future.*

The Left was aroused too by events in Greece, which were also debated at the conference. Early in December the Athens police fired on and killed demonstrators. In the House Churchill, a friend of the King of Greece, justified sending troops to support the authorities on the grounds that the Communists were trying to seize power. Bevan and others maintained that by supporting one faction Britain was interfering with Greek sovereignty. When our troops became involved in heavy street fighting *The Times* too was roused: 'The British Government and the British Army have associated Britain with what is everywhere condemned as Fascist action.' A young RAF officer wrote home from the Middle East: 'About Greece: I don't know what the general opinion is at home, but that out here is that it seems singularly strange that we, supposedly fighting for democracy, should force upon a "liberated" people an autocratic and unpopular government, and then commence to sacrifice our own troops in a fight against the common people of the land who have risen in protest at what must appear a peculiarly unjust and high-handed action on our part.'

Churchill himself went out with Eden to Greece on Christmas Day and imposed a non-Communist provisional government on the people. The Greek Civil War was not an issue that died. In June at one of Quintin Hogg's first big campaign meetings in Oxford nearly every sentence was interrupted by cries of 'Greece! Greece!' Even some of Churchill's admirers, like the writer Compton Mackenzie, thought it was bloody-mindedness in compensation for having to be nice towards the Russian Communists. To many, Churchill stood for the old world of kings, princes and overlords, supporting people like Prince Umberto in Italy rather than the resistance forces that had fought so bravely against overwhelming odds. He was betraying the European revolution, of which some people at home already saw themselves as part. Above all, he was the wrong man to establish close bonds with our great ally the Soviet Union, whose friendship was the key to world peace. Instead he was truckling to America too much. That was not the way for Britain to be a genuine post-war equal in the Big Three.

Meanwhile at home things were warming up. All over the country Parliamentary candidates were being adopted. The chairman of the Conservative Party, Ralph Assheton, in a Leeds speech after the Labour Party conference, warned against nationalization and bureaucracy, a theme that Churchill used at his Party conference in March 1945 to try and drive a wedge between the Labour leaders. Labour had adopted a nationalization programme, he declared, 'much to the disgust of some of their leaders' and their sweeping proposals would destroy 'the whole of our existing system of society'. We were faced with 'the creation and enforcement of another system . . . borrowed from foreign lands and alien minds'. For his part he was prepared to bring into the government that would follow the Coalition 'men of goodwill' from any or no party. Some thought it was a bid for the support of Bevin, who had defended Churchill over Greece.

Bevin soon made his position clear at a Labour Party meeting in Leeds:

The Tories are saying that the Labour Party has not got the men to govern. Believe me, if I were to join them, you would be surprised at the virtues which would be attributed to me in tomorrow's Press. A lot of the Tory propagandists seem to have forgotten that I am a member of the Labour Party. I have been a member through all its vicissitudes. I have witnessed its ups and downs, the treachery of some of its leaders in the past . . . As far as I am concerned I still abide by the Party decision – whatever

it may be. Those of us in the Trade Union Movement know
how to accept majority decisions.

Bevin went on to endorse in detail the nationalization proposals
adopted by the annual conference. He was not going to enter a
Ramsay MacDonald 1931 type pact. Labour was united for the
fight.

What a fight it was going to be, judging by the Chelmsford by-
election. This was the last, spectacular triumph of Common Wealth,
which had applied for affiliation to the Labour Party and been refused. Chelmsford was a contest between two RAF types, Wing-
Commander Millington, who continued his bomber squadron duties
as long as possible and Flight-Lieutenant Cook, an admin officer
from London. The latter was a poor candidate, uttering platitudes
like: 'The only weakness of the League of Nations was that it
hadn't any strength.' With such inadequate material, the Conservatives fought the election on Churchill, plastering his picture
everywhere. Millington did not expect to win. CW had only two
full-time workers at Chelmsford, a large sprawling constituency.
Loyal and devoted supporters, however, came down from London
to help. Local converts were recruited, many of them middle-aged
ladies with tremendous energy and organizing talents. They arranged a thorough canvass of the agricultural workers, militant in
their Union, who were glad to vote for genuine opposition. All the
effort, what the *Express* described as 'the Common Wealth circus',
converted a Conservative majority of 16,624 into a Left-wing victory of 6,431.

At the declaration of the poll, with the Lord Lieutenant's wife
in tears, Millington said: 'Chelmsford has voted for a new way
of living.' Churchill cabled Eden, then in San Francisco at the
founding conference of the United Nations: 'The by-election at
Chelmsford, making all allowances for special conditions, airborne
v. chairborne, etc, shows clearly how impossible it will be for us to
hold office for a moment longer than is necessary after our Labour
colleagues have been called out. It seems to me most likely that
electioneering will begin the moment after the end of the German
war, and you will probably find it in full swing before you return . . .' Two days later Hitler committed suicide. The new world
was apparently not far off.

After VE Day, 8 May, there was a strong possibility of a snap
election, something like a repeat of Lloyd George's Khaki Election

coup of 1918. On 11 May Churchill again cabled Eden: 'There is a consensus of opinion on our side that June is better for our Party.' Eden agreed that on balance it was better than October. The same day, as Attlee was also in San Francisco, Churchill saw Bevin and Morrison about the date of the election. Churchill admitted that he was under heavy pressure from his own party, actually Beaverbrook and Bracken, 'to take it quickly'. He was personally unhappy about this. It was a bitter thought that, having been a national leader for so long and having been so kindly treated by all, he would soon be attacked and spoken ill of by nearly half the nation. What he wanted was a continuation of the Coalition so that a unified British government could play a strong role, especially necessary after the death of Roosevelt, in international affairs. The Japanese still had to be defeated and the Russians had not been co-operative since the Yalta conference he had attended in February.

One of his supporters was R. A. Butler, who thought a continuation of the Coalition until at least the end of the Japanese war was in the national and Party interest. For the good of the country it could complete its programme of social reform. In the Party the policy on which he had been working as head of the Post-War Problems Committee was not yet fully worked out and had not got down to the constituencies, where the organizations were in a parlous state. If there were an early election the result would be disastrous. After he had put this point of view to Churchill, Beaverbrook reproved him: 'Young man, if you speak to the Prime Minister like that, you will not be offered a job in the next Conservative government.' Butler replied: 'That doesn't really affect me: for if we have an early election, there is not going to be a Conservative government.'

Labour and the Liberals were in favour of an October election. By then Churchill's war prestige would be a dwindling asset; a large number of Servicemen would have returned home; the electoral register would be brought up to date; and the annual Prolongation of Parliament Bill would be due for renewal anyway. Morrison thought that neither the country nor the Labour Party would swallow any further extension. Bevin, it seemed, was impressed by Churchill's arguments and was prepared to go on with the Coalition until the end of the Japanese war. The decision, however, rested with Attlee.

On his return from San Francisco he and Churchill met. They agreed that they would like to maintain the Coalition until the defeat of Japan, with an election following the final victory. Both recognized though that their own parties might not be prepared to wait. So that a decision on the date could be reached Churchill set out his options in a letter to Attlee. Ruling out the idea of an October election, he offered either the Coalition continuing until the defeat of Japan or an immediate dissolution and a July election. To make the Coalition proposal more acceptable to his Labour colleagues Attlee, after consulting Bevin, got inserted into the draft a sentence promising that the Government would do its utmost to implement the White Paper propositions on social security and full employment. The letter, dated 18 May, was ready for discussion at the Labour Party conference then assembling in Blackpool.

Before the conference opened the National Executive met in the Town Hall to discuss the letter. Attlee and three minor members of the Executive were very much on their own in wanting the Coalition to continue. Bevan, Morrison, Shinwell (who in 1935 had won Seaham from the 'traitor' Ramsay MacDonald), and the Chief Whip, Whiteley, all warned that neither the conference nor the Parliamentary Party would stand for it. Before them was the greatest political opportunity in Labour's history. It could not be cast aside. The majority opinion was for an October election and it was left to the War Cabinet ministers, Attlee and Morrison (Bevin was not interested), to draft a reply to Churchill to that effect.

On Whit Monday, 21 May, as the crowds sunned themselves on the Blackpool beaches, in the Empress Ballroom at the Winter Gardens a united Labour leadership faced 1,100 eager delegates. In private session they endorsed the Executive's view with only two hands raised against. Attlee sent his reply to Churchill, who rejected the compromise of an October election and stated that he would resign straight away. On 23 May he drove to the Palace, tendered his Government's resignation and agreed to form a Caretaker administration. Parliament would be dissolved on 15 June ready for an election on 5 July. Next day, in active trading on a declining London stock market, Industrials fell almost three points.

At its dissolution Parliament had set some records. Lasting nine years, six months and twenty days, it was the longest United Kingdom Parliament ever and the fourth longest in British history. Its like had not been seen since the English Parliaments of the seventeenth century, the Long and Pensioners' Parliaments of Charles I and II. It had spanned three monarchs and three Prime Ministers. During the first half of its life it had tried to avoid war, in the second half to win it. *Punch* celebrated its end with an E. H. Shepard cartoon of two crocodiles, one Labour and one Conservative, embracing and shedding tears with a small Liberal crocodile on the ground between them. The caption was: 'FAREWELL Since there's no help, come let us kiss and part.'

Churchill did in fact shed tears. On 28 May he held an 'At Home' at No 10 to thank the members of his Coalition. Hugh Dalton was there:

> Standing behind the Cabinet table, now draped as a buffet, he addressed us all, with tears visibly running down his cheeks. He said that we had all come together, and had stayed together as a united band of friends in a very trying time. History would recognize this. 'The light of history will shine on all your helmets.' He was sure that, if ever such another mortal danger threatened, we would all do the same again. He went on to say that, when he went to meet Stalin and Truman, he wanted to take with him 'My good friend, Clem Attlee' to show that, whatever happened in the election, we were a United Nation.

The country was in the meantime under a Caretaker Government. Its Ministers were mainly Conservatives, with the Liberal Gwilym Lloyd George and some 'Independents' like Sir John Anderson, Sir James Grigg and Lord Woolton. Churchill's old critic Leslie Hore-Belisha, the new Minister of National Insurance, got the Family Allowances Act on to the statute book and some of the other outstanding Coalition bills were hastily passed into law. But these were mere gestures towards a new world. Since its conference at Blackpool Labour's blood was up.

After making their decision to fight, the delegates had spent three days discussing the Party policy as set out in *Let Us Face The Future*. Herbert Morrison presented it, promising 'great changes in our time' and the cheers echoed for minutes on end through the Winter Gardens. The delegates were changed too. As one said: 'The round belly and the gold Albert are gone.' From the platform the view was not of 'a sea of white heads' but of enthusiastic young men and women, to whom red-headed Ellen Wilkinson in the chair gave preference at the microphone. Among them were many service candidates like Captain Raymond Blackburn, who had left Com-

mon Wealth and was now up for the King's Norton division of
Birmingham; from the Navy Lieutenant Jim Callaghan, who was
to gain Cardiff South; Major John Freeman, the Desert Rat fresh
from the surrender of Hamburg three weeks before, standing for
Watford; Captain Roy Jenkins contesting Solihull in the hope of
joining his father, Arthur, the Member for Pontypool; Squadron
Leader John Pudney, with the impossible constituency of Sevenoaks.

Lieutenant David Packham, who had the neighbouring impossible
constituency, East Grinstead, emphasized the fact that the serviceman did not want to be regarded as an ex-serviceman when he
came out of the Army but as a civilian. Servicemen's views had
been shaping for a long time. 'Two years ago,' he said, 'when I was
in Africa, the main topic was not the war, but the things we wanted
after the war – a cottage and kids – chocolate and chicken. After
escaping from prison I decided that it would be useless to fight
for peace in time of war unless one was prepared to fight for peace
in time of peace . . . so I became a Labour candidate.' One service
candidate was Air Vice-Marshal H. V. Champion de Crespigny.
When introduced, Fred Burrows of the National Executive said:
'I can't believe it. Either that's not your name or you aren't a
Labour candidate.' The Air Vice-Marshal was in fact the candidate
for Newark.

Still wearing uniform, Major Denis Healey, the candidate for
Pudsey and Otley, who had just flown in from Italy, made a pas-
sionate speech: 'The Socialist revolution has already begun in
Europe, and is already firmly established in many countries in
Eastern and Southern Europe . . . The upper classes in every
country are selfish, depraved, dissolute, and decadent. . . . The
struggle for Socialism in Europe has been hard, cruel, bitter, merci-
less and bloody . . . After paying this price our comrades won't
let go.' Bevin was with him: 'I am not a recent convert to friendship with the Soviet Union'. His watchword was 'To Moscow, not
Munich'.

When the delegates called for action, Morrison was on his feet,
quickly followed by Bevin, shouting 'Forward!' MacDonald, 1931
and coalition were in the distant past. Ahead was the bright future.
The delegates had the will to win, to build the new Jerusalem. As
they left, the closing words of Ellen Wilkinson's speech were still
ringing in their ears: 'Fight clean, fight hard and come back with
a solid majority for a Labour Government.'

12

The Thunder Of The Captains

One beautiful summer evening during the election campaign Margaret Cole was driving back from a meeting at Streatham, where she had been speaking, when suddenly the driver of her car could go no further. Huge crowds of people blocked the pavements and the road. A motorcade with Churchill at its head had passed through only minutes before. With a ready-made crowd, Margaret Cole held an impromptu meeting of her own. When she returned to her car an old man stepped out of the crowd and took her by the arm : 'Don't get me wrong, lady. I only came to see the bugger, not to vote for him.'

Certainly there was a great desire to see in the flesh the man who had stood firm and rallied the nation in 1940, the great leader, the historic figure. Wherever he went during the campaign crowds flocked to see him. On an informal visit to his constituency before the campaign proper the word soon got round and, as if by magic, the roads on his route were lined by cheering people waving handkerchiefs and holding small children up to see the doughty champion pass by. It was like the triumph of a Roman general. During a three-hour stay despatches were brought from Downing Street to his hotel at Loughton.

Inevitably, Churchill was to be the dominant personality of the election and the temptation to latch on to his heroic and already legendary status proved irresistible. The Conservatives appealed to the electorate with his record, as though that were the same as theirs. Was it not a patriotic duty to support the man who had led us to victory in Europe, the 'man with the big cigar' as the words of a popular Flanagan and Allen song had it? 'They know they can't win without me', Churchill had confided to Ernest Bevin. About half the prospective Conservative candidates had a picture of Churchill on their election addresses, with a letter of support from him printed below. If accused of cashing in on a great name, they were unrepentant. Stephen Benson, the candidate for Upton, roundly asserted: 'I shall always try to cash in on Churchill because I think he is worth cashing in on.'

They realized too late that their opponents could also cash in on him, particularly as a crowd-puller. On Richmond Green, in the wake of a Churchill walkabout in aid of his former Parliamentary Private Secretary, Brigadier George Harvie Watt, Labour supporters distributed a leaflet listing Socialist measures Churchill had advocated in wartime speeches but now omitted from the Conservative manifesto. In the Ladywood division of Birmingham the Labour candidate, Victor Yates, followed him round the constituency, saying to the crowds: 'Now you've all cheered the old man it's time for somebody else to win the peace.' He met with even louder cheers. The cheers for Churchill many felt were no more than a victorious warrior's deserts, though others considered this was less than the truth. At a May Day rally in West Leyton the Labour Member, A. E. Bechervaise, remarked: 'Ordinary people won this war. It is not Mr Churchill's victory', an observation repeatedly made from Labour hustings throughout the campaign.

Labour's attitude to Churchill was conditioned by four bad memories, four events sufficiently remote in time to have been elevated to the status of folk myth. In 1910, as Home Secretary, he had been responsible for ordering troops to South Wales, where there was considerable industrial unrest. By 1945 this was commonly represented as Churchill having ordered troops to fire on Welsh miners, an event that never occurred. In 1919, as Secretary for War, he had lent British troops to the anti-Bolshevik armies in Russia. This was considered a bloodthirsty attempt to make war on Socialists at the moment the rest of the world was having its first taste of peace in five years. Labour speakers throughout the campaign were able to draw the parallel between events then and the intervention in Greece in 1944, quoting from a full page in *Your MP* anti-Russian remarks made by Churchill since 1919. In 1925, as Chancellor of the Exchequer, he returned to the Gold Standard, an act which many Labour stalwarts considered made him personally responsible for the Depression and all the bitterness of the 1926 General Strike. His leading part in organizing the emergency measures to defeat the strike and his advocacy of the firmness with which they should be applied was the fourth black mark against him in Labour eyes. For them it was quite impossible to regard him as the man of the people now depicted by his Party.

Nor, despite his anti-Munich stance and thirties calls for re-armament, was it altogether possible for Labour voters to disentangle him from pre-war Conservative foreign policy. Had he not had kind words to say for both Franco and Mussolini in his time, words that *Tribune* was only too ready to quote back at him throughout the campaign? If Labour supporters remembered his close association with Lloyd George and the foundation of the Welfare State in the years before the First World War, they would no doubt have dismissed it as irrelevant in the light of his subsequent behaviour. Even within his own Party his virulent attacks on Conservatives in that early period were still remembered as the act of a man who could not be trusted. His wife was supposed never to vote anything but Liberal. Consistency had never been Churchill's strong point and in any examination of such a long political career it was only too easy for opponents to make capital out of his shifting views.

As well as all this, Churchill was never as popular with the forces as he was with the civilian public. His disposition to see himself as Marlborough reincarnate resulted in many attempts at autocratic and amateur soldiering that caused resentment among the officers, even when they were brave enough to ignore his dictates. Field-Marshal Alan Brooke, Chief of the Imperial General Staff, in 1944 bemoaned the fact that Churchill's orders had no practical bearing on the fighting. The men often saw little more to Churchill than a man with an idiosyncratic way of speaking. At the moment of final victory British soldiers in Holland listening to Churchill's broadcast speech were seen to mimic the cadences once thought so rousing and now felt to be behind the times.

Of all this his Conservative supporters seemed totally unaware and remained sure that he was their key to easy victory. Churchill himself was no fool and on more than one occasion seems to have had doubts about his capacities as a peacetime Premier or even his ability to win an election. As early as 1940, while reassuring Anthony Eden on his claims to the future leadership, Churchill had insisted that he was already an old man and that he would never repeat the mistake of Lloyd George in carrying on as a post-war leader. Although he had been leader of his party since Neville Chamberlain's death he had been successful in hiding this role from himself and a great many others. He used every propaganda device at his disposal to create the legend of a national warrior figure. His somewhat melodramatic proclivities led to secret sessions of Parliament and calls for votes of confidence that were frequently unnecessary.

They also led him into sartorial fantasies. While Joseph Stalin liked to be photographed smoking a pipe and wearing a homespun peasant blouse, Winston Churchill preferred to face the camera wearing uniforms of high-ranking officers in the various services, to none of which was he strictly entitled. In Churchill's view government was essentially a presidential affair. In the general election it was a mistake. The Conservatives reported finding many who believed that, no matter which party won the day, Churchill would remain Prime Minister. Some Labour supporters, like H. G. Wells, increasingly saw the old man as deluded by some kind of *fuehrerprinzip*. Service voters who, now that demobilization had just begun, increasingly dreamed of a return to Civvy Street, had had more than enough of uniforms, particularly those of high-ranking officers. While Churchill did not campaign in uniform, calendars and diaries for 1945 bore many a photo of him in the role of some kind of military supremo, an ever present reminder that the choice was between this and Clement Attlee. And whoever saw Attlee tricked out in gold braid, with rings on his sleeves?

Attlee, with his owlish spectacles that did little to hide his strabismus, the toothbrush moustache and the unattractive rasp in his voice that could come perilously near a drone, was frankly unprepossessing. Yet many voters must have recognized in this Stanmore solicitor the quintessential committee man, have seen him as a mirror image of the quiet and unassuming chap found on so many of the committees that had proliferated throughout the war, the fellow who took the minutes in a laboriously tidy hand or who could call a meeting to order when friction threatened, the chap who could guide them unerringly through a lengthy agenda. To many he was unquestionably the man for the moment, the right one to tackle the already intimidatingly long post-war programme.

Like many such men, Attlee had become a leader by accident. The Parliamentary Labour Party elected him in 1935, when George Lansbury's extreme pacifist views made him no longer acceptable in the role. At the time there seemed no alternative among the thinned ranks of the Party and most of them thought of his accession as a stopgap measure. The war prolonged his leadership, while membership of the Coalition Government increased his importance and influence, though many on the Left considered he allowed himself to be overshadowed by Churchill and other Conservatives in the Coalition. Up to the very beginning of the election campaign there was much serious heart searching in the Labour Party about whether Attlee was really the right man to lead them into what was clearly going to be a very vigorous and hard fought campaign.

Jim Griffiths found that one of his leader's outstanding characteristics was his virtually old-world correctness. After the events of 1935 Lansbury and Attlee never spoke ill of each other but always behaved with almost exaggerated courtesy. To many it hardly seemed the right style to fight such a champion as Churchill, who had never been inclined to pull his political punches. In 1943 Harold Nicolson had ruminated in his diary on the unsuitability of Attlee to deal with great events and confessed he found it impossible to convey the absurdity of that small man. Churchill himself was supposed to have made a petty remark at the time of the election to the effect that Attlee was 'a sheep in sheep's clothing', while Attlee himself once confessed that until middle age the limit of his ambition had been to be mayor of some minor London borough. To Margaret Cole he was a man who could have done with more imagination and certainly lacked panache, but was nevertheless better than most people thought.

If he was misunderstood this may have been because he was no spendthrift with words. His colleagues used to say of him he would never use one syllable where none would do. Ernest Millington found him intelligent but inhibited: 'He never argued. He would listen and listen and listen and then he would decide. But he never argued.' Jim Griffiths experienced the same sort of thing: 'Attlee made very firm decisions when they needed to be made and stuck to them. They always seemed sudden because he concealed the thought processes that led to them. I think he came to these decisions while he sat there doodling.' Jim Cattermole, the paid Labour Party agent for the whole of Birmingham, met him for the first time when arranging a campaign meeting at the Town Hall.

'I've been looking at this agenda,' said Attlee, 'I see you've got me down to speak for forty-five minutes. Why's that?'

'I thought you'd like forty-five minutes.'

He shook his head: 'Any politician who needs more than twenty minutes to say what he has to say isn't worth listening to.'

He was nothing if not shrewd and precise. But he was also shy and, though he was always loyal to the Labour Party, many of its members thought his Socialism less than avid. For *Tribune*, Attlee brought 'to the fierce struggle of politics the tepid enthusiasms of a lazy summer afternoon at a cricket match'. One of the few non-political subjects on which Attlee could become animated was cricket. He was also judged to have consistently under-played his position and opportunities. 'He seems determined to make a trumpet sound like a tin whistle', complained the same writer. This criticism had been occasioned by Attlee's attendance at the San Francisco Conference, an action seen as a crowning blunder in that it served the purpose of ostentatiously identifying Labour with Tory foreign policy without the Tories paying any price for it. Many on the Left saw it as an unnecessary agreement to serve as lieutenant to Anthony Eden. *Tribune* concluded its thunderous rebuke with: 'The whole affair is painful, humiliating and hurtful to the Labour Party. At no time has Mr Attlee stood so low in the estimate of his followers.' The piece was unsigned but might have been written by Professor Harold Laski, who the year before had not flinched from writing to Attlee accusing him of actually enjoying the Coalition and who, after the Party conference of 1945, again wrote to inform Attlee that his leadership was a grave handicap. The Labour leader, however, had little time for Labour intellectuals and, though professing to regard Laski as a great teacher, considered him 'hopeless' when it came to practical matters. In later years Attlee could not be persuaded to rate Laski at this time as more than 'a slight irritation' to him.

In any case there was really no alternative to his leadership once Ernest Bevin had made it clear he was not interested. Herbert Morrison may have yearned for the post but once the imminence of an election campaign became an established fact he was absorbed in preparing for it to the extent that, master tactician though he was alleged to be, his assault on the leadership was crassly mistimed. The movement closed ranks behind Attlee for the campaign, all misgivings forgotten, as it slowly became clear that something in his unassuming style made crowds warm to him. After Churchill's grandiose motorcades there was something reassuring about the man in the crumpled suit who pottered along in a small family car that was driven by his wife. They would have endorsed Donald Soper's view of him: 'He was extraordinarily anonymous but a man of tremendous resolution, a man who was at ease with himself in that he knew what he wanted. He was never unduly concerned as to what other people thought of him.'

The Conservative candidate who, speaking in Birmingham, sneered that the contest was between Churchill, the National lion and Attlee, the Socialist mouse, had forgotten that in Aesop's fable it was the mouse who was able to deliver the lion from a tight spot. In fact the campaign seldom resolved itself into a fight between the two disparate personalities but was soon understood as a conflict between a flamboyant personality whose policies seemed non-committal and a committed policy advocated by a man who seemed to lack personality. Churchill's name appeared on the cover of the Conservative declaration of policy. Attlee's name was not mentioned anywhere in the Labour manifesto, which was seen as a programme to be tackled by a team. In a campaign speech made at the end of June, Attlee declared: 'Labour could form a team infinitely stronger than the Tories. In the Tory team after Churchill and Eden, who comes next?' There was much substance in the charge and it was further driven home by the fact that throughout the election Eden was a sick man.

Anyone attempting to answer Attlee's question at the time could really have only put forward the names of R. A. Butler and Brendan Bracken. Butler, despite his Education Act of the year before, was still relatively unknown, although he had been MP for Saffron Walden for sixteen years. Something of a Churchill protégé, he had been made Minister of Labour in the Caretaker Government so he became responsible for carrying out Bevin's demobilization plan. Mindful of this, he included in his election address a 'Special Message to Serving Men and Women'. Most of it was painfully stiff and formal, with the air of some official government handout, and struck an unfortunately ingratiating note when it reminded the reader that he had helped Mr Bevin frame a Further Education Scheme whereby those whose education or technical training had been interrupted by the war could obtain a substantial grant. Service voters who thought more about demobilization than anything else were going to prefer the genuine article to a mere 'helper'. Unlike Bevin, Butler seemed to prefer to hold what cards he had tight to his chest rather than fling them on the table with a challenging air.

If Butler's introvert nature hid his considerable gifts and even gave him a cold and calculating air, Brendan Bracken, with his unruly mop of red hair and mischievous grin, was the complete extrovert. He had been an almost unqualified success at the Ministry of Information, which had drawn much adverse criticism until his arrival. There he had shown a ruthless way with bureaucracy that many in the main parties might have emulated with profit. To Bracken that was what being a Minister was all about. Yet neither was he the creature of the Prime Minister. Indeed Churchill's remarkable tolerance of the volatile Bracken occasioned all kinds of rumours, including one that he was his natural son, given credence by a superficial facial resemblance but totally without foundation. The fact that in the three years before 1945 he was clearly one of Churchill's ablest Ministers won him no friends, even in his own Party. The old guard, particularly, disliked and distrusted him and considered him to be, in effect, a crook. This distrust was also echoed on the Left, which at the start of the campaign was convinced that if there were to be any Tory stunts they would emanate only from Lord Beaverbrook and Brendan Bracken. Indeed, there were some who thought that Beaverbrook dreamed of grooming Bracken to be the next Prime Minister.

In May 1945 the two of them were reported to have been urging a snap election on Churchill 'because by autumn unemployment will increase due to slackened war production and housing problems will be worse than ever so they are moving quickly while they are able to cash in on Churchill's war prestige'. Later Churchill's broadcast 'Gestapo' speech was attributed to 'the evil genius of Lord Beaverbrook and Mr Bracken'. At the beginning of June 'London Diary' in the *New Statesman* noted: 'I expect Brendan Bracken to be involved in any Tory stunts. He will be good at this sort of thing. He always says that which will please, amuse, cajole or sidetrack those to whom he is talking. No one is ever quite sure what he really thinks.' These are, of course, characteristics that many might consider virtues in a politician. Bracken's virtues, however, were to be obscured when he unexpectedly became a figure of fun after Churchill made him First Lord of the Admiralty in the Coalition Government. In a presumably unguarded moment of hyperbole during a campaign speech, Beaverbrook called him the greatest holder of that office since Churchill. Gilbert Wilkinson, the *Daily Herald* cartoonist, in a humorous comment on Conservative attitudes twisted this to 'the greatest since Nelson'. By the end of the week the *New Statesman* leader had it as 'the greatest Sea Lord there has ever been.' To make matters worse, the speech was made to a naval audience at Chatham dockyard. The unrepentant Beaverbrook went on to say that Bracken was, moreover, 'the best man for any job in a good government'.

There were few other names. Some may have been aware of a stormy young petrel called Captain Quintin Hogg, who seemed ready to embrace certain radical, if not Socialist solutions, when it suited him. There was also Harold Macmillan. Probably the only other well known name in the Conservative ranks was that of L. S. Amery who, so legend had it, had once been ducked by Churchill when they were at Harrow together. Born in India, he had remained Secretary of State for that colony throughout Churchill's administration and had drawn up the plan for its self-government. Sadly, he was probably better known to the public because his son John had espoused the enemy cause, apparently without remorse, and now awaited trial for treason. In some quarters this reminded voters that Conservative families in the pre-war years had frequently taken too uncritical a view of Nazis and Fascists.

If the colourful Churchill made most of his team appear nonentities, the anonymous Attlee headed a group of lively, well-contrasted characters whose names were well known to the public. Biggest among them at the time, in physical stature as well as reputation, was Ernest Bevin, who now found himself fighting his first election. He had come into the Coalition through an uncontested by-election as part of the electoral truce. This was necessary because he was the most powerful man in the trade union movement and his authority was indispensable in implementing industrial conscription without incurring the hostility of the Left. In this he was phenomenally successful but there were many in the Party who were resentful and suspicious of his Rightist leanings.

The Observer, however, saw him as the 'first British statesman to have been born a working man and remained one', and this was probably how the British electorate saw him. His war work had much to do with factories and machines but he had been born a country lad in Somerset and first worked as a farm labourer on leaving school at the age of eleven. He had a forceful and blunt manner of speaking that he liked to represent as a virtue, though it could be graceless and coarse, as in his unnecessary insolence to the inoffensive Lansbury in 1935. Not for Bevin the courtesy of an

Attlee. His pride in being a true son of toil also led him to believe that it did not matter that he was unable to put two sentences together containing the proper number of verbs properly conjugated. With him consistency counted for more than coherence. He flaunted his lack of education. His single-minded hammering away at what he wanted as a trade union official had early earned him the title 'Dockers' KC'. When he became chairman of the TUC General Council in 1937 he showed none of the finesse a chairman's role calls for but an authority, power and dynamism on a Churchillian scale. In the war this was an asset, justly celebrated in a Transport House booklet circulated during the election called *Ernest Bevin And His Work In Wartime*.

Jealous of him was Herbert Morrison, whose detestation was returned in full measure. As tiny in stature as Bevin was big, Morrison, with his one good eye and jaunty Edwardian quiff, a gift to cartoonists, was probably as little activated by great moral principle. To these two, politics was a career where personal ambition manipulated them as easily as they manipulated others. In writing the Party manifesto and shaping and organizing the campaign, Morrison was sure his foot was now firmly on the ladder that led to personal supremacy, all the more so in that he had always enjoyed such planning almost for its own sake. He was reputed to have a vision of democracy as a succession of London Passenger Transport Boards, while his sole concern about Hell, it was once said, would be wondering whether there was an increasing demand for it in the marginal parishes. Yet the image the public had of Morrison was not of a manipulator, though 'planner' – then a term of approval – might have been acceptable. The son of a London policeman, he liked to project the image of a lovable, chirpy Cockney sparrow.

There was not much lovable or chirpy about the tall, austere figure of Stafford Cripps, but neither could there be any doubt about the moral principles motivating his politics. For him Socialism was a practical expression of Christianity. Somewhat aloof, he had led a rather sheltered life, having been a delicate child who endured poor health and then, after a spell at Winchester, going on to study patent law. This was not perhaps the best branch of the law to qualify a man for dealing with people, and some claimed he always had to grit his teeth to give a working man a hearty slap on the back. Convinced of the rightness of whatever cause he took up,

Cripps could be a difficult man for colleagues to work with. The Labour Party had expelled him for advocating a Popular Front and as the campaign began he had but recently been welcomed back to the fold. He was always followed by the idealists in the Party and, though he may have lacked the common touch, was enormously respected by all.

Expelled along with him and other Popular Front advocates had been the young Welshman, Aneurin Bevan. The son of a miner, he had gone to work in the mines at the age of thirteen and was elected MP for Ebbw Vale in 1929. He did not choose to be Labour in the way of a Cripps or even a Morrison. He was born into the Movement. He first gained some kind of national notoriety with his Commons attacks on Churchill and the Coalition Administration, which were amplified in his own writings and his editorship of *Tribune*. By 1944, whenever the message went round Westminster that Bevan was to speak the Chamber would fill, for even his enemies would come to hear him. Able to think quickly on his feet and loving the cut and thrust of argument, he soon became the speaker most in demand at Labour campaign meetings. Although he had a slight stammer, many discovered a beautiful quality in the voice and limpid speech. His personality came over as warm and caring. He was a man to whom words and facts and people mattered. His popularity incited his opponents to a fury in which they caricatured him as a Socialist cad who had stayed at home dodging National Service while the True Blues had got on with the job of thumping the Hun.

Beside the tremendous crowd-pulling magnetism of Bevan the other personalities were small stars in the Labour heaven. But they were still stars. There were the smiling, rather jolly features of the voluble Hugh Dalton, whose heart was in the right place as even his worst enemies would admit; Jim Griffiths, a Welsh miner MP, who could speak with passion and compassion, rated by all those who came in contact with him a totally lovable personality; Arthur Greenwood, the Party treasurer and vice-chairman of the Parliamentary Labour Party, who had gone to Attlee and put forward the name of Beveridge to compile that report; and John Strachey, whose name was so widely known from his books. With such a strong team it is a wonder that any of them ever entertained any doubts about the result of the contest. Only Bevan made anything like an accurate prediction.

The Liberal Party, on the other hand, was convinced that its hour was at hand. Its fortunes, shattered so cruelly over the years, were about to be restored. True, Lloyd George, the greatest Liberal of the century, had died in March, but was it not many years since the old man had been truly with them? Was not, in any case, Beveridge a new name to conjure with, the one on everybody's lips? Admittedly he was only the chairman of their campaign committee, not the Liberal leader. That was Archibald Sinclair, who served in the Coalition as Minister for Air. Some said he was the most unpopular Minister in the Government, with an annoying habit of answering questions in the House in an unnecessarily heated and rhetorical manner. Many Liberal MPs were among his bitterest critics and considered that he had for years taken no significant part in their Party activities. Others, like Frank Byers, saw this as a selfless dedication to his wartime job, which excluded his Party and turned his hair from jet black to silver in the space of three years. He had an aristocratic, somewhat testy manner in personal relationships but was striking and well dressed in his appearance, the sort of man it was believed who might attract the female vote. On a public platform, though not in the Lloyd George class, he was a considerable spell-binder.

Inside the Party the Radical Action Group was active, including among its members a future party leader, Clement Davies. Working very closely with Aneurin Bevan, they favoured an anti-Tory coalition at the general election. Transport House was rigid in its isolationism. Liberal, Common Wealth, ILP and Communist advances were alike unwelcome and spurned. The Conservatives, on the other hand, were by no means averse to sheltering and welcoming to their colours odd groups and individuals, be they National Liberals, Unionists or Independents.

Apart from Ernest Millington few of the Common Wealth candidates were widely known to the electorate, but the Party was thought to have more chance of electoral success than the Communist party, whose best known member was Willie Gallacher. The only Communist MP, he had started work in a Lancashire coal mine at the age of twelve, was now a pillar of the Scottish Co-op and away from politics wrote plays and short stories. The Party secretary, Harry Pollitt, who had opposed Communist branding of the war in 1939 as an imperialist conflict, was less well known. One small boy happily off on a day trip to Skegness saw the words

'Attlee or Pollitt for PM' chalked on an engine in Lincoln station. When he asked what this meant, his father was at a loss to tell him.

Churchill too must have been at something of a loss when, instead of being returned unopposed for his constituency as Labour had agreed, he discovered his candidature was to be disputed by a one-man party. Alexander Hancock arrived from Northampton on nomination day to register as the Independent candidate for Woodford. After the initial surprise local people were at first rather superior. 'It was inevitable', said a writer in the *Walthamstow Guardian*, 'that somebody should oppose Churchill: the chance of overnight fame was too great to be missed.' An earlier possible candidate was Trooper William Douglas-Home. The national Press called Hancock a farmer but the National Farmers' Union pointed out that he was not one of their members. Hancock was aged forty-eight and, after serving in the Navy during the First World War, had become a boot manufacturer, prospering enough to retire and buy a farm that his two sons ran for him.

Asked whether the thought of Churchill as an opponent daunted him, he replied: 'He is beneath my contempt.' When asked how he would pay for his campaign he retorted: 'Tell them I am ready to spend more money than anybody else.' He had a plan which he claimed was based on his long interest in the welfare of humanity. He was not interested in politics or personal publicity. He seemed, however, to enjoy giving interviews to Indian and American newspapers and being filmed for the newsreels. He wanted to outline his Plan to the public and printed a version of it in the local Press in a curious typographic farrago of capitalized words that had an eighteenth-century look about it. It might have been from Lemuel Gulliver in Brobdingnag. The British began to feel a little better about his presumption. After all, he was no more than that ever popular character, the English eccentric. When his agent said he had already had many offers of help, nobody paid much attention.

If Hancock looked amateur, so to modern eyes was the national campaign. In this election as in no other the politicians knew the electorate had to be taken seriously and spoken to directly, for the electors had come to hear them. There was no sitting at home with the election brought unceasingly and monotonously to one's fireside. The elector had to go out to the election, to go and find it, and he was well advised to go early if he wanted a seat at a meeting, no matter which party was holding it. This gave a sense of occasion, which has been lacking from every election since. The parties used no marketing men to produce policies they believed the public wanted, or public relations and advertising agencies to concoct unbelievable 'images'. Had anybody thought of them, such ideas would probably have had short shrift from a public whose wartime experiences had given them a nose for truth. It was the politicians themselves and the new men who fretted to take their place that the public wanted to meet, to hear and to dispute with.

13

Battle Of The Hustings

Early in the campaign *The Times* published a letter from the Liberal candidate for Ilford North, Lady Rhys Williams, which reminded all candidates that the Butler Education Act passed the year before gave them the right to use school premises for election meetings. This action was not prompted simply by a desire to be informative but by an experience that had befallen her local party. The Ilford County High School for Girls had been booked for a Liberal meeting, though the headmistress had expressed doubts because the hall would be used throughout that week for the School Certificate exams. Doubts turned into a problem when the chairman of the school governors telephoned Lady Williams to tell her that the Liberals could not have the hall. He was not impressed by the fact that Lord Samuel had been engaged to speak. Under law, the chairman said, election meetings could only be held in elementary schools.

Hurriedly consulting her solicitor, Lady Williams found this was no longer the case and that the new Education Act did in fact permit the use of secondary schools for electoral purposes. The headmistress, however, remained unimpressed and withdrew her previous permission, convinced that the upheaval such a meeting might cause would prove too upsetting for her examination candidates. The local Conservatives, anxious no doubt to snatch a Pharisee's mantle and demonstrate that they 'were not as other men', piously declared that, though they too had booked a meeting at the school, they would be happy to withdraw without fuss. An appeal to the local Education Committee and an undertaking from the Liberals to supply six men to tidy up and replace desks after the meeting finally removed the impasse. Lord Samuel was able to appear to the sound of prolonged applause and to declare that the war had been due to Tory foreign policy.

The whole incident illustrates how unprepared on a practical level the country was for an election and how the difficulties this created were usually solved by a little goodwill, co-operation and commonsense. The habit of working together could still assert itself even when those who did so might now find themselves on opposite sides of the political fence. The need to use schools for meetings, particularly in London, was acute. In Ilford the Town Hall could not be used by any party because it was occupied by the Food Committee Staff absorbed in their task of allotting new ration books. Not far away in Leytonstone there was concern that even small church halls might not be available. These were now crammed to the roof with the furniture and belongings of those unfortunate enough to have been bombed out by the recent VI and V2 rocket attacks. To begin with, the idea of open air meetings did not seem to be relished.

Halls were not the only things in short supply. A special issue of petrol to candidates did not ameliorate the shortage of cars. Paper, too, presented a problem. There was no special provision of paper for candidates and certain sizes of envelope were totally unobtainable. There was no choice but for election addresses to be brisk and to the point.

Moreover, all the party organizations were run down. Hugh Dalton confided to his diary doubts about the 'old agent' and 'poor organization' at Stockton, feelings that existed in other constituencies too. Since the redoubtable Marjorie Maxse had left Conservative Central Office to organize evacuation schemes the Conservative organization in the country had fallen into disrepair and decay. Not only did the parties encounter tremendous difficulty in getting men out of the Services and industry quickly enough to stand as candidates but to be election agents as well. Perhaps it was not surprising that the quality of the candidates left something to be desired. Frederic Mullally, who acted as deputy agent in Swanage where he had a cottage, found much lacking among the 'new Socialists' who suddenly came forward: 'They were mostly solicitors and lawyers who were quite frankly climbing on the band wagon. Some of them had been to public school or in the Guards but they knew nothing at all about Labour Party history or about speaking. Oh, they'd read the Labour Party guide to public speaking that told them how to answer questions but when the supplementaries came they were utterly at a loss.'

In much the same way as Mullally had been summoned to help the Labour cause so was journalist James Wentworth Day called to Newark to take over from the agent, who – the Conservative candidate complained – 'had only one tooth and a yellow complexion'. Another Tory, E. D. O'Brien, shared hustings with a candidate who had never made a political speech in his life and whose agent had no experience of the job.

Nor were the Liberals in any better condition. Frank Byers, contesting Dorset North, found there was no organization at all:

> We had to start absolutely from scratch in a council house. We went to Sherborne, Gillingham and so on and literally built the whole thing up overnight. We organized the thing under great difficulties and I think a lot of other constituencies were the same. Violet Bonham Carter's constituency in Somerset didn't seem so bad as it might have been. We put a tremendous amount of work in. We had very little literature. Everything was out of date. We just had an election address. We built a good local organization up from scratch by finding people who had worked for us before. They hadn't had an election since 1937. The Conservative organization was certainly no better than ours. Their candidate made all sorts of excuses for not coming down. One bunch of their canvassers was telling the electorate he was in the Far East, another said he was in Germany and couldn't get back. Actually he was somewhere like Catterick.

No wonder the *New Statesman* observed: 'Six years of war have stiffened our political joints. Election tactics and procedure are a novelty to millions. Most citizens under thirty have never been called on to vote, and the older electors have only known nine years of Party government since 1916. The election will reveal how far our traditional political institutions have been affected by ten years of Fascism and war.' There were glum predictions about a poll of less than fifty per cent. Yet within a week the outlook had changed. From such unpropitious beginnings there evolved what many were to remember all their lives as the most exciting general election of the century.

The first signs came with the well attended meetings that all parties found they could command. One Liberal agent explained to a *Times* reporter that after five years of war people were 'meeting-starved'. At last they could go out untroubled by bombs or blackout and contemplate the future. Another Liberal agent at Ilford, bemused by the huge crowd of over a thousand crammed in to hear Sir Archibald Sinclair declare Sir William Beveridge to be

F

'a new prophet in Israel', wondered whether the large audience was there 'out of a concern for politics or a treat to go to an evening meeting after all these years'. The Labour agent in the same constituency declared his party had found very deep interest among the electors: 'People have taken it seriously and tried to work things out.' His Conservative counterpart also expressed 'astonishment at the very large number of people attending our meetings, exceeding anything in the election history of the town'.

Unquestionably there were excitement and exhilaration but, though the national Press preferred to highlight such fervour and frenzy as they could find, local newspapers were repeatedly impressed by the solemn and serious approach of the electorate and their earnest and sincere desire to get it right. After all, was not this what they had been fighting for? An editorial in *Time And Tide* also referred to this mood: 'There is not a sign of apathy or cynicism among the electorate . . . due in part to a keen awareness of our grave responsibilities at this period of crisis in the history of civilization, which will demand the undivided service of the best brains and characters in the country . . . it is a profoundly serious mood, which challenges the politicians to summon the selflessness, breadth of vision and honesty of purpose which the times – and the electorate – demand.'

But the earnestness and enthusiasm were not confined to becoming part of an audience at meetings. Eager amateur help was soon forthcoming for the party organizers. The Labour Party in particular benefited from servicemen home on leave ready to address envelopes, post bills, and canvass. In a way the very unpreparedness for a political fray necessitated improvization and helped the electorate to think of it as 'their' election. Dennis Howell, Labour deputy agent in Birmingham West:

There had never been such response as we had. The organization was non-existent, but miraculously the atmosphere was such, the expectations of a Labour victory were such, that we probably had more volunteers and certainly a better spirit of winning that I've ever met since. We did a leaflet based on *Your MP*, picking out all the Birmingham ones and reproduced their voting records and extracts from their speeches. We got that into the factories. We decided to have our meetings on street corners and in schools. Our candidate Jim Simmons had spent all his life on the stump, a wonderful propagandist.

In London at Leyton West, where most unusually a detailed election campaign had been drawn up twelve months previously, disaster seemed to threaten at the last moment. Reg Underhill, demobbed from the NFS and now working at Transport House, was the local agent: 'We'd had to close the Central Committee room because it got bombed about but we kept the wards going. When the election came nobody could get time off to be Leyton West election agent. I was wanted at Transport House. Another colleague was needed by the Clerical Workers' Union. Eventually the job was shared between three of us, a triumvirate.'

The Conservatives seem to have had less voluntary assistance than the other parties and were not slow to complain that the Savings groups, Spitfire Week type of activities run by union officials in the factories gave them an unfair advantage regarding organization. The Communists had always been highly organized. Common Wealth from its leaders down was a band of theorists who, according to Wilfred Brown, had little idea of filing or the routine of running an office, let alone an election campaign.

Yet enthusiasm was the order of the day and young people, not merely servicemen, thronged the committee rooms. Nor were their activities confined to addressing envelopes. Schoolboys of fifteen and sixteen went canvassing and discussed ideology on the doorstep and were seldom rebuffed. A teenage Clive Jenkins was much in demand as a speaker at meetings in South Wales. That the parties should have been eager to use young people is no mystery. Demobilization had scarcely begun and every hand was needed to push the rusty machinery into action.

Undoubtedly, for all the seriousness of approach, it was an election of genuine passion, probably the last time *The Red Flag* and *Jerusalem* were to be sung at meetings with fervour and without embarrassment. The emotional appeal to young idealists is apparent but it was really something more than that. Young people had been able to read about politics for years without being able to take any part. Suddenly, though the ultimate participation with a vote was still denied them, they could actually play a part. They could be committed and energetic after monotonous years of hearing about other people's deeds. The photographs and newsreels of Belsen released in April 1945 had sickened young people as much as any and made them acutely aware of what this country's fate had so nearly been. Most of them were determined that never again would the world head for such waste and destruction as war imposed. Many of these voteless election helpers later became the young parents of the Aldermaston marches. Above all, the election was a chance for young people to express themselves. For a brief while nothing in the world was so exciting as to master the details of, or discuss, or simply sell the party manifesto of their choice.

The Labour Party manifesto *Let Us Face The Future* was largely the work of Herbert Morrison, with considerable help from Jim Griffiths. Apart from its content, it was quite the best looking of the party manifestos. On the cover was a large red V, a device cheekily lifted from Churchill's wartime repertoire and indicating inevitable victory. It was well printed and laid out and written in no-nonsense, easy to understand terms. It stressed that food, work and homes were the main issues and the *New Statesman* declared it was 'remarkably clear and precise on domestic issues'. It also said that to achieve Labour's aims 'we need the spirit of Dunkirk and the blitz sustained over a number of years'. The document cost twopence (less than 1p) and there was no difficulty in selling it.

Mr Churchill's Declaration Of Policy To The Electors, price one penny, was at once less impersonal and more woolly. It conceded that certain controls would have to remain, particularly in housing, but any kind of control of industry was rejected. Fine phrases did little to obscure that Churchill was not thinking about the future in the detailed way his opponents were. For this he cannot altogether be blamed, since throughout the election period his time was much taken up with foreign policy in preparation for the Potsdam conference on the future of defeated Germany. Indeed, he scarcely had time for his own constituency, where the campaign was conducted by his wife.

The Communist manifesto appeared in June at about the same time as Churchill's and was not, in essence, so different from *Let Us Face The Future*. It favoured defeating the Japanese, nationalizing coal, electricity, steel and transport, and looked forward to higher wages and a shorter working week. It was more specific about foreign policy than Labour, in deploring Churchill's policies in Greece, Belgium and Italy. There was also to be a Soviet-style five-year plan in which industry would be modernized.

The Liberal manifesto was not over specific about foreign policy beyond defeating the Japanese. Though it advocated a new deal at home, especially in matters of social security and social justice where the Party had the authority of Beveridge to back its sincerity, it admitted a strong case for nationalization of railways, electricity and coal without producing any details of how and when that should be done. This had the effect of making the Liberals look like a hesitant party that did not really know its own mind, an impression strengthened by the internal squabbles that soon broke out. In a moment when incisive and decisive policies were called for it never really looked adequate.

On 7 June Sir William Beveridge had gone to Penzance to talk about his famous plan. He took the chance to announce to a packed hall that they should 'save Mr Churchill from his dreadful friends by letting him come back to Parliament and have as few Tories or Liberal Nationals to hamper him as possible'. The sitting member for the constituency, Captain N. A. Beechman, was a Liberal National but this did not prevent Beveridge from warming to his theme and insisting that the Liberals under Sir Archibald Sinclair and the Liberal Nationals under Ernest Brown were very different creatures. The latter, Beveridge insisted, were 'really only Tories in disguise'. Nor did he flinch from examining Beechman's voting record where it had been cast against the Liberal Party.

A fortnight later Beechman, as though eager to prove Beveridge's point, flourished a letter he had received from Winston Churchill: 'It has come to my notice that in certain parts of the country Sinclair Liberals are receiving active support of Socialists and Communists and in other parts they are representing to the electors they stand in support of me. I wish to make it plain Sinclair Liberals are in opposition to me.' The candidate for Ilford North, Lady Rhys Williams, rebutted Churchill's claim that a vote for Sinclair Liberals was a vote for Socialism. 'A Liberal vote,' she insisted, 'is not a wasted vote. A large number of free independent Liberal MPs, free to vote as they wish on every issue, is invaluable.' At Camborne, Isaac Foot insisted: 'If the price of Mr Churchill's leadership means consent to that Tory majority again governing the country, it is a price no Liberal could pay.'

But the damage had been done. Churchill had successfully split the Liberals in a way he had conspicuously failed to do with the Labour Party. Any divergencies in the Labour ranks were successfully hidden, even though Transport House continued to cold shoulder all advances from radical and progressive allies. On many occasions, however, care was taken to avoid splitting the Left-wing vote in constituencies, though it was usually the smaller parties that gave way to help Labour, not excluding the Communists. Able Seaman Douglas Long shared a platform with Harold Wilson opposing Commander Stephen King-Hall at Ormskirk. Soon many Labour agents were full of praise for Communist energy in implementing Labour instructions without making political capital for themselves.

An exception to this amity was the Sparkbrook division of Birmingham, where L. S. Amery was opposed by a Labour candidate and by Palme Dutt for the Communists. Dutt received a letter of support from Bernard Shaw, who throughout the campaign wrote a number of letters to candidates whom he regarded as most truly progressive, no matter what their party. To Dutt, after claiming to have helped found the Labour Party, Shaw wrote:

> I think it has blundered badly in putting up a party candidate to oppose you at Sparkbrook. It has created a situation in which a vote for the Labour Party is a vote against Labour, a vote against India, a vote against Russia and a vote for Imperialist capitalism in the person of its most thoroughgoing prominent representative . . . Mr Amery is an exceptional and formidable opponent and is in possession of the seat. To put up against him a commonplace competitor is to trifle with a very important occasion . . . You call yourself a Communist. So do I. So would all the others if they understood that our practical British Communism has saved us in the war in the West, just as Russian Communism, which Russia learnt from England, has saved us in the East.

As part of his campaign Dutt issued a pamphlet on the Bengal famine. 'The price of Mr Amery's incompetence and reactionary indifference is too high,' it thundered. 'One and a half million corpses call to Sparkbrook electors to register their verdict on Mr Amery.'

Though speakers and audiences alike frequently returned with relief to the various manifestos, this kind of excursion was by no means infrequent. They often centred round Churchill's ingratitude, revealed by his denigration of erstwhile colleagues, men whom only recently he had been glad to have sustaining him. His remark that he welcomed the election because now he did not have to consider men like Morrison was particularly resented, since it was felt that

Morrison had frequently had to shoulder thankless tasks on the home front while Churchill glamorously toured the war areas.

There were, too, a great many diversions about how demobilization should be conducted and what the demobilized man wanted. The Conservative candidate at East Grinstead was sure they did not want any ideological change in the country they knew and loved, only practical changes. He cited Mulberry Harbour as a splendid achievement of private enterprise, which could surely be emulated in housing. Nationalization would only bring hordes of officials, red tape and denial of choice. Most Conservatives were convinced that the Labour Party was dedicated to controls for no good reason. Oliver Lyttelton, Conservative candidate for Aldershot, declared that the Labour Party wanted queues to be permanent. Ernest Bevin tartly reminded him that before the war there had been twenty years of queues – outside the labour exchange. When Beaverbrook's newspapers had first advocated in April an end of wartime controls Bevin had retorted that this was to advocate 'get rich quick anarchy'. It was Bevin too who rebutted Sir John Anderson's advocacy of a cheap money policy by maintaining it would mean 'an orgy of speculation'.

Clearly, Bevin at least favoured all manner of economic and financial controls and this helped the Conservatives to regard Labour as an authoritarian party. Earl Winterton opened his campaign by announcing Socialist policy would lead to 'totalitarian tyranny'. Before the election campaign had even begun, Ralph Assheton back in April had insisted that Socialism must be rejected outright because Karl Marx had been a German. A fusion of these two lines of thought found apotheosis in Churchill's first broadcast election speech on 4 June.

After a few words about Socialists regarding 'controls of every kind as though they were delectable foods instead of wartime monstrosities', the Prime Minister startled thousands of listeners by announcing: 'No Socialist system can be established without a political police . . . They would have to fall back on some sort of Gestapo.' His idiosyncratic pronunciation of foreign terms gave the word a soft 'g' and accented the final syllable. For good measure he rounded off by declaring nest eggs of savings, however small, stood in danger of shrinking once exposed to Socialism and recalling how he had to rebuke Arthur Greenwood two years previously for saying pounds, shillings and pence were 'meaningless symbols'. In the Carlton Club Quintin Hogg declared that the speech had cost their Party a quarter of a million votes.

The Times next day thought that even the most enthusiastic would be the first to feel a little disappointed with the change circumstances had forced upon Churchill and was first the following day to commend Attlee for the mild nature of his reply. Progressives were shocked at what they had heard and their kindest comment was that the old man's sense of history seemed, for once, to have deserted him. Attlee himself said 'the voice was Churchill's but the mind was Beaverbrook's', a remark which led many to think subsequently that the speech had been written by Beaverbrook. But Churchill wrote his own speeches. This was no exception. Kingsley Martin wrote in the *New Statesman*: 'I am sure there must be people who liked Churchill's broadcast. I just don't happen to have met them. Civil servants, middle-class Liberals and men in the street have expressed to me something like real grief. They thought their hero a bigger man than he now wants to be.' With something of this grief, Vita Sackville-West wrote to her husband, Harold Nicolson, asking 'What has gone wrong with him?' On the day after the speech, however, another diarist of the period, 'Chips' Channon, encountered Attlee in a House of Commons lavatory and thought he looked shrunken and terrified.

Certainly there was no lack of Conservative candidates ready to repeat Churchill's accusation. At Epping the Conservative Lieutenant-Colonel A. P. Wise affirmed: 'Fascism is only Socialism with a dirty shirt.' Captain Harold Balfour at Portsmouth went one further and declared that Stafford Cripps and Mosley had the same policy. 'The Socialist State of Cripps is to be the same as the Fascist state of the blackshirts,' he avowed and supported this with quotations from Mosley in 1931 and from Cripps's book *Problems Of Socialist Government* on the subject of a General Powers Bill. At St Ives, Sir Edward Evans, a hero of Scott's last Antarctic expedition and of the First World War as 'Evans of the *Broke*', asked a Liberal National rally: 'Are we to throw overboard what we have won for the new Gestapo of Whitehall?'

From the outset of the campaign Labour had warned its supporters to be wary of Conservative 'stunts' designed to frighten the electorate. The Party remembered the Zinoviev letter, which had sealed the fate of Ramsay MacDonald in 1924. As though in honour bound the stunts were duly provided. The first was the

'National' Socialists scare, which probably reached its nadir with those Conservative election addresses that had printed boldly on them the words 'Remember Belsen!'

The second came in the diminutive shape of Professor Harold J. Laski, the Jewish professor of political science who had been first a Fabian and then a member of the Labour Party. Nine years after joining the Party, in election year he became its chairman. As such he felt obliged to tell the leader of the Party, Clement Attlee, who was, he argued, in an unprecedented position, what policy line he should take in the Party's interest. Conservatives throughout the campaign made much of what they saw as Laski's 'meddling', though Attlee steadfastly ignored it. Matters moved a stage further though when Laski appeared in support of the Labour candidate on the hustings at Newark.

Journalist James Wentworth Day, annoyed by the defensive stance of his Party and over-reliance on Churchill's prestige, declared to the Conservative for whom he acted as agent that he was 'determined to throw a brick into this pool of complacency'. He intended questioning Laski on his advocacy in print of bloody revolution should constitutional means fail. The candidate refused to accompany Day, claiming a prior engagement at the local Working Men's Club, so Day sailed into battle alone, having first made sure that the meeting would be covered by national Pressmen. Laski seems to have been taken by surprise and did not give a very good account of himself, with the result that a letter appeared in the *Nottingham Guardian* suggesting Laski was a bloodier revolutionary than he found it convenient to admit. The *Daily Express* was quickly on to the story and its editor, Arthur Christiansen, unabashedly admitted later that he was convinced he had given the Conservatives a weapon as good as the Zinoviev letter, an impression Brendan Bracken seemed to share. He assured Christiansen the Conservative Party would never forget him.

For a while Laski's name was enough to heighten the temperature at any campaign meeting. At West Walthamstow, Charles Curran proclaimed: 'You know who the Conservative leader is. But who is the Labour Party's? Not Mr Attlee it seems but Mr Harold Laski. I don't suppose there's a constituency in the country would elect Mr Laski. But there he sits on top of the Socialist machine cracking the whip over Mr Attlee.' At Stratford, London, G. D. Roberts KC apostrophized his listeners: 'Are we going to have a Labour Party

F*

leader saying what we are going to do, directed by the hidden hand
of Mr Laski?' Roberts was met with prolonged protests from the
hall. He pointed to one of those his remarks had affronted: 'A
man who behaves like you at a public meeting is not fit to have a
vote. I have seen your kidney before. I expect you were shouting
"Open a second front now" as though it were a tin of sardines and
then went on strike.' Roberts's heckler, clearly upset, stood and
claimed that he had been bombed out during the blitz as had
many others in the East End. 'Some of the finest people in the
world,' he affirmed. 'The best thing you can do in fairness to your
candidate is to sit down. I am not a Labour Party member or a
Bolshie. I am just a common working man and I don't want to
be insulted by you or anybody else.'

The incident well illustrates the dignified rejection of outdated
Right-wing hauteur. Ordinary people were declaring their new
status. When Roberts persisted in claiming that not only Attlee but
Bevin and Morrison must take their orders from Laski there was
more and louder uproar. In the words of a local reporter: 'After
trying to take up the threads of his address, which he had scarcely
begun, Mr Roberts sat down.' Laski was not made more popular
with his opponents when he made the observation, much quoted on
Labour hustings, that Britain had suffered two Norman conquests,
the first under William the Norman, the second under Montagu
Norman, the inter-war governor of the Bank of England. A fellow
Jew and prominent Labour peer, Lord Strabolgi, defended Laski in
a speech at Walthamstow: 'The Laski business is a bundle of false-
hoods. He is brought up to create an anti-Semitic feeling because
he is a Jew.' Harold Macmillan's palpably preposterous dubbing of
the professor 'Gauleiter Laski' did little to erase the impression.

The temperature cooled somewhat when Laski took out a writ
against both the *Daily Express* and *Nottingham Guardian* over their
assertions about his advocacy of violence. He observed: 'Accusa-
tions have been levelled against me showing a singular inability to
understand the conditions upon which any man or woman in this
country is permitted to be a member of the Labour Party'. The
Labour Party felt constrained to make an official pronouncement
that never in its history had it advocated the pursuit of violence to
achieve political aims. The sigh of relief was almost audible and
Hugh Dalton, who was aware from his own constituency of agi-
tation against businessmen who were Jews, wrote in his diary:

The Laski affair was most irritating . . . A plausible new bogy. It is a pity his name was Laski, and not Smith, and that he was not a Member of Parliament . . . A further fuss, as to whether the little fool said that in any circumstances we should 'use violence' – I always find it rather comic that this contingency should have been discussed by this puny, gloomy, short-sighted, weak-hearted, rabbinical-looking little chap! – has been stopped for the moment by the issue of writs, a very sensible move. But I have a sort of suspicion that here too he said something he should not.

Voters and candidates came face to face and swept away many an illusion. Jennie Lee was only allowed in her committee rooms once some puritan stalwart had been convinced that she was not Gypsy Rose Lee, the strip-tease queen and, in his eyes, scarlet woman of quite another sort. Canvassing for votes was one of the exciting experiences for many and took some people into strange new territory. This did not, however, include the barracks at Aldershot, where Tom Wintringham was standing as Common Wealth candidate with the backing of Liberals, Labour and Communists against Conservative Oliver Lyttelton. No canvassing was allowed in military areas, even though many civilians lived there. Nevertheless, half of Wintringham's indoor work was being done by soldiers.
Wilfred Brown, another Common Wealth candidate, dared to venture inside Buckingham Palace to canvass:

I met a low level person who said, 'You can't see the staff here. Impossible.' I said, 'But they have a right to see their prospective candidate.' So he went away and a more senior official appeared. He said in a rather offhand way, 'No. You can't see them. It's impossible.' I said, 'I insist.' Then a very senior man appeared, charming. He said, 'This is terribly difficult. I agree you've got the right. Absolutely. But it would be embarrassing in all sorts of ways,' which he explained. 'I'm asking you not to pursue it.' He handled me very well. A wise man. Not like the furious little man in Dolphin Square who came down, ripped the leads out of my car and tried to go for me.

Most popular of all were the meetings that usually had a holiday, even a fairground atmosphere, almost as though the heady togetherness of VE Day were going to be extended for ever. This was aided by the fact that meetings could take place almost anywhere

at any time. Hugh Dalton addressed fifty meetings in his own constituency alone. David Stark Murray at Richmond addressed eighty-
nine meetings and in addition agreed to call at the homes of anyone
who could guarantee an audience of at least twenty, an offer so
popular he lost count of the number that took place. Meetings
were held in fields, in squares, all kinds of open spaces, outside
factory gates at noon and outside pubs as they closed. The public
coming out of a more formal meeting that had been held in a hall
would often continue the discussion till near midnight, breaking up
at last to go home in twos and threes still passionately discussing
all they had heard. These late night meetings seemed natural enough
as the wartime daylight saving measure of British Double Summer
Time was still in force and during the campaign the light did not
fade till almost eleven o'clock.

Those meetings held inside halls frequently ran out of seating
and many would be forced to stand, often packed shoulder to
shoulder. At Conservative meetings a Union Jack would drape the
speaker's table and behind him there usually hung a giant portrait
of Churchill, with the Prime Minister's own slogan 'Vote National'.
Nobody was actually being asked to vote Conservative. Meetings
closed with the singing of the National Anthem. On the other hand,
as an indignant reader complained to the *Birmingham Mail*: 'The
Labour Party on every possible occasion ignores the National
Anthem, which has nothing to do with party politics and is the
natural end of any meeting, and substitutes *The Red Flag*.' The
Brighton Evening Argus observed with an air of mild surprise that
the innovation of a collection taken at the end of a meeting of any
party was now universally accepted. The dedicated, however, obviously put a smaller sum – if anything – in the box of their opponents.

A meeting at Battersea was addressed for the Conservatives by
Lord Beaverbrook, who spoke for about fifty minutes after a ren-
dering of *Land Of Hope And Glory* on the organ. Unfortunately,
as he ignored the microphone most people could not hear him. The
audience grew restless and heckled. In the middle of a long
anecdote about himself and the development of the Mosquito aircraft someone shouted: 'Why don't you tell us about the Three
Bears?' When asked why his newspapers did not publish news as
impartially as *The Times*, he said he would answer questions 'afterwards'. The chairman at the meeting reproved the hecklers for

their 'unmannerly, caddish rowdyism' and Lord Beaverbrook never did answer the question.

Churchill, who was later to have the most disastrous mass meeting of the campaign and was content for the most part to ride in motorcades and smile and wave his cigar, had little time to address meetings, though he did in fact set the mood for the small, packed, intense meetings. At the very beginning of the campaign, when Churchill paid a flying visit to his constituency to ensure that the local party machine was in working order, he had addressed his followers at the West Essex Conservative Club in Wanstead, denying that his was a political speech or that he was starting his campaign. This did not inhibit him from delivering what he no doubt hoped would be a pre-emptive blow: 'I am very sorry our Labour and Liberal friends could not stay with us to finish it off, as many of them wished to do. I do not reproach them but someone has to carry on the show.' This sally was greeted with laughter and even when the polls were closed many Conservatives still had not realized they had nothing to laugh about.

Like all elections it had its vogue words and phrases. Labour could induce a shiver among its followers with the words 'vested interests' and conjure up visions of a sinister group with a term like 'profiteers' or 'the cement ring'. Conservatives responded with chilling tales of a 'Socialist caucus'. Since a thoughtful approach was what the electors demonstrated and what they most wanted to see in their candidates, slogans were nothing like as popular as they have since become, were indeed regarded as no substitute for a policy. Those that did appear were mostly in the wake of Churchill's royal progress.

In the East End of London 'Cheer for Churchill and Vote Labour' was popular. A variant used in Labour loudspeaker vans was 'Cheer Churchill now for Victory but don't vote for him on Thursday'. In the jewellery quarter of Birmingham, not known for its Labour support, appeared the whitewash recommendation of the Labour candidate 'Jim Simmons 22 carat'. In Ilford, Conservatives complained of the calumnies opponents had proclaimed in creosote, less easy to remove than whitewash. Perhaps the most esoteric cry of all was the Conservative one bawled at Hugh Dalton: 'What about Dalton in 1938?' He had no idea what was meant by it and apparently nor did anyone else.

When it was all over, most people were convinced that housing had been the most important single issue. 'We want premises, not promises,' Charles Curran had proclaimed early in the campaign. Ernest Bevin had just promised to build four to five million houses 'in very quick time.' Duncan Sandys retorted that this was nothing but 'extremely quick election trickery' and pointed out that a limiting factor was the amount of building labour available. Churchill himself returned to this theme on the great eve of poll rally that he had been persuaded to address at Walthamstow. Twenty years before he had been badly heckled at the same spot but, secure in the adulation accorded him on his campaign tours and which had reached its high spot when the Conservative candidate for Jarrow had begged his presence with a telegram telling him 'Tyneside would like to touch the hem of your garment', he did not hesitate to return to the great stadium.

Once again crowds packed the route, but the stadium revealed great blocks of seats unoccupied. Moreover, it was soon obvious that considerable sections of the crowd were decidedly hostile. Some observers felt that faced with a hostile crowd the great Churchill went to pieces. A Canadian reporter declared he simply dare not tell the truth of what had happened because his countrymen, who idolized Churchill, would not believe him and he would be sacked. Certainly New Zealand papers expressed shock at his reception. From the very first moment things did not go well. Churchill had to shield his eyes with his hat from the rays of the setting sun and he was soon greeted with booing. He began: 'I want to congratulate London as it is the first great speech I have made' – hastily correcting himself – 'the first important gathering I have addressed in London, upon her wonderful record in the war.' He paused and asked: 'Would you like to boo that?' Nobody did. But he had far from won his audience to his side. At the mere mention of Russia there were prolonged cheers and soon Churchill was offering his audience 'another two minutes for booing if you like'. When a section of the crowd on his right started calling 'We want Labour' as he began to talk on housing, he turned in their direction and called: 'Again?' Once more the cry went up 'We want Labour' and he was able to quip: 'That is exactly the trouble. We want the labour.'

The official story claimed that he sat down to an ovation greater than the stadium had ever heard. But clearly something had gone wrong. It may not have been complete *débâcle* but Charles Curran, who had arranged the rally, had confidently predicted all 50,000 seats would be filled. In fact fewer than half that number were taken. Arrangements for relaying the speech to expected crowds outside had to be cancelled. The Churchill cigar and V sign were noticeably absent and Walthamstow may have instigated the first real doubts about his campaign's success. Outside, as the meeting dispersed, the Labour Party distributed their leaflets. Reg Underhill in a borrowed car narrowly avoided the anger of Churchill supporters who tried to overturn it.

In other eve-of-poll meetings up and down the country excitement reached fever pitch and often boiled over into something like frenzy, in which the line between the comic and the ugly could be very thin indeed. At Faversham as a soldier in uniform vainly tried to put a question, only to be repeatedly snubbed in the heavy handed manner that seems to have been favoured by many chairmen at Conservative meetings, uproar broke out. For a while nobody could be heard until a gas fitter's mate leaped upon his seat and yelled: 'Let the man what's fought for his country get up and speak.' There was instant silence, the kind in which a pin might have been audibly dropped. The soldier spoke. At Ilford, the Conservatives were so ill-advised as to hold a meeting to hear Sir John Anderson while neglecting to make clear that admission would be by ticket only. Hundreds of angry, disappointed electors milled about in the street outside. When the chairman rose to open the meeting they began an angry knocking at the doors and a policeman had to be called to restore order before the meeting could continue. But even those who had gained admission by ticket were not disposed to restore order inside the hall, where it was soon obvious that constant heckling was beginning to bother Anderson. Finally two sailors burst in through the doors, took up positions in the front of the hall and tried to organize the eager questioners in the audience.

There was a similar scene at the Conservative meeting in East Grinstead, where for a while members of the audience were answering each other's questions. Not far away at Horsham only the Liberal had anything like a quiet reception. Pandemonium erupted at the Labour meeting when a woman in the audience accused the candidate, A. F. H. Lindner, and his wife of being German. He had in fact been born and brought up in Hungary. His wife was British. At Croydon, Conservative candidate Sir Herbert Williams lost his temper with an interrupter and personally offered to throw him out bodily. He was not much mollified when his questioner pointed out that he was a serviceman seeking a serious answer. At Aldershot, Oliver Lyttelton made the mistake of thinking that he could mock Sir Richard Acland by reading the Common Wealth manifesto aloud. His listeners refused to let him stop and called eagerly: 'Go on. Go on. More.' At Woodford Mrs Churchill toured the constituency on the eve of poll and addressed six meetings, which went off in an orderly way. Elsewhere, things were a deal more heady and electors mostly wended a reluctant way home as the last midnight of the campaign approached, which for most was to remain the most vivid, vital and valid political experience of their lives.

Few had been frightened by the Gestapo, Laski and nest egg scares, though they had certainly been roused. Basically the Left had offered a short term, reasonably detailed programme of planning and the Right had been for a removal of as many controls as possible. The Labour manifesto had been available before any others and it was offering fifty years of ideas argued and refined throughout the grim twenties and thirties and carefully prepared throughout the latter months of the war. This enabled Labour to move to the offensive from the outset and, in the political phraseology of the time, to recommend 'fair shares for all' rather than what seemed 'get rich quick profits for the vested interests of the cartels preferred by the old gang'.

Sadly, the national Press seemed mainly unaware of this and found its main enchantment in Churchill's royal progress and saw him as a conquering hero who must surely come to power again. The exceptions were the *Daily Herald*, the *Daily Mirror* (thought by some on the Right to be run by Jews) and the *Manchester Guardian*. The *News Chronicle* strove for objectivity and intended to run a series by members of its staff on *Why I Vote Labour, Tory, Communist, Liberal* and so on. Then the Liberal newspaper discovered that there was nobody on its staff who proposed to vote Liberal. Among the periodicals the *New Statesman* supported Labour, though sometimes in a qualified way, quite lacking in the wholeheartedness displayed by *Tribune*. With a wide circulation in Scotland there was also *Forward*, which brought off the scoop of Bernard Shaw's only article on the election: *The Fancy Ball On The Fifth*. He saw it as 'a muddled masquerade' in which Beaverbrook played for the votes of idolaters in need of a fuehrer and the Liberals played for the vote of the middle class snobbery. He castigated Beveridge for assuring electors that he was not a Socialist though he advocated social reform. Nor did he spare the Labour Party, which he saw playing the old party game.

The Press generally lacked humour in its treatment of the campaign and the fact that cartoonists Low and Vicky were both ill and drew no comment on the fight is as much regretted by the historian now as the participants then. Hearing that the popular newspaper columnist A. J. Cummings was also ill caused Kingsley Martin to muse on 'a malignant spirit working against Labour in the election'.

In fact there was quite a different spirit abroad and, though they may have regretted that the fights and the fun of the last three weeks were over as they heard the chimes at midnight on that polling eve, most of the electors as they woke next morning would certainly have agreed with the Labour candidate for St Ives. His helpers were up early and posted bills throughout the constituency with the confident assertion: TODAY YOU MAKE HISTORY!

14

All On A Summer Day

Polling day, 5 July, dawned warm and sunny. It was to be one of the hottest days that month and in parts of Scotland the temperature rose to seventy-five. In some constituencies the polling stations were open as early as seven am, in others not till eight am. One early morning voter at Upton in East London found his enjoyment of the already cloudless skies suddenly curtailed when, calling in to vote on his way to work, he discovered that he was not on the electoral list while his baby of a few weeks was. A twelve-year-old evacuee schoolgirl recently returned to London from Sussex was on the electoral register at East Grinstead, where her former guardians had been bombarded with literature for her. Throughout the country many residents found that they had no vote at all.

The election was fought on a new register compiled without sufficient manpower. Its basis was the issue of current ration books. At the beginning of June a woman had written to the *New Statesman* complaining that she was not on the electoral register because she had been omitted from the Food Office returns, which had been completed while she was on holiday. There was no redress. It had been understood and reluctantly accepted that many serving with the forces would lose their vote but the disfranchisement of civilians had not been expected to run into thousands. Many had moved away from industrial centres because of bombing, some very recently to escape the V1 and V2 rockets. To make confusion worse, twenty-five new constituencies were created by splitting in two the larger constituencies.

Among such seats being contested for the first time were Eton and Slough, Heston and Isleworth, and Woodford, whose Conservative candidate, Winston Churchill, found himself without a vote. He was not on the lists for his home in Westerham, for Chequers or Downing Street. His name had been left off the register in error. He had been abroad at a conference in the summer of 1943, when the buff identity cards from which the register was compiled were exchanged for new ones. A new card had been issued but Churchill's old one had not been given up. Bertrand Russell, on the other hand, complained in a letter to *The Times* that he had been given a vote to which, as a peer, he was not entitled.

Some electors were legally entitled to more than one vote. The universities returned their own candidates and all graduates were eligible to vote for them whether or not they qualified for a vote elsewhere. Election was by a system of proportional representation and since most of the electorate were not resident in the university seats there could be no question of electioneering or even canvassing. In this gentlemanly atmosphere, progressive candidates were felt to be at a disadvantage, especially as the voting paper was posted to each elector. Younger graduates tended to be more mobile, spread all over the country or abroad, and perhaps less likely to notify their changes of address to the university authorities. The greater number of older voters, like country parsons, established schoolmasters and other professional people, were more settled and more likely to be firmly on the register. Oxford and Cambridge in particular were felt to reflect reactionary opinion.

Businessmen also qualified for an extra vote in the constituency where their business was located. Right-wing newspapers urged them to ensure that this vote was used. London Conservatives issued in March a circular advising directors and employers that this extra vote was obtainable simply by renting a room in their company's premises, a move seen by at least one Labour MP as a 'slick and somewhat shady incitement to misuse the franchise laws'. Though Herbert Morrison thought it 'a bit near the line' he took no action. Watching his opponent's tactics in Birmingham, Jim Cattermole became aware that local businessmen were phoning Conservative Headquarters for instructions on which of the city's constituencies would find their second vote most valuable.

In two-Member constituencies electors were entitled to two votes, which could cause confusion. The *Brighton Evening Argus* made it clear: 'You can vote for two candidates. You cannot vote twice for one candidate. If you put more than one cross against a candidate's name it just means kisses, not votes.'

Because of fixed holidays like Wakes Weeks some constituencies in the North and Scotland did not poll until a week later, 12 July. At Nelson and Colne, which was to return Sydney Silverman, polling was staggered over three Thursdays, finishing on 19 July. In the country as a whole there were almost 1,700 candidates to choose from. Only once before, in 1929, had there been more. The Conservatives and the Labour Party contested almost every seat, but the Liberals fought in less than half. They had hoped to field 500 candidates but claimed that a July election made it impossible to find more than 306. The Communists had meant originally to put up forty-two candidates but halved this number on deciding that they should limit their efforts to industrial areas where they might find more support. Elsewhere they advised their supporters to vote Labour. Common Wealth, flushed with by-election successes, felt confident enough to send into the fray two more candidates than the Communists. Ever since the Chelmsford victory many, like the *New Statesman,* saw it as 'more than just a splinter party'. There were thirty-five Independents, sixteen of whom were standing in the university seats. Transport House agreed that thirty-three Co-op candidates should stand and Jimmy Maxton led four ILP stalwarts besides himself into the fray.

War records had often been a touchy subject during the campaign and, if this were seen only as synonymous with joining the forces, the Conservatives seemed on stronger ground. Over three quarters of their candidates had fought in either the First or the Second World War. Of the twenty-two MPs killed in the Hitler war twenty-one had been Conservative. There might have been more had not all Conservative MPs and candidates serving abroad been recalled to England in January 1945. The Labour candidates numbered less than half the figure of fighting men in the Conservative ranks, a fact quickly seized upon as evidence of lack of patriotism. Men like Aneurin Bevan and Michael Foot were constantly denigrated as cowards who had stopped at home to miss the fighting and then had the cheek to criticize those who had stood up in battle.

Indeed, very few in the Labour Party were exempt from this Tory charge of being 'unpatriotic'. The Conservative candidate for Ilford South, Major E. J. Boulton, destined for defeat, observed at one of his meetings that it was 'scandalous that Bevin and Greenwood should demobilize themselves to fight an election while others were still serving'. Labour resented the Conservative supposition that it alone was the patriotic party. When the same Major Boulton was introduced at another campaign meeting as 'having served in

Egypt, the Western Desert and Italy', a voice from the hall was heard to observe tartly: 'So did a great many others.' With futile cries of 'Is this free speech?', the interrupter was ejected bodily.

According to the regulations a candidate could not appear upon the hustings in uniform although he might so appear in a photograph on the cover of his election address. Frank Byers, the Liberal candidate for North Dorset, called himself 'Lieutenant-Colonel' on his election address because he was fighting another Lieutenant Colonel: 'I didn't see why I should be outranked.' Under War Office regulations service candidates were placed on an unemployed list and forfeited the month's pay and allowances for the period between nomination and declaration days. This was hard on those with no other income, in practice usually Labour candidates. No serviceman was allowed to make speeches at an election meeting while in uniform, but he was permitted to ask questions, and many frequently did.

The Conservative candidates also included among their number far more businessmen and people of private means than did Labour. Something like half of them came under this category. At Braintree, Essex, Tom Driberg in his fight against Major Melford Stevenson, later to win renown as a reactionary High Court judge, linked private wealth with the Conservatives-in-uniform issue. More Conservative MPs had been killed, he said, 'because the Conservative Party consists of young men who can afford to go into politics at an early age and there are a large number of young Conservative MPs. It is a defect in the Labour Party that most of their MPs are on the older side; they come from working class families and work their way up through trade union branches.' Challenged on why he had 'not lifted a finger for his country in the war', Driberg defended himself vigorously: 'I could have got into uniform, and held a comfortable non-combat job in Whitehall had I wished. As I did not happen to be a lawyer I could not have been made a Deputy-Judge Advocate.' Loud laughter greeted this spirited sally at Melford Stevenson before Driberg continued: 'But I could have got a job on one of the newspapers, and called myself a Brigadier-General.' More laughter greeted this observation that many of the Conservative candidates held jobs which afforded more or less bogus military rank, the sort of rank that W. E. Williams of ABCA had so offended them by refusing. Driberg went on: 'I chose the job I was most fitted to do and I have been told by many servicemen that was the right thing to do. In a total war it is not only those in uniform who serve their country.' This was an attitude that many of the electorate, their thoughts already turning from war to peace, were only too eager to endorse.

Those with votes were often prepared to go to remarkable lengths to make sure they were not wasted. At Ilford South two electors arrived from Newcastle and another from Thorpe Bay. H. G. Wells, who had seemed to despair of mankind in his last work, *Mind At The End Of Its Tether,* now summoned enough optimism to rise from his deathbed and vote Labour. Strapped to a stretcher, he was driven to the polling booth for what was to be the final political act of a life that had so often embraced Socialist causes.

He was lucky to get the lift. Throughout the campaign candidates had felt the lack of transport. Drivers were entitled to only fifteen gallons every three months but election candidates found themselves entitled to a special allocation of 500 gallons. In the two Ilford constituencies it was reported that although there was plenty of petrol for the campaign the supply of cars was decidedly short. The local Conservative parties estimated that they could muster 150 cars but all the other parties doubted whether they could find that many between them. Nevertheless Lady Rhys Williams, the Liberal candidate for Ilford North, had hit upon the idea of a committee room on wheels, which she used throughout the campaign. In Preston Julian Amery and Randolph Churchill drove on polling day from nine in the morning till nine at night in a cavalcade of cars, which was loudly cheered wherever it went and which must have made them doubly regretful that their earlier idea of a parade of elephants had been frowned upon. Candidates in more rural areas and legitimately in possession of more petrol than anybody else must frequently have felt some of Christopher Hollis's delight as he drove from one Wiltshire village to another along empty roads that seemed to him like 'riding through the avenues of Heaven'. The weather on polling day itself was good enough to favour a 'carless' party.

Of those voters who did get to the polling booth it seems to have been mainly Conservative voters who spoiled their papers, usually due to an excess of zeal. A supporter in Folkestone proudly informed Party workers she had indicated her approval of the Conservative candidate by putting a large V as well as a cross against his name. A few were disgusted at not finding Churchill on their ballot papers. Most, however, stopped considerably short of the woman who announced in the national Press: 'I intend to write across my ballot paper "God Save the King" and nothing else. If a million voters did this the moral effect would be profound.'

Those who could not appear in person at the polls included thousands upon thousands of servicemen scattered abroad. They were enabled to vote either by appointing a proxy or by post. The despatch of postal vote forms to all forces overseas had begun on 26 June and they were to be returned to the United Kingdom by 22 July at the latest. The voting forms were flown out from and returned to five airfields: Blackbushe, Croydon, Down Ampney in Gloucestershire, Lyneham in Wiltshire, and Prestwick. Within a week of despatch the first forces postal votes began to arrive back in special mails from Army Post Offices overseas. These mails always travelled by air and bore the words 'ELECTION' on the letter bag label. Once in this country, the contents went to the appropriate distribution offices and received priority at all stages to ensure that they were in the hands of the returning officers at the earliest possible moment.

It had been assumed even before the election began that the forces vote would be almost entirely for the Left. The day the result was known many Conservatives found some consolation in the thought: 'Of course it was the service vote that did it.' Supporters of all parties seem never to have questioned this assertion. In its crudest non-political form it may be seen as a rebellion of conscripted servicemen against the discipline and bull of 'them', the officer class. Did not the class system operate more obviously and more senselessly in the forces than anywhere else? Could a conscript not see, after all, that many of the officers whose orders he must obey were in fact no brighter than himself? For many, too, the change of environment and chance to travel must have transformed their outlook. Would for instance an agricultural lad whose family had never travelled far and who had always been content to vote for the farmer or the squire's party still be content to continue in that tradition?

Moreover, nothing so preoccupied a conscript as getting out of the Army and he would have been justified in thinking that the men of Whitehall were getting ready to transfer him to the Asian front. Some of his mates were already on their way and Yorkshire mills were busy making ant-proof socks for jungle use. Demobilization had begun on 18 June under a scheme devised by Ernest Bevin. There seems to have been little criticism of the scheme among the troops and Emanuel Shinwell considered it was responsible for hundreds of thousands of service votes going to Labour. There must have been some suspicion that the Conservatives under their 'warrior' Prime Minister might be tempted to suspend the scheme. The non-political British Legion recommended that candidates of all parties be closely questioned about priorities in housing and jobs for ex-servicemen.

All these reasons and more were enough to create the assumption that the forces' vote would be massively and overwhelmingly Left. Aneurin Bevan, in a cogent analysis of the Labour victory, was to write: 'Another profound influence in the election was the Service vote. Owing to the nature of the election it was possible to estimate how the Services voted, and the universal admission is that it went overwhelmingly Labour.'

In fact, it was not as overwhelming as all that. We cannot know what Bevan based his 'estimate' on but it certainly needs some qualification. To begin with a large number of servicemen did not vote for the simple reason that they were not legally entitled to. Though men were conscripted at eighteen they had no vote until they were twenty-one. In June 1945 there were 4,531,300 men and women over twenty-one in the Forces. Of these, 2,895,000 had their names on the special electoral register. This means that, had every single one of these recorded a vote, there would have been just under three million in a total electorate of some thirty-three million. In the event nothing like every one of those on the register recorded a vote. Votes cast by proxy or by post numbered only 1,701,000 – under sixty per cent of the Service register and less than forty per cent of those originally eligible. The national average poll was over seventy per cent.

There were, of course, special and even bizarre reasons why a number of votes may never have reached England. War still raged in Asia. All kinds of enemy activities, including those of *kamikaze* pilots, may have delayed or destroyed votes. Even in Europe things were not easy. Some servicemen, such as those trying to bring order to the chaos of what had till recently been enemy-occupied zones, found that their mobility and the lack of communications denied them an opportunity to vote.

There was also a hard core of apathy, sometimes allied to a sort

of political fatalism, that no amount of ABCA sessions was able
to overcome, justifying W. E. Williams's view that his scheme was
limited in its influence. It was exemplified in the attitude of Canon
Collins's batman, who declared that, though he was a Socialist, he
would vote Tory because he felt that his future employers would in
some way discover which side he had supported and sack him if
they disapproved. But there were many more who had no intention
of voting at all, simply because they were incapable of summoning
sufficient interest. It was a source of worry to the Left for months
before the election and the subject of much correspondence in
Tribune, where at the end of an article describing a mock election
on board a troopship, which had been won by Labour, the writer
averred: 'The common contention that troops and officers are not
interested in politics is sheer nonsense. It is a question of presentation, of relating politics to daily life.' This was the sort of view
officially accepted by Labour leaders and one which made it easy
for them to maintain later that the forces' vote had won them the
election.

As far as they were concerned unreceived votes were due to the
slackness of the responsible officers. In May it was being claimed
that the Royal Navy was a particular villain in this respect and
there were at least four ships where commanding officers had failed
to display notices about the regulation on voting. By June there
were plenty of stories about officers who were not merely indifferent
to their men voting but positively hostile. A description of one incident in Belgium was fairly typical: 'Nearly 1,000 men were
assembled on parade. The OC arrived and without any prelim-
inaries barked: "All those who don't want to vote, fall out". It
should be noted that (a) the parade was timed for just before dinner
on Sunday, and the men were eager to have their meal and get out
and (b) that although it was raining and there was ample space for
inside parades, this one was held outside. Not surprisingly about
forty per cent fell out. The barest instructions were then given the
men on the filling in of application forms.'

A further insight into the political orientation of such a camp
and its almost invincible ignorance in that regard is provided by
the same informant: 'Scarcely one man in a hundred ever sees
a newspaper unless he buys outside the camp the *Daily Mail Continental Edition* or the *New York Herald-Tribune*. The men still
get plenty of routine training – including gas-mask drills – yet no

attempt has been made to educate the men on the need to exercise their right to vote. There are plenty of new posters coming in on non-fraternization, but not a single poster of any description dealing with this vital general election.' When General Slim told Churchill that ninety per cent of the troops in Burma would vote Labour and the other ten per cent would not vote at all he too contributed to the myth of the crucial Left-wing vote of the troops. No doubt his, like others', was a pardonable exaggeration based upon the intensity of feeling expressed by those Servicemen who did vote Labour. Because of enemy action, maladministration, and apathy, however, the service vote was not crucial to the outcome of the election nor was it necessarily as Left as both main parties have always contended.

Probably much more vital to the outcome and important as never before was the female vote. Not only had women been conscripted into the forces and industry, where their experience must of necessity have been widened and they saw the desirability of controlling in some degree decisions that affected them, but the woman who had been left behind at home was not forgotten either. Indeed, the *Daily Mirror* ran a whole campaign specifically aimed at her. It had begun with a reader's letter from a wife who wanted to know how she should vote on behalf of her service husband. Some people thought the letter was a fake but Philip Zec, the *Mirror's* cartoonist at the time insists that it was genuine:

> The letter arrived after the whole campaign was conceived and just happened to illustrate our point perfectly. Herbert Morrison and Harold Laski with all the Labour bigwigs had laboured for days and nights over an election campaign to turn out nothing but a load of rubbish. Herbert knew it was no good and sent for the *Mirror's* editor, Guy Bartholomew, who recommended me. I asked for seven days but I was baffled at first. My sympathy was always with the chap on the sharp end of the stick, the serving soldier. I thought how can we do something for him? How can we vote for him? Bart shouted: 'That's it. You've got it. Vote for *him*.' So I did twelve posters in three days. Pictures of soldiers, airmen, old age pensioners with the words 'Vote for him'. Not 'Vote Labour' but 'Vote for him'. And that's what thousands of housewives did. I'm convinced it was really they who won the election for Labour.

Once the votes had all been collected and the polling booths closed down at nine pm there was to be no quick release from the tension and uncertainty. The votes were not to be counted until three weeks later. This was to enable time not only for service votes to be collected from as far away as India and Burma but also for a rigorous checking to avoid the duplications possible with direct and proxy votes.

Churchill tacitly admitted the possibility of a Labour victory by taking Clement Attlee with him on 17 July to Potsdam, a suburb of Berlin, where he was holding talks with Truman and Stalin. Eden had been in charge of the Government at home from 10 July, enabling Churchill to snatch a few days at Biarritz to recuperate from election stresses. Their followers had plenty of time to ruminate on what the contents of the ballot boxes would reveal and, though some admitted to a twinge of anxiety, there was remarkably little doubt that they would remain inviolate. They were under constant police supervision. Margaret Cole did, however, encounter a European friend who scoffed at her naïveté in assuming that nobody would tamper with the seals.

One candidate who was assumed to have done some tampering of her own was the outsize Labour candidate for the Exchange division of Liverpool, Mrs Bessie Braddock. Impatient at the wait, she sought the goodwill of a local dog track owner for the services of his chief assistant, R. A. Russell, reputed to be a genius with figures. During the campaign he conducted elaborate research and on polling day collected more information. After the polls were closed he disappeared to concentrate on his calculations.

That same night, to the astonishment of the Party workers around Mrs Braddock, he congratulated her on becoming the new Member. 'Are you sure?' she gasped. He was. When she informed the town clerk the next morning he maintained that since all the service votes were not in such a calculation was impossible. This did not stop Bessie Braddock touring the constituency announcing the result from a loudspeaker van. The Press refused to believe it; the Conservatives scoffed at what they regarded as a belated 'stunt'. Russell told the town clerk before the official count began that he estimated Mrs Braddock had won by 620 votes. He erred on the side of caution. She was in fact returned by 655 votes, the first Labour MP ever for the Exchange Division as well as the first woman to represent a Liverpool constituency.

Those who had no mathematical wizard to come to their aid –

political betting had not yet been introduced – could only conjecture how well they and their parties had done. Few seemed to have got it anything like right. Harold Macmillan and R. A. Butler had from the early years of the war faced up firmly to the possibility of a Labour victory when peace came. The Duke of Devonshire was sure of it. On the other hand, Sir Walter Citrine, general secretary of the TUC, frequently expressed the view right up until the election that Churchill and the Conservatives would win easily. Robert Boothby told Compton Mackenzie that Labour would sweep the country. Churchill, though he had told the King confidently at the beginning of the year that the new government would have a substantial Conservative majority, had his moments of private doubt. To his doctor he had said: 'I am worried about this damned election. I have no message for them now.'

Labour leaders scarcely seemed confident of victory. Attlee himself rated his Party's chances as no more than 'fair' though he did think it would be 'a close run thing'. The possibility of defeat and lost deposits had been squarely faced by Transport House, which had arranged for candidates to insure their £150 deposits through the Co-op Bank for a premium of £10 each. Ernest Bevin, however, thought Labour would 'just win' while Herbert Morrison was reasonably 'optimistic'. For the Party as a whole Hugh Dalton was pessimistic, foreseeing a Conservative majority of some eighty seats. Aneurin Bevan had on the other hand nothing but optimism, rooted in a certainty held for many years that Labour would be returned to power, although his wife, Jennie Lee, was not so sure. Margaret Cole wrote that long and dismal experience and the memory of what had happened in 1918 combined to make delegates to the Labour Party conference sceptical of their own impressions. It seems this scepticism was hard to remove in many quarters. Even those Party workers who had been sure of a Labour victory had usually anticipated nothing on the scale of what actually occurred. Liberal HQ confidently predicted that their Party would secure eighty to a hundred seats, thus making them a considerable moderating force in any party alignments.

The *Financial Times* Index during the three-week wait remained reasonably steady, indicating a faith in business circles that the Conservatives would be returned. The only argument among the political correspondents was over the actual size of Churchill's majority. Hardly a newspaper gave a thought to the possibility of his Party losing power. None took the realistic stance of the *New Statesman* in summing up the campaign: 'Nobody can foretell the result. There have never been so many imponderables. For instance, what is the effect of nightly electoral broadcasts? How many would feel they were ungrateful if they did not vote for Churchill? There were 296 three cornered contests. No one under thirty-one has ever voted before. Many are disfranchised, many constituencies transformed since war because of an influx of war workers.' Few seemed to have noticed that the Gallup Poll published in the *News Chronicle* had consistently shown a Labour lead since 1943. Even the paper's political correspondent did not notice it on the eve of the poll.

One group of detached observers was German prisoners of war. Karl Schrade, son of a Marxist but disillusioned by meeting ordinary Russians, was trying with broken English to persuade farm labourers to vote Conservative in the national interest. He and his fellow prisoners could see the way things were going: 'The feeling generally in our camp – there were about 4,000 of us there – was that the Labour Party might get in. We got that feeling from the Forces we were in contact with – our guards and in the aerodrome camps where we went – and the people we were working with on the farms all over Lincolnshire. You don't generally associate agricultural areas with the Left.' The conquered seemed more in touch with public opinion than most of Fleet Street.

15

The Time's With Labour

On 26 July, declaration day for all the seats except the universities, the *Daily Express* leader said: 'There are reasons for expecting that by tonight Mr Churchill and his supporters will be returned to power.' In general the enthusiasm of the Conservative Press had steadied. Beaverbrook was the optimist, confident his hero would have a majority of over sixty. Churchill was not so sure. Before leaving Potsdam on the twenty-fifth he told his doctor, Lord Moran, of the bad dream he had that night: 'I dreamed that life was over. I saw – it was very vivid – my dead body under a white sheet on a table in an empty room. I recognized my bare feet projecting from under the sheet. It was very life-like . . . Perhaps this is the end.' Back on home ground, he went to bed the next night feeling confident but started out of his sleep before dawn on 26 July with 'a sharp stab of almost physical pain', convinced that the election had gone the wrong way. He fell back to sleep, however, until nine am, getting up later to put on his siren-suit and go to the underground war-room in the Downing Street annexe. There he sat surveying the constituency charts that had been put up in place of the strategic maps.

The first Labour gain was Salford South. In the first half hour four more gains were registered. At ten twenty-five came news of the first Ministerial defeat. The Secretary for Air, Harold Macmillan, had lost his old Stockton seat to a young Army Education Corps captain, George Chetwynd, by the decisive margin of 8,664 votes. 'That lifted hope high at once,' recorded Hugh Dalton, who was awaiting his own result in the same county at Bishop Auckland. Hopes went even higher with the defeat of Brendan Bracken at Paddington North. The First Lord of the Admiralty had fallen to another Labour soldier, Sir Frank Mason-Macfarlane. It was the end of Bracken's political career. Among the crowd at the declaration was seventeen-year-old Richard Clements, a future editor of

Tribune: 'It was unusual for the results to be read out in the middle of the day and the crowds were immense. I can remember the long faces of all the Tories. We were jubilant. Marched around singing and cheering. It was the same all over London.'

In the second city things were not going well either. Another Cabinet Minister, Leo Amery, lost the Sparkbrook division of Birmingham after thirty-four years. The city, the solid Conservative home of the Chamberlains, was going Left. It elected its first woman member, Mrs Edith Wills, a down to earth, honest-to-God, working class woman, Co-op all her life. Captain Raymond Blackburn was so overcome with excitement at gaining the King's Norton division with a 12,298 majority that he leaned out of the Council window cheering, waving his Labour colours, shouting 'We're in, we're in' to a deserted square. Altogether Labour won ten of the thirteen Birmingham seats.

In the two-Member constituency of Preston the bad news softened the personal blow for Leo Amery's son, Julian, defeated with Churchill's son, Randolph. They consoled themselves that they had done better than average. Churchill suffered another family setback when his son-in-law, Duncan Sandys, fell to a Labour man called Chamberlain at Lambeth Norwood. All over the country people were able to catch up with the news when the BBC started broadcasting the results at eleven am. Labour's top men were doing well in London. Attlee, returned for Limehouse, was cheered with other East End victors at the People's Palace, Stepney. In the line-up Phil Piratin, the Communist who, profiting from local disputes, captured Mile End from Labour, appeared between Attlee and his wife in Press photographs. Syndicated in the USA, they cannot have helped Labour's image. Morrison comfortably won what had been thought by those with less electoral nous the marginal of Lewisham East. By eleven-thirty Bevin had beaten Brigadier Smyth VC at Wandsworth Central. George Woodcock of the TUC was just one of those surprised: 'I thought Labour would do well but I'd never voted for a successful candidate in my life. We'd had nothing to live on but moral victories all our lives. I was absolutely lifted that morning.'

The suburbs were going Left too, places like Barnet, Bexley, Chislehurst, Dulwich, Eton and Slough, Harrow East, and Mitcham. Wimbledon was explained at the time by the high proportion of the service vote. Diehard Sir Herbert Williams lost Croydon South.

Flight-Lieutenant Reginald Maudling failed to win the new constituency of Heston and Isleworth. This kind of result seemed
already to herald a new dawn for many. Wilfred Brown, the CW
candidate for Westminster St George's, was relieved. He had succeeded in losing to Baldwin's son-in-law. Having stood at the last
moment in place of somebody else he had spoken himself hoarse
in a concentrated effort but had spent the three-week gap worrying
that he might have won. He was concerned about the six factories
he had to manage. The one London constituency in which Labour
did badly was Hammersmith North, where the official candidate
forfeited his deposit for polling less than one eighth of the total
vote. Topping the poll was the Independent Labour lawyer, D. N.
Pritt. Among his congratulations was a cable from the head of the
Communist government in North-West China, Mao Tse-Tung.

Churchill's wife Clementine and his daughter were at his new
constituency of Woodford for the count. The surprise was not that
Churchill was elected but that his Independent opponent, a stranger
to the constituency with a policy only he could understand, polled
over 10,000 votes. In his old constituency, Epping, Churchill had
had a majority of over 20,000. Mrs Leah Manning, the 1945 Labour
candidate, remembers her count: 'When the constituency boxes
were opened, I was well down – radiant smiles from the Tory candidate's wife. But when the soldiers' vote came to be counted, my
pile crept up and up. I was well in, by a majority of over a thousand. The Tory wife burst into hysterical weeping; the Liberal wife
rushed across to give me a hug and a kiss; and, as soon as the
declaration had been read to the waiting crowds, the Epping boys
rushed across to the Parish Church for a peal of bells.'

At noon, independent Lord Woolton, the preacher of 'fair
shares', wrote to Churchill expressing his regret at events and asking if he could be honoured by being allowed to join the Conservative Party. Woolton was 'shocked at the prospect of the new
Britain under nationalization'. Meanwhile Clementine was on her
way from Woodford to join Winston in the map room. At lunch
with Beaverbrook and Bracken she tried to comfort him: 'It may
well be a blessing in disguise.' To which he retorted: 'At the
moment it seems quite effectively disguised.'

On the one o'clock news it was clear that the Conservatives were
out and that Labour would have a clear majority over all other
parties. The Conservative Party chairman and landed proprietor,

Ralph Assheton, lost Rushcliffe (Notts) to Labour. Rural strong-holds were falling. That majority was still growing. On the Stock Exchange dealings were down, with Industrials falling over three points and Home Rails nearly two. In Constitutional Clubs throughout the country the results were being heard in stunned silence. At Chatham the Conservative Club had thrown its premises open to men in uniform: 'We were all in there listening to the results of the radio. As each Labour victory was announced a great cheer would go up. As the place filled the cheering got louder and more frequent. Eventually we were quietly asked to leave.' In Southern England that day heavy rain was accompanied locally by thunder. The heavy rain often kept down the size of the waiting crowds. It did not stop Lieutenant-Colonel King's supporters carry-ing him shoulder high through Falmouth. He was Cornwall's first Labour MP.

There were some bright spots for the Conservatives. Eden was back at Leamington with a handsome majority. Butler held Saffron Walden and Oliver Lyttelton beat the CW candidate, Tom Wintringham, at Aldershot. Captain Ernest Marples gained Wallasey from an Independent. Barnstaple was a Conservative gain of what had been Acland's CW seat. Quintin Hogg held Oxford against Frank Pakenham. Earl Winterton, Horsham's MP since 1904, was back as Father of the House. In his constituency a senior scholar at Christ's Hospital, Bernard Levin, hung a red flag out of his window. As well as the two largest majorities, in Antrim, the Conservatives also had the distinction of the smallest: four at Worcester and six at Caithness. Their biggest fillip was their victory over a Liberal, Sir William Beveridge, at Berwick-on-Tweed. It was a cheerful moment for Churchill and delegates at the BMA's annual conference in London applauded loudly.

Outside people formed long queues to buy the evening papers. 'Huge Majority' said the news bills. Barbara Wootton, returning to London by coach kept seeing them: 'I couldn't ever see which Party because the coach was going so quickly. This was a tremen-dous tension.' On the set of *Pink String And Sealing Wax*, a Victorian melodrama being filmed at Ealing Studios, the Socialist actress Mary Merrall with her period skirts hitched up, a cigarette in the corner of her mouth, was studying the paper and listening to the radio, absolutely cock-a-hoop. She and Robert Hamer were so surprised and excited at the extent of the victory that they burst

G

out laughing at the long face of the unseated Macmillan staring out from the *Evening Standard*. At Widnes, Lancs, the employees in Bolton's copper factory, who had been organized during the war by the young Jack Ashley in the Chemical Workers' Union, were jubilant. They chalked the latest figures in large letters near one of the furnaces, and enjoyed changing them as more sweeping gains were broadcast.

A favourite method of displaying the national results was on ladders or 'thermometers', often used in wartime Savings Weeks. Each Party was given its own 'thermometer', perhaps displaying the caricatured head of its leader, which notched up as the temperature rose. In Manchester those high up on Kemsley House had by late morning attracted a great crowd stretching hundreds of yards along Hanging Ditch and Corporation Street. Another crowd in Cross Street was watching those on the front of the *Manchester Guardian* and *Evening News* building. There was much cheering and jeering as the figures climbed and some trouble with the police because at exciting moments – as when Flying-Officer Harold Lever defeated the sitting Conservative at Manchester Exchange – the crowd surged forward and obstructed traffic. As Attlee was going up and up leaving Churchill behind, the Co-op Youth Movement was dancing in a side street. 'The young people are going to have it better,' commented an old woman.

Everywhere announcements passed with little violence. The only exception was Londonderry, where club-waving police dispersed crowds disputing a Conservative's victory over an Irish Nationalist candidate. One defeat that raised a loud cheer from Manchester to the Cocos Islands was of Sir James Grigg, the unpopular Secretary for War. Other ranks everywhere rejoiced. At the Rifle Depot in Winchester there were cries of mock drill from the Barrack blocks: 'Move to the Left in threes, Left turn.' The officers' mess was full of gloom. At Bomber Command HQ Squadron-Leader L. John Collins remembers: 'The war was practically ended, but the looks on the faces of those officers, particularly the senior ones, as it became more and more certain that the Labour Party would win a landslide victory, grew sadder and sadder. To the Establishment at High Wycombe the Labour Party victory was a disaster which so overwhelmed them that they could hardly believe their ears. Was it for this, they seemed to be saying to themselves, that the war had been fought and won?' Another Left-wing officer saw a disaffected group in the Eighth Army: 'The Polish officers in particular were sad at Churchill's defeat. They were upper class Poles who'd been dispossessed. They were quite openly very anti-Soviet, highly reactionary and pro-Churchill.' His Ministers fell, as *The Times* put it, 'in swathes'. Altogether twenty-nine members of the Caretaker Government, thirteen of them of Cabinet rank, lost their seats.

During the afternoon, Churchill, who at lunchtime had stubbornly felt like not resigning, sent a message to Attlee at Transport House, conceding victory, congratulating him and telling him that he was tendering his resignation at seven pm. His recommendation to the King would be to invite Attlee to form a Government. Attlee was then with Bevin, Morrison and the Party secretary Morgan Phillips. Morrison, ambitious for the leadership, believed that Attlee should not accept the invitation to the Palace until the Parliamentary Labour Party had met to elect its leader. Bevin, suspicious of Morrison as always, backed Attlee. While Morrison was out of the room taking a call from Cripps, whom he claimed as a supporter, Bevin said: 'Clem, you go to the Palace straightaway.' Attlee, sure of his constitutional position, took a detour via the Great Western Hotel, Paddington, where he had tea with his family.

At six pm Churchill left the map room to get ready for his audience with the King at seven. As his Rolls drove through the Palace gates some of the small waiting crowd cheered. Alone, grave in the back seat, Churchill raised a smile and gave his V sign. In the formal words of the Buckingham Palace announcement, he 'tendered his resignation as Prime Minister and First Lord of the Treasury and Minister of Defence which His Majesty was graciously pleased to accept'. For the King 'it was a very sad meeting'. As consolation he offered Churchill, confirmed as Leader of the Opposition, the Order of the Garter but Churchill felt it was not the right time to accept an honour. Five minutes after he left, at seven-thirty pm, a small family car went into the Palace. At the wheel and wearing a bright red hat was Violet Attlee and beside her the quiet, balding Clem. They were almost unnoticed. Presenting himself to kiss hands Attlee looked, in the King's words, 'very surprised indeed.'

From his half-hour audience Attlee went straight to Central Hall, Westminster, crammed with Labour Party workers. His voice resonant with pride, he announced: 'I have this evening accepted His Majesty's Commission . . .' The reception was thunderous.

People leaped on to chairs, shouted, cheered, whistled. Morrison was not quite so pleased. Only minutes before Attlee's arrival he had been canvassing MPs for a vote by the Parliamentary Party to settle the leadership. He was now presented with a *fait accompli*. It was the moment Party workers had dreamed of for over half a century: an absolute landslide. As Attlee told them: 'This is the first time in the history of the country that a Labour movement with a Socialist policy had received the approval of the electorate.' He went on: 'Our first task is to finish the war with Japan.' He pledged that 'our fighting men will get all the support they need'. Bevin said the Government would 'speak as a common man to the common man in other lands'.

Earlier Laski, calling himself 'the temporary head of the Socialist Gestapo', had received the first big ovation of the evening when he told the jubilant members: 'This great victory for Socialism will bring a message of hope to every democracy all over the world.' He asserted that the new Government 'will enter into full friendship with the Soviet Union, be in a position to do full justice to our Spanish comrades, and will give no help to decaying monarchs or obsolete social systems'. Outside supporters chanted 'We want Clem' and 'We want Attlee' until the new Prime Minister addressed them briefly from a balcony. The victory rally broke up with the singing of *The Red Flag*. Attlee and his wife had to fight their way out of Central Hall. 'We are on the eve of a great advance in the human race', he had told the Press. He now had to take the first practical steps. The international situation was the most pressing. With Stalin and Truman (reported by BBC correspondent Richard Dimbleby to have cancelled a post-Potsdam meeting in London because of the result) awaiting the resumption of the Big Three talks, Attlee asked Eden to call on him. Eden had dined at Number 10 with Churchill and his family, leaving the young ones trying to cheer the old boy up. Soon after ten pm, when asked his opinion, Eden advised Attlee to return to Potsdam no later than Saturday 28 July, taking his Foreign Secretary with him. After the meeting Eden was disappointed to hear that his own successor was likely to be Dalton not Bevin.

No such weighty matters of state were troubling Attlee's supporters, nor were they having any truck with the Opposition. For them it was VE night again. Weather permitting, there were bonfires, singing, dancing, street parties. At one of them in staid Harrow

East fourteen-year-old Jim Higgins, intoxicated with the thought of a workers' revolution, got drunk for the first time. An over generous Labour Party enthusiast gave him a half-pint of gin. Jim was ill for days. The rain did not stop Labour enthusiasts, with the help of a long ladder, climbing the Chamberlain clock in the jewellery quarter of Birmingham. They got soaked but it was worth it to plant the red flag.

At the hurriedly organized celebration in Aberavon Labour Club the plaster bust of Keir Hardie, who had been MP for Merthyr, was brought from the secretary's office. As it was carried in people cheered the tiny figure, only a few inches high, thirty years after his death. This time Llanelly produced Labour's biggest majority, 34,117 for Jim Griffiths. In South Wales there was a vicious delight at the defeat of the Tories. At the same time, even where the legend of Tonypandy lived, there was a widespread sympathy for the personal ignominy Churchill had suffered. His total rejection was regarded in many places as an act of ingratitude, if not treason. Not only Margaret Roberts (later Thatcher) was 'amazed'. One Conservative family felt it was like the fall of France, Singapore and the sinking of the *Prince of Wales* all rolled into one.

It seemed that G. K. Chesterton's 'Secret People' had at last spoken. At Claridge's Beaverbrook had arranged a large party. He announced to his guests: 'This occasion was intended as a victory feast. In the circumstances it now becomes a last supper.' As with his fellow propagandist Bracken, it was the end of Beaverbrook's career inside politics. He did, however, have one consolation of the day. His son, Group-Captain Max Aitken, was among the new Conservative MPs. Back in his penthouse after that sad supper Beaverbrook telephoned Arthur Christiansen, who had put the *Express* to bed and gone home exhausted. As he gave his boss the latest news, Christiansen broke down, suffering from acute shock, his professional pride wounded. The *Express* had failed.

The news was broken to the Red Dean by the First Secretary of the British Embassy at a dinner in Prague. The Dean's fellow traveller said: 'Everything is going to change'. This caused consternation among some of the Embassy staff. The First Secretary was very depressed and gave the impression that almost the end of the world had come. He probably feared Socialism on the Soviet model, especially as the Dean was returning from the Soviet Union,

where he had been an official guest with Mrs Churchill for the two
Aid to Russia Funds they had run during the war.

The following day, 27 July, Churchill, who had had a heavy
postbag of letters of sympathy, held his farewell Cabinet at noon,
a pretty grim affair. Meanwhile Attlee was having problems in
forming his Cabinet. Morrison, who over-estimated his own capa-
bilities, wanted the Foreign Office. So did Dalton. At the Palace
the previous evening, when the King asked Attlee whom he intended to make Foreign Secretary, he replied that he had been
thinking of Dalton. The King suggested that Bevin would be a
better choice. For his part Bevin wanted to be Chancellor of the
Exchequer, a point he had made to Attlee that afternoon. Sure
that he was staying on the home front, he and his wife Flo had
their bags packed for a holiday in Devon. Whatever Attlee did, he
knew it was better to keep Bevin and Morrison in separate com-
partments. Attlee first refused Morrison's claim to the Foreign
Office and then, with the help of his Chief Whip, persuaded him to
accept the office of Lord President of the Council and Leader of
the House. In addition he was to have overall responsibility for the
economy. This would keep him fully occupied with the kind of
organization and planning at which he excelled.

Before lunch Dalton managed to see Attlee and was told that
'almost certainly' he would be offered the Foreign Office and that
he should get his bag packed for Potsdam. He was even given
advice on the most suitable clothes to take. Attlee had lunch with
his wife, who had spent the morning doing some shopping and
clearing up odd jobs like her Red Cross and National Savings work
at their Stanmore home. He took a lot of notice of Violet and
Dalton believed they talked the whole matter over. Certainly Attlee
changed his mind. At four pm he rang Dalton: 'I have been re-
considering it. I think it had better be the Exchequer.' After that
the loyal but disappointed Bevin accepted the Foreign Office, where
there was a vacancy for a Palmerston. He was the kind of 'heavy
tank' Attlee wanted to stand up to the Russians, who were 'be-
having in a perfectly bloody way, telling us nothing but setting up
puppet governments all over Europe as far West as they could'.
His blunt forcefulness would soon have the opportunity of exerting
itself. The next day they were due back at Potsdam.

The other three key appointments Attlee made were Sir Stafford
Cripps to the Board of Trade and, as routine rewards of Party

eminence, Arthur Greenwood to the nebulous position of Lord
Privy Seal and Sir William Jowitt as Lord Chancellor. Having
established a skeleton Cabinet, he asked the Caretaker Ministers to
stay at their desks for a few more days so that 'the King's govern-
ment might be carried on'. The following morning, Saturday 28
July, the new Ministers went to the Palace to kiss hands and receive
their seals of office. Dalton noted: 'The King hadn't much to say
and seemed quite resigned to the new situation . . . Then from the
Palace to the Beaver Hall. How apt a meeting place! Near the
Mansion House. A magnificent scene. Hundreds of new Members.
My eyes are full of tears. Our dreams have all come true at last.
And great numbers of young men in whom I have taken an interest
for years have all come thronging in together. Ernest Bevin moves
and Arthur Greenwood seconds a vote of confidence in and thanks
to Clem Attlee. Great applause and enthusiasm and greetings
everywhere.' If there were any lingering doubts about the leadership, that settled them.

Attlee replied and handed this first meeting of the Parliamentary
Party over to Morrison, now firmly in his place as the deputy
leader. He and Bevin then left for Potsdam, where Stalin – the
remaining leader of the original Big Three – was astonished to see
them. He could not comprehend a democratic victory producing
such a decisive change. Churchill's doctor Lord Moran, certain
that he would be back, had left his luggage at Potsdam. Churchill
moved into Claridge's.

On 1 August when he entered the Commons, met to elect the
Speaker, his supporters got up and sang *For He's A Jolly Good
Fellow*. In reply a backbencher put his Welsh miner's heart into
The Red Flag. Herbert Morrison looked uncomfortable. So did
some of the new Labour MPs. They did not know the words. There
were, however, enough who did to join in and raise a lusty sound.
The Conservatives were aghast. Oliver Lyttelton began to fear for
his country. Things soon quietened down though and the two
sides of the House unanimously re-elected a Conservative, Colonel
Clifton-Brown, as Mr Speaker. After being traditionally dragged
to his chair he wryly remarked that he hoped he had been elected
Speaker of the House and not director of some musical chorus.
The House was already beginning to exercise its moderating influence on the revolution.

The next day, 2 August, Attlee flew back from Potsdam with

Bevin and at Number 10 set about completing his ministerial appointments. Before they were announced *The Economist* commented: 'Two-thirds of the Parliamentary Labour Party are newcomers and the old stagers are not numerous enough to fill a Government. Moreover, many of the old familiar faces are very old and all too familiar. Mr Attlee's only possible course is boldness in experimenting with men . . . the dangers attaching to the new Government are not those of red revolution and rashness but of incompetence and sluggishness. The risk is not that the Labour Party will change British society too much but that it will change itself too little.'

In the event the twenty-strong Cabinet was, with one exception, unexciting. All the old hands (a quarter of them former miners), many of them weary from war work, were appointed. Their average age was sixty-one, five years older than the Caretakers they succeeded. The exciting exception was Nye Bevan, at forty-seven the youngest member of the Cabinet. From Number 10 he went straight to the *Tribune* offices, where the paper's assistant editor Frederic Mullally realized the significance of the appointment:

Attlee had sat down with Ernie Bevin and quite coldly and calculatingly decided they'd give Nye the Ministry of Health, which then included Housing. And housing was the absolute Number One issue. They didn't want Nye behind them sniping at them and they reckoned this would keep him quiet. They thought he'd make a mess of it and they could sack him and that would be the end of Nye. That day in the office it was pointed out to him what they were up to. He knew perfectly well of course. He wasn't worried . . . Before he left I said to him 'Now, Nye, suppose you bring forward policies we disapprove of. Do we attack you in the paper?' He looked at me and said 'If I've got policies you disapprove of I want the paper to attack twice as hard as it would with anyone else.'

The rest of the appointments ran true to form. Only three of the new £600 pa MPs were made Junior Ministers. One of them was Harold Wilson.

It did not seem like the beginning of a new era, the atomic age. On 16 July a plutonium bomb had been successfully exploded in the New Mexico desert. A report and pictures of this cataclysmic event were rushed to Truman in Potsdam. When shown them, Churchill described the event as 'the Second Coming in wrath'.

Together they agreed the bomb should be used against Japan, the final decision resting with Truman. Stalin was told of its existence and remained unmoved. Russia was not at war with Japan. On 26 July, the day the British election results were declared, Truman, Churchill and Chiang Kai-shek of China issued an ultimatum to Japan: unconditional surrender or face destruction. The bomb was not mentioned. Churchill was aware what the ultimatum meant when he issued his valedictory message to the British people that same evening. Buried in the middle of it was a hint: 'I regret that I haven't been permitted to finish the work against Japan. For this, however, all plans and preparations have been made and the results may come quicker than we hitherto had been entitled to expect.' He knew it could be only a matter of days. He must have realized too that if the election had been held over the atomic bomb would have given him and Attlee the date they both wanted. The poll would have been in October.

Churchill's farewell statement came out at the same time that Attlee in Central Hall Westminster, was promising to prosecute the war against Japan. Although he had been at Potsdam he did not know of the bomb's existence. The day he returned to Potsdam, 28 July, the Japanese rejected the Three-Power ultimatum. The Americans were anxious to save their own boys' lives and stop any Russian advance in the Far East. On 2 August, the day Attlee flew back to Britain, Truman sanctioned the use of the bomb.

The first – 'thin man' – was dropped on Hiroshima on 6 August, Bank Holiday Monday, with devastating effects: a city and perhaps 300,000 people destroyed. Russia declared war on Japan, to begin on 9 August. That day the second bomb – 'fat boy' – was dropped on Nagasaki: another city devastated and an untold number killed or missing. Within twenty-four hours three things happened: Japan agreed to unconditional surrender; Keynes warned the Cabinet that Britain was practically bankrupt; and an inner Cabinet stumbled into the assumption that Britain as a major world power must have its own bomb. In London VJ Day, 15 August, coincided with the opening of the new Parliament. Both were fairly sober celebrations. After a two-week session during which some fine sentiments on the King's Speech were expressed the House went into recess for six weeks. The revolution was going to take its time and would not really start until October, anyway.

G*

16

Middle And Left

'Britain has undergone a silent revolution', wrote the editor of the *Manchester Guardian*, whose leaders were hovering in the political centre. He went on: 'Throughout the country, in country no less than in town they swung to the Left. And when they voted Left they meant it. They had no use for the middle-of-the-road Liberals; they voted Labour and they knew what they were voting for . . . Many bad things have been made an end of. It is the kind of Progressive opportunity that comes only once in every few generations – in 1832, in 1868, in 1885, in 1906.' On the other side of the country for the *Yorkshire Post* it was 'in some ways . . . nothing less than a grave disaster'. To the Right-wing weekly *Time and Tide* it was 'a Conservative rout'. Certainly there was no mistaking the will of the electors. When all the results were in Labour had a majority of at least 146 over all other parties. With a higher poll it could have done even better. People foresaw a generation of Labour rule. The only place where the Conservatives were entrenched was the less and less relevant House of Lords. Some enthusiasts believed there would never be another Conservative government. The revolution had come.

To a few Conservatives it was perhaps as well. Walter Elliot, defeated at Kelvingrove, expressed his feelings in a private letter: 'Politically and personally this is one of the Best Things that ever happened. There are two good Continental comments: "Ingratitude is the mark of a great nation" (French); and "England knows well how to take leave of a great man" (Italian). These are not remarks of cynicism – they are remarks of envy. There is, first of all, the fact that the nation has provided itself without the slightest strain or effort with an alternative Government. Next, that it has solved the problem which all the world boggled at of "What to do with Winston?"' Alec Dunglass (later Douglas-Home), who lost Lanark to a former stationmaster, was philosophical about the Labour victory. Had it not occurred 'there might well have been a degree of violence which would have been bad for us all', he wrote in a letter.

The City at first prophesied disaster. On the morning after, the *Financial Times*, with the 'largest circulation of any financial journal in the Empire', opened its leader: 'The City, with the nation, was shocked by the political landslide revealed yesterday. A substantial marking down of Stock Exchange prices was traditionally precautionary rather than due to selling pressure. Significant of the importance attached by the world to stable Government in Britain was the unsettlement spread abroad as the certainty of a Socialist Government became plain.' A week later 'Chips' Channon noted: 'My shares have declined by £5,000 in value since the Labour Party came in.' After another week, however, he was able to record: 'The Stock Market has recovered and is actually soaring. Evidently it does not fear the Socialist Government now that the first shock has worn off.'

In New York the immediate market reaction was bearish. Stock losses ranged from one to over three points. There were fears that a controlled economy in Britain would lead to an Anglo-American disagreement on international trade. A link was also lost in that Churchill was half American. The *Washington Post* expressed the widespread sympathy for 'the man who piloted Britain through her darkest hour', now dropped 'with a shattering bang'. By comparison Attlee was colourless, if not unknown. Most Americans, however, were prepared to give him and his Party a chance. By July they themselves were getting used to the idea of Roosevelt's apparently colourless successor. Old-timers remembered the way Woodrow Wilson had been repudiated, like Clemenceau in France. Labour too had articulate friends in universities and in the Press. The formerly anti-British *Chicago Tribune* concluded its leader: 'Needless to say, Americans, with the fewest exceptions, will hope for the success of the new government. Those of us who do not share the Socialist outlook can, at least, rejoice that the election marks a wholesome reduction in the influence of the aristocracy in government.' Among the fewest exceptions was Representative John E. Rankin of Mississippi, to whom Churchill's defeat showed 'a Communist trend that should be a warning to the American people'. Such remarks were the cue for US security services to monitor the activities of the new Left-wing MPs.

In the Dominions the main reaction was sympathy for Churchill. *The Toronto Globe and Mail* felt 'the United Kingdom has lost in the world of leadership to satisfy a domestic ideology'. Churchill's position was more understandable following the defeat the month before of the Canadian Premier, Mackenzie King, who lost his own seat with the counting of the service votes. Pointing out that Labour had 'gained a truly national mandate', *The Sydney Morning Herald* was at pains to emphasize that 'the reverse is not personal to Mr Churchill'. It was also noted that for the first time Labour Governments would be in full power in three of the five self-governing units of the Empire: the United Kingdom, Australia and New Zealand. In New Zealand sympathy towards Churchill was expressed alongside concern over post-war trade policies. Observers took comfort from Bevin's emphatic declaration at the Blackpool conference that Empire preference must be maintained.

In South Africa the *Rand Daily Mail* commented that 'the verdict is due not to personal but to permanent political factors'. It was a paradox. 'Had the British public voted as Mr Churchill wished them to do, they would in fact have returned to power a number of men whose policies were the opposite of his own before the war and led directly to the desperate situation which he himself so brilliantly remedied. Asked to vote for Mr Churchill, they were in fact being called upon to vote for the Conservative party machine – which is a very different proposition . . . It is probably correct to say that, for several years past, Britain has been a predominantly Labour-minded country ruled by Governments of a different political complexion.' The Afrikaans *Die Burger* took a similar view, drawing added comfort from the poor performance of the *Engelse Kommunistiese Party*.

Indians were pleased at the defeat of Amery, coming within a fortnight of the failure of the Viceroy's constitutional conference at Simla. The basic feeling in the Congress Party, however, was that the new government, like the old, would do little towards advancing independence. Azad, the Congress president, on holiday up in Kashmir, sent a telegram of congratulations to Attlee and Cripps expressing the hope that now Labour had come to power it would fulfil the pledges it had always given to India while in opposition. Attlee replied that Labour would do its best to arrive at a right solution and Cripps cabled that India would not be disappointed. Nehru, not two months out of detention, and Gandhi were unhappy about this exchange of telegrams. They were both sceptical about Labour's intentions. The Arab world was not happy either because of Labour leanings towards unrestricted Jewish immigration from war-torn Europe into Palestine.

The European reaction was mainly favourable. To the Prime Ministers of Norway, Sweden, Denmark, Italy and Belgium it was a major advance for Socialism. The Belgian Premier, challenged in Parliament for preventing King Leopold's return 'against the will of the people', interrupted his reply to read the first results. They offered hope to people all over Europe. In France de Gaulle's personal regime, at odds with Churchill, was expected to give way to a Left-wing majority at the next election. The Socialist leader Leon Blum had already proclaimed 'democracy's right to be ungrateful' to a great wartime leader. Moscow radio gave a reserved welcome. In the British Zone the Germans looked forward to forming their own political parties and trade unions. Left-wingers in Greece, where public demonstrations were banned for four days, were confident that there would soon be a change in their government. Ignoring the police, they stopped cars in Athens and chalked 'Attlee' on them. Labour was expected to show little tenderness to the thrones of Greece and Italy.

The country where the biggest change was expected was Spain. Reuter reported from Madrid that Franco supporters were 'flabbergasted', business circles depressed and high military officers stupefied. The controlled Press, which had predicted a Conservative victory, was silent. General Franco and his Cabinet met on the evening the results were declared. In Mexico City the large Spanish Republican colony rejoiced. The president of the Spanish liberation junta declared: 'The defeat of Churchill, who supported Franco in Spain, brings great satisfaction to all the Spanish Republicans. It means that chances for restoration of the Republic in Spain are greatly improved.' Internationally, many commentators felt that the overthrow of Franco – who had staged a solemn requiem mass for Hitler – and total victory over Fascism were not far off. Those on the Right feared that Labour's victory might prejudice the prospect of the Spanish monarchy being restored. Changes were also predicted in the corrupt military government of the Argentine. In Portugal Mario Soares, a Socialist student, felt a tremendous joy and a new hope for his fellow democrats.

The international impact of the Labour landslide was all the greater for being a surprise. At home both parties took a few weeks to recover and begin to see the event in perspective. Perhaps that is why it was never given a label, like the Khaki Election of 1918 or the Zinoviev Letter Election of 1924. It was not the biggest landslide of the century. The Liberal victory of 1906 and the Conservative ones of 1918 and 1931 were all bigger. What had clearly occurred in 1945 was a major decisive and apparently permanent shift in British politics. Why? An obvious immediate explanation was the service vote, young, idealistic, presumed overwhelmingly Labour. In some constituencies candidates were well aware that it was decisive. The service vote, however, was by no means a uniform proportion of the votes in every constituency, high for example in Ilford and low throughout Cornwall. In total it did not amount to the number of votes separating the two major parties, let alone account for the strong swing of the pendulum. Something much more fundamental had happened.

On declaration night a Moscow radio commentator attributed the change to 'wartime movements of population'. The wartime dispersal of industry was one aspect of the change. More basic was the redistribution of the industrial population that had been steadily going on between the wars, the movement of people from the west and north to the south and south-east. They were crossing an unseen boundary that had existed from prehistoric times, a line that divided the civil from the military areas of Roman Britain, Roundheads from Cavaliers, agricultural England from the Industrial Revolution. The new invaders, reversing the movement of population during the Industrial Revolution, came from areas where the Labour Party was strongest. They brought with them ideas and a way of life that were not immediately accepted. Slough landladies put notices in their windows 'No Welsh'. The exiles from the old distressed areas took some time to make themselves at home in Slough, Birmingham, Dagenham and a host of other places where there was work. Gradually they settled into their new communities and a better way of life but they had not left their memories behind. They helped to convert some of the deferential working and lower middle class voters who had been stolidly Conservative. Welshmen outside Wales and shipwrights far from the north-east enjoyed taking their long revenge with the help of their new workmates.

Some moved to rural areas, where they gave more heart to agricultural workers moving Leftwards. The mechanization of agriculture and the development of transport had contributed to the urbanization of the countryside. It was no longer the squire's exclusive fief. No agricultural labourer was elected but Labour made a long overdue breakthrough in rural areas, especially in the Eastern Counties. There were also gains in Buckinghamshire, Hampshire, Hertfordshire, Kent and a few seats in the West Country. The difficult areas were the rural-cum-residential ones of Cheshire, Dorset, Surrey, Sussex and parts of the North and East Ridings.

Here the middle classes did not join forces with the agricultural workers in a less class conscious electorate. Elsewhere class, which had formed the basis of the British party political system since the beginning of the century, was clearly less important. Labour was now respectable. It had won support from the floating voter, the politically unattached from the dormitory and suburban areas. They may not have voted for Socialism but they did want greater social justice. The fight for this by the Labour Movement had been an uncertain political struggle for nearly twenty years, ever since the bitter failure of the General Strike of 1926. In that industrial action the Government had had the strike-breaking support of the middle class. Wise heads within the Labour Movement learned the lesson that strategy had to be shifted from the industrial to the political front and that victory could only be achieved with middle class support. A revolution without them was impossible. Many of the sons and daughters of those who had defiantly kept the public services going in 1926 had now voted Labour.

The Labour MPs they had helped elect were mainly like themselves, middle class, professional people with some property and education. 'Why,' said one MP's wife visiting the new House, 'it looks almost like a Fabian Summer School!' She was right. Over half those on the Labour benches were Fabians. By profession the largest group was lawyers, followed by university and school teachers, journalists, company directors or businessmen, managers or technical men, medical practitioners, farmers and shop owners. Richard Crossman, Maurice Edelman, Michael Foot, Hugh Gaitskell, Christopher Mayhew, Alf Robens were just some of the men in the new array of talent. Denis Healey was not elected and became secretary of the Labour Party's International Department at £7 a week. The new breed easily outnumbered the manual workers, the miners, transport and general workers, railwaymen, and employees from the distributive trades. Two-thirds of the Labour MPs were taking their seats for the first time, bringing youth to the Parliamentary Party. The average age dropped from fifty-six to forty-three. Of the twenty-four women elected twenty-one were Labour. Unversed in the ways of Westminster the new entrants may have been, but many of them had had experience in local government and public affairs. Occupationally, they were not a cross-section of the nation. One of the aspects of the landslide was to reduce the Parliamentary importance of the trade unions. Less than a third of those elected were union sponsored.

A writer in the *New Statesman,* the middle class journal of the Left, said with justification: 'Labour is no longer a class party; it is a national party. It is not revolutionary: it is in itself a popular front, and it is pledged to a practical and constructive and comprehensible policy.' He went on: 'The voters did not want a minority government. To them the Liberals seemed divided between disguised Conservatives and Socialists who were too timid to face the logic of their own thinking.' Their vote went up but they were reduced to a dozen seats, over half of them in Wales. Lady Megan Lloyd-George was re-elected for Anglesey, the only Liberal woman, but her father's former seat at Caernarvon Boroughs was lost to a Conservative. Their well known candidates, Sir Archibald Sinclair, Sir Percy Harris, Sir William Beveridge, Lady Violet Bonham Carter, were massacred. Clem Davies took over the leadership. One of those elected, in a straight fight with a Conservative, was Lieutenant-Colonel Frank Byers, a future Liberal leader: 'Nobody in his wildest moments could have thought that Archie Sinclair would lose his seat. He was leader of the Party. Or Dingle Foot. These were the people we expected to be joining . . . We genuinely believed we'd get eighty to a hundred seats. If we had we might have had a Liberal-Conservative coalition.' Instead the Party, seeking its identity, became prone to Left and Right factions. One small side effect of the election was to end the official link between the editor of the *Manchester Guardian* and the Liberal Party, without diminishing the paper's radicalism.

Small parties did as badly as the Liberals. The electors no more wanted extremes than a wobbly centre. By adding Mile End to Willie Gallacher's seat of West Fife the Communists doubled their representation, but elsewhere they performed poorly. A notable failure was of the Party secretary, Harry Pollitt, at Rhondda East.

In all, their twenty-one candidates polled just over 100,000 votes, fewer than CW. Of CW's twenty-three candidates sixteen, including their leader Sir Richard Acland, forfeited their deposits. Their one success was Chelmsford, where Ernest Millington was returned, unopposed by Labour. He took the Labour Whip and CW, reduced to a rump in Hampstead, contested no more Parliamentary elections. The ILP held their three former seats in Glasgow. Two of them, which had a strong personal following for the dying Jimmy Maxton and the Rev Campbell Stephen, were not opposed by Labour. For the ILP it was to be the last Parliament.

In a few cases personality counted for more than party and some better known Independents like Vernon Bartlett, W. J. Brown and Denis Kendall succeeded in beating both Party machines. It was the last Parliament until 1970 in which Independents were to figure. Altogether fourteen were elected, half of them for university seats. One of them was the writer A. P. Herbert, who defeated G. D. H. Cole at Oxford. At Cambridge Dr Charles Hill and J. B. Priestley were both defeated. The only Independent woman elected, Eleanor Rathbone, represented the Combined English Universities. The twelve university seats were to be abolished along with the 'business' vote. Plural voting, a privilege enjoyed by a minority, came to be regarded as an undemocratic anachronism. Other splinter groups made little showing. All the Scottish and Welsh Nationalist candidates were defeated, as were the Trotskyites, National Democrats, National Labour, Independent Christian, Anti-Hanging and others. Two Irish Nationalists were returned. Henceforward it was apparently the day of the big battalions.

Those most anxious to recover their strength were the Conservatives. Their 398 seats had been reduced to 213 (only one represented by a woman). On the day of his defeat Churchill appeared to be taking it with humour. The shock was delayed. He was deeply wounded that he had been deprived so sharply of the power and the limelight that meant so much to him. 'Tomorrow, no despatches' was his sad, terse comment on the day. He felt he had occupied Number 10 for the last time. In later years he used to say to his Australian opposite number, Sir Robert Menzies: 'They dismissed me, they dismissed me.' For this the only cure was to return. 'Chips' Channon, surprised by his own survival at Southend, predicted 'the Socialist regime will soon come to grief: I give it three years, and then we shall be returned to power; but do we deserve to be?'

Beaverbrook drew a distinction: 'It was Churchill that I was endeavouring to return to office, and not his Party. The unpopularity of the Party proved too strong for the greatness of Churchill and the affection in which he is held by the people.' Some days later he expanded on this theme, recognizing that society had changed: 'Once the middle class had been made up of small, self-employing business men, whose national political interest lay with the Conservative industrialists or the Liberal exporters and merchants. But now, to an increasing degree, the middle class is composed of salary-earners, whose relationship to the capital structure is precisely parallel to that of the wage-earning proletariat, although on a higher financial plane and whose future is conceived in terms of pensions, like the worker rather than investment like the capitalist.'

These were the people who had to be convinced that there was a new Conservative Party, still led by Churchill but reorganized and reformed, younger, pragmatic, a party of Right Progressives more representative of the country at large. Top-hatted Sir Waldron Smithers, the MP for Orpington who wanted the country to be governed according to the Ten Commandments, was not typical. The concept of 'the class born to rule' was dead. Much money and effort were to be spent in creating and projecting a modern image. The fight was for the middle ground of politics.

17

The Bloodless Revolution

Richard Dimbleby's prediction was wrong. Truman did visit Britain on his way back from Potsdam to the States. On 2 August he and the King met for two hours on board the British cruiser *Renown* at Plymouth. By way of introduction the President said: 'I hear you've had a revolution.' 'Oh no,' replied the King, 'we don't have those here.' On his journey home Truman was to cause a much more momentous event. From the cruiser *Augusta* he was to give the order for the first atomic bomb to be dropped on Japan. Hannen Swaffer disagreed with the King: 'I took my flat above Trafalgar Square to have a front view of the revolution. But when it came, in 1945, nobody noticed it.'

Hopes were high. It seemed that Marx's prophecy might be fulfilled: 'Britain is the only country in Europe where the inevitable social revolution might be effected by peaceful and legal means.' The new day was apparently dawning. But the effort was one-sided. The weary public, worn out by the national war effort, in one last gesture had heaved the problems over to a Labour Government saying 'Now get on with it', and had sat back to take it easy at long last, to get on with leading their own lives.

Unfortunately it was a new world. Britain had sold off assets, got into debt, accepted Lend-Lease to win a military victory. At the time of Dunkirk the nation had stood alone in the world against Hitler. That was a great victory for morale and also an economic defeat from which we did not recover. As soon as the war ended we were fighting a different battle. It was now called economics and was fought with different rules for new stakes. The nation was faced with a double expense: the cost of rebuilding its war-damaged economy and the enormous expense of social change. These coincided with a low point of our national wealth. The position quickly worsened. Soon after getting back to Washington, in mid-August President Truman without warning signed an order

ending Lend-Lease. Britain, facing economic ruin, bought time by
negotiating on unfavourable terms an American loan. Many
Americans felt they were paying for the extravagant and alien
doctrine of Socialism.

The strains were felt within the Labour Government. It boldly
aimed to implement Beveridge in full within three years, bringing
it into operation on 5 July, 1948, the third anniversary of the great
electoral victory. As an initial step, Jim Griffiths, the Minister of
National Insurance, decided to pay out the first family allowances
on August Bank Holiday Tuesday 1946. He had to get the money,
£59 million, from the Chancellor, Hugh Dalton. At the Party's
June conference in Bournemouth Dalton announced to the delight
of their supporters that he was giving the £59 million 'with a song
in his heart'. Privately he said: 'I tell you, Jimmy boy, it gives me
sleepless nights, sleepless nights.'

An answer was an increase in productivity and exports but that
would take time and the producers were weary from the war. Their
wartime sense of community, the feeling of all being in it together,
ebbed away. Even though the trade unions were well represented in
the Cabinet, the Government failed to bring home to people the
message that revolution had to be worked and paid for. There
was the danger that Bevan had foreseen, 'a general lethargy of the
collective will'. It soon dawned on people that it was not going
to be share and share alike. Personal material considerations began
to come to the fore. There was a fight for higher wages.

The strains of day to day living in the austere, more severely
rationed post-war world began to tell. People resented the shortages,
privations, controls and restrictions, especially when they shivered
during the fuel crisis of the 1947 winter. The fact that it was the
worst winter since 1880 was for some just another historical excuse
and the last straw. Income tax was a burden and they saw opportunity and affluence abroad. They emigrated. For those who
wanted to avoid Socialism, Australia and New Zealand were out.
Dollars for the USA and Canada were not to be had. India was
independent. The equable places left were Southern and East
Africa.

Meanwhile the Government pushed on with its programme.
Apart from nationalizing iron and steel, it did everything it
promised. Perhaps though the legislation was closer to the letter
than the spirit of *Let Us Face The Future*. The notable exception

was the creation of the National Health Service. This established the principles that health was a basic human right, that everybody must have access to whatever was needed for the cure or prevention of disease, and that the highest possible standard of treatment should be equally available. It was the change that brought the most obvious public benefit. Other changes were not so exciting. Nationalization, much of it of Cinderella industries, did not produce the fundamental social changes expected. The European revolution had got frozen in the Cold War. To those on the Left and to the Right, Bevin was a good Conservative Foreign Secretary.

At home the revolution was bloodless, without passion. The atmosphere was one of reasonably efficient dullness, characterized by Attlee himself. When Parliament was dissolved in 1950 it had accomplished much in the way of legislation. Nevertheless Richard Crossman observed in a Fabian lecture that same year: 'All the obvious things have been done which were fought for and argued about. And yet, mysteriously enough . . . the ideal, the pattern of values, has not been achieved. We have done them, we have created the means to the good life which they all laid down and said, "If you do all these things, after that there'll be a classless society." Well, there isn't.' It looked as though the King in Buckingham Palace had been closer to society than Hannen Swaffer overlooking Trafalgar Square.

Acknowledgements

For permission to reproduce extracts, acknowledgements are due to the following publishers and literary agents:

CASSELL & CO LTD
for the telegram quoted in Chapter 11 from p533 of the *Eden Memoirs* (1965) by the Earl of Avon.

WM COLLINS SONS & CO LTD
for extracts from *Diaries and Letters 1939-45* (1967) by Harold Nicolson, and for the Walter Elliot quotation in Chapter 16 from *A Companion of Honour* (1965) by Colin Coote.

CONSTABLE & CO LTD
for the quotation in Chapter 15 from *Winston Churchill, The Struggle for Survival* (1966) by Lord Moran

LESLIE FREWIN PUBLISHERS LTD
for the extract in Chapter 15 from *Faith Under Fire* (1966) by Canon Collins

VICTOR GOLLANCZ LTD
for Leah Manning's recollection in Chapter 15 from her *A Life for Education* (1970)

HAMISH HAMILTON LTD (THOMSON NEWSPAPERS LTD)
for extracts from *The Art of the Possible* (1971) by Lord Butler, and from *Beaverbrook* (1972) by A. J. P. Taylor

WILLIAM HEINEMANN LTD
for the quotation in Chapter 6 from J. B. Priestley's *Postscripts* (1940)

DAVID HIGHAM ASSOCIATES
for the extract from Launcelot Hogben's letter in Chapter 7 from *The Life, Letters and Diaries of Kingsley Martin* (1973) by C. H. Rolph published by Victor Gollancz Ltd

SIR EDWARD HULTON
for extracts from *Picture Post*

MACMILLAN, LONDON AND BASINGSTOKE
for the extract in Chapter 2 from *The Last Enemy* (1941) by Richard Hillary.

A. D. PETERS & CO LTD
for the extract in Chapter 10 from *The Adventure of Reconstruction* (1945) by Lord Woolton, published by Cassell & Co Ltd

The Society of Authors on behalf of the Bernard Shaw Estate.

PROFESSOR C. H. WADDINGTON
for the extract from his *The Scientific Attitude*, published by Penguin Books (first edition 1941)

GEORGE WEIDENFELD AND NICOLSON LIMITED
for extracts from *Chips Channon Diaries* (1967) by Sir Henry Channon

For permission to quote from Hugh Dalton's diaries we are indebted to the late Anthony Crosland MP

Press – UK

Birmingham Mail
Birmingham Post
Brighton Evening Argus
Common Wealth Review
The Cornishman
Croydon Advertiser
Daily Herald
East Grinstead Observer
The Economist
The Essex Chronicle
Evening Standard

Financial Times
Ilford Recorder
Manchester Evening Chronicle
Manchester Evening News
The Manchester Guardian
New Statesman and Nation
News Chronicle
Punch
Radio Times
Stratford Express

Time and Tide
The Times
The Times Literary Supplement
Tribune
Walthamstow Guardian
The West Briton
West Sussex County Times
Yorkshire Evening Post
Yorkshire Post

Press – Overseas

AUSTRALIA	*The Sydney Morning Herald*	NEW ZEALAND	*The Dominion*
CANADA	*The Montreal Gazette*	SOUTH AFRICA	*Die Burger Rand Daily Mail*
	Toronto Globe and Mail	UNITED STATES	*Chicago Tribune*
FRANCE	*L'Humanité Le Monde*		*Los Angeles Times*
MALTA	*Times of Malta*		*New York Times*
			Washington Post

We should like to thank the following:

Organizations

BBC Written Archives Centre
British Film Institute
Communist Party
Conservative Research
   Department
Co-operative Union Ltd
Fabian Society
Labour Party
Ladbroke & Co Ltd

Meteorological Office
National Liberal Club
Northern Ireland Labour Party
Post Office
Public Record Office of
   Northern Ireland
Society of Motor Manufacturers
   and Traders Limited
Spotlight Directory

Libraries

Birmingham City
British Library of Political and
   Economic Science
Crawley, Sussex
Croydon
Daily Mirror
King's College, London
Leeds

Manchester
The Mitchell Library of New
   South Wales
Newham
Redbridge
Trades Union Congress
Waltham Forest
Westminster

The manuscript was typed by Ann Haines

Index